Study Guide (Chapters 1-15)

Financial & Managerial Accounting
EIGHTH EDITION

OR

Corporate Financial Accounting
EIGHTH EDITION

CARL S. WARREN • JAMES M. REEVE • PHILIP E. FESS

Prepared by

Carl S. Warren
Professor Emeritus of Accounting
University of Georgia, Athens

James M. Reeve
Professor of Accounting
University of Tennessee, Knoxville

THOMSON

SOUTH-WESTERN

Australia · Canada · Mexico · Singapore · Spain · United Kingdom · United States

THOMSON

SOUTH-WESTERN

Study Guide to accompany Financial & Managerial Accounting, 8e, Chapters 1-15 or Corporate Financial Accounting, 8e

Carl S. Warren, James M. Reeve, Philip E. Fess

VP/Editorial Director:
Jack W. Calhoun

VP/Editor-in-Chief:
George Werthman

Publisher:
Rob Dewey

Executive Editor:
Sharon Oblinger

Developmental Editor:
Erin Joyner

Marketing Manager:
Keith Chassé

Production Editor:
Heather Mann

Manufacturing Coordinator:
Doug Wilke

Technology Project Editor:
Sally Nieman

Media Editor:
Robin Browning

Design Project Manager:
Michelle Kunkler

Production Services:
Mary Hartkemeyer

Illustrator:
Matsu

Cover Designer:
Michael H. Stratton

Printer:
Thomson West
Eagan, MN

For permission to use material from this text or product, submit a request online at http://www.thomsonrights.com. Any additional questions about permissions can be submitted by email to thomsonrights@thomson.com.

For more information contact South-Western, 5191 Natorp Boulevard, Mason, Ohio, 45040. Or you can visit our Internet site at: http://www.swlearning.com

CONTENTS

1   Introduction to Accounting and Business

QUIZ AND TEST HINTS

The following hints may be helpful to you in preparing for a quiz or a test over the material covered in Chapter 1.

1. Terminology is important in this chapter. Do the Matching exercises included in this Study Guide. Expect multiple-choice, true/false, or matching questions to include the terms introduced throughout the chapter. For example, you should be able to distinguish between the different types of business organizations, identify business stakeholders, and distinguish between financial and managerial accounting. Pay special attention to the terms beginning on page 2 to the end of the chapter. These terms will be used frequently throughout the remainder of the text.

2. Know the accounting equation: Assets = Liabilities + Owner's Equity. Be able to compute one amount when given the other two. For example, if assets equal $100,000 and liabilities equal $60,000, owner's equity must equal $40,000. Be able to determine the effect of change in the basic elements on one another. For example, if assets increase by $10,000 and liabilities decrease by $5,000, owner's equity must increase by $15,000.

3. Be able to record business transactions within the framework of the accounting equation. Use the illustration on pages 15–18 as a basis for review and study. Pay particular attention to items that are increased and decreased by transactions a through h. Note the introduction of new terms such as account payable, account receivable, revenue, and expense. These new terms are highlighted in color in the text.

4. Be able to describe each of the financial statements listed on page 19. You may be required to prepare a short income statement, statement of owner's equity, and balance sheet. You will probably not be required to prepare a statement of cash flows.

5. Review the summary data for NetSolutions on page 18. Trace the numbers into the statements shown in Exhibit 6 on page 20. Know the format of each statement such as the number of columns and placement of dollar signs. Some of the numbers in Exhibit 6 appear on more than one statement. Sometimes a quiz or a test question will provide partially completed statements, and you will be required to complete the statements. Recognizing amounts that appear on more than one statement will aid you in answering this type of question.

MATCHING

Instructions: Match each of the statements below with its proper term. Some terms may not be used.

A. account form
B. account payable
C. account receivable
D. accounting
E. accounting equation
F. assets
G. balance sheet
H. business
I. business entity concept
J. business stakeholder
K. business strategy
L. business transaction
M. capital stock
N. corporation
O. cost concept
P. differentiation strategy
Q. dividends
R. ethics
S. expenses
T. financial accounting
U. Financial Accounting Standards Board (FASB)
V. generally accepted accounting principles (GAAP)

W. income statement
X. liabilities
Y. low-cost strategy
Z. managerial accounting
AA. managers
BB. manufacturing
CC. matching concept
DD. merchandising
EE. net income
FF. net loss
GG. objectivity concept
HH. owner's equity
II. partnership
JJ. prepaid expenses
KK. proprietorship
LL. report form
MM. retained earnings
NN. retained earnings statement
OO. revenue
PP. service
QQ. statement of cash flows
RR. unit of measure concept
SS. value chain

_____ 1. An organization in which basic resources (inputs), such as materials and labor, are assembled and processed to provide goods or services (outputs) to customers.

_____ 2. A type of business that changes basic inputs into products that are sold to individual customers.

_____ 3. A type of business that purchases products from other businesses and sells them to customers.

_____ 4. A business owned by one individual.

_____ 5. A business owned by two or more individuals.

_____ 6. A business organized under state or federal statutes as a separate legal entity.

_____ 7. An integrated set of plans and actions designed to enable the business to gain an advantage over its competitors and, in so doing, to maximize its profits.

____ **8.** A strategy wherein a business designs and produces products or services of acceptable quality at a cost lower than that of its competitors.

____ **9.** The way a business adds value for its customers by processing inputs into a product or service.

____ **10.** A person or entity who has an interest in the economic performance of a business.

____ **11.** Individuals authorized by the owners to operate the business.

____ **12.** An information system that provides reports to stakeholders about the economic activities and condition of a business.

____ **13.** Moral principles that guide the conduct of individuals.

____ **14.** A specialized field of accounting concerned primarily with the recording and reporting of economic data and activities to stakeholders outside the business.

____ **15.** A specialized field of accounting that uses estimated data to aid management in running day-to-day operations and in planning future operations.

____ **16.** The authoritative body that has the primary responsibility for developing accounting principles.

____ **17.** A concept of accounting that limits the economic data in the accounting system to data related directly to the activities of the business.

____ **18.** A concept of accounting requiring that economic data be recorded in dollars.

____ **19.** The resources owned by a business.

____ **20.** The rights of creditors that represent debts of the business.

____ **21.** The rights of the owners.

____ **22.** Assets = Liabilities + Owner's Equity

____ **23.** An economic event or condition that directly changes an entity's financial condition or directly affects its results of operations.

____ **24.** The liability created by a purchase on account.

____ **25.** Items such as supplies that will be used in the business in the future.

____ **26.** A claim against the customer.

____ **27.** The amounts used in the process of earning revenue.

____ **28.** The amount a business earns by selling goods or services to its customers.

____ **29.** A summary of the revenue and expenses *for a specific period of time,* such as a month or a year.

_____ **30.** A summary of the changes in the retained earnings in a corporation for *a specific period of time,* such as a month or a year.

_____ **31.** A list of the assets, liabilities, and owner's equity *as of a specific date,* usually at the close of the last day of a month or a year.

_____ **32.** A summary of the cash receipts and cash payments *for a specific period of time,* such as a month or a year.

_____ **33.** A concept of accounting in which expenses are matched with the revenue generated during a period by those expenses.

_____ **34.** The form of balance sheet that resembles the basic format of the accounting equation, with assets on the left side and the liabilities and owner's equity sections on the right side.

_____ **35.** Shares of ownership of a corporation

_____ **36.** Distributions of earnings of a corporation to its owners (stockholders).

_____ **37.** Net income retained in a corporation.

FILL IN THE BLANK—PART A

Instructions: Answer the following questions or complete the statements by writing the appropriate words or amounts in the answer blanks.

1. An organization in which basic resources (inputs), such as materials and labor, are assembled and processed to provide goods or services (outputs) to customers is a(n) _____.

2. A business organized under state or federal statutes as a separate legal entity is a(n) _____.

3. A person or entity that has an interest in the economic performance of a business is called a(n) _____ _____.

4. An information system that provides reports to stakeholders about the economic activities and condition of a business is _____.

5. Moral principles that guide the conduct of individuals are called _____.

6. A specialized field of accounting that uses estimated data to aid management in running day-to-day operations and in planning future operations is called _____ accounting.

7. A concept of accounting that requires that economic data be recorded in dollars is the _____ _____ _____ concept.

8. The resources owned by a business are called _____.

9. The rights of the owners are called _____ _____.

10. Assets = Liabilities + Owner's Equity is the _____ _____.

11. Carson offered for sale at $75,000 land that had been purchased for $45,000. If Zimmer paid Carson $70,000 for the land, the amount that Zimmer would record for the purchase of the land in the accounting records is _____.

12. The liability created by a purchase on account is referred to as a(n) _____ _____.

13. If liabilities are $85,000 and owner's equity is $45,000, the amount of the assets is _____.

14. If assets are $375,000 and owner's equity is $295,000, the amount of the liabilities is _____.

15. The amount a business earns by selling goods or services to its customers is called _____.

16. If operations for an accounting period resulted in cash sales of $60,000, sales on account of $150,000, and expenses paid in cash of $195,000, the net income or (net loss) for the period is _____.

17. A summary of the changes in the owner's equity that have occurred *during a specific period of time*, such as a month or a year, is the

    _____ _____ _____ _____.

18. The owner's equity at the beginning of the period was $19,000; at the end of the period, assets were $98,000 and liabilities were $41,000. The owner made no additional investments or withdrawals during the period. The net income or (net loss) for the period is _____.

19. The form of balance sheet that resembles the basic format of the accounting equation, with assets on the left side and the liabilities and owner's equity sections on the right side, is called the _____ form.

20. If total assets increased by $85,000 and liabilities decreased by $9,000 during the period, the amount and direction (increase or decrease) of the period's change in owner's equity was _____.

FILL IN THE BLANK—PART B

Instructions: Answer the following questions or complete the statements by writing the appropriate words or amounts in the answer blanks.

1. A type of business that changes basic inputs into products that are sold to individual customers is a(n) _____ business.

2. A type of business that purchases products from other businesses and sells them to customers is a(n) _____ business.

3. A business owned by one individual is called a(n) _____.

4. Individuals whom the owners have authorized to operate the business are called _____.

5. A specialized field of accounting primarily concerned with the recording and reporting of economic data and activities to stakeholders outside the business is called _____ accounting.

6. The authoritative body that has the primary responsibility for developing accounting principles is the _____ _____ _____ _____.

7. A concept of accounting that limits the economic data in the accounting system to data related directly to the activities of the business is the _____ _____ concept.

8. The rights of creditors that represent debts of the business are called _____.

9. An economic event or condition that directly changes an entity's financial condition or directly affects its results of operations is called a(n) _____ _____.

10. Items such as supplies that will be used in the business in the future are called _____ _____.

11. A claim against the customer is called a(n) _____ _____.

12. If owner's equity is $46,000 and liabilities are $34,000, the amount of assets is _____.

13. If assets are $98,000 and liabilities are $32,500, the amount of owner's equity is _____.

14. The amounts used in the process of earning revenue are _____.

15. A summary of the revenue and expenses *for a specific period of time*, such as a month or a year, is called a(n) _____ _____.

16. If operations for an accounting period resulted in cash sales of $90,000, sales on account of $40,000, and expenses paid in cash of $135,000, the net income or (net loss) for the period is _____.

17. A list of the assets, liabilities, and owner's equity *as of a specific date*, usually at the close of the last day of a month or a year, is called a(n) _____ _____.

18. If total assets increased by $21,500 and owner's equity increased by $8,000 during a period, the amount and direction (increase or decrease) of the period's change in total liabilities was _____.

19. A summary of the cash receipts and cash payments *for a specific period of time*, such as a month or a year, is called a(n) _____ _____ _____.

20. The owner's equity at the beginning of the period was $46,000; at the end of the period, assets were $99,000 and liabilities were $22,000. If additional capital stock of $10,000 was issued and dividends of $8,000 were paid during the period, the net income or (net loss) for the period is

_____.

MULTIPLE CHOICE

Instructions: Circle the best answer for each of the following questions.

1. Accountants employed by a particular business firm or not-for-profit organization, perhaps as chief accountant, controller, or financial vice-president, are said to be engaged in:
   a. general accounting
   b. public accounting
   c. independent accounting
   d. private accounting

2. A type of business that changes basic inputs into products that are sold to individual customers.
   a. service business
   b. manufacturing business
   c. merchandising business
   d. proprietorship business

3. The accounting concept that requires economic data be recorded in dollars.
   a. cost concept
   b. objectivity concept
   c. business entity concept
   d. unit of measure concept

4. The amounts for recording properties and services purchased by a business are determined using the:
   a. business entity concept
   b. cost concept
   c. matching principle
   d. proprietorship principle

5. Another way of writing the accounting equation is:
   a. Assets + Liabilities = Owner's Equity
   b. Owner's Equity + Assets = Liabilities
   c. Assets = Owner's Equity – Liabilities
   d. Assets – Liabilities = Owner's Equity

6. If total liabilities increased by $20,000 during a period of time and owner's equity increased by $5,000 during the same period, the amount and direction (increase or decrease) of the period's change in total assets is:

   a. $20,000 increase

   b. $20,000 decrease

   c. $25,000 decrease

   d. $25,000 increase

7. A business paid $6,000 to a creditor in payment of an amount owed. The effect of the transaction on the accounting equation was:

   a. an increase in an asset and a decrease in another asset

   b. a decrease in an asset and an increase in a liability

   c. a decrease in an asset and a decrease in a liability

   d. an increase in an asset and an increase in owner's equity

8. The total assets and the total liabilities of a particular business enterprise at the beginning and at the end of the year are stated below. During the year, dividends of $30,000 were paid, and additional capital stock of $25,000 was issued.

	Assets	Liabilities
Beginning of year	$290,000	$190,000
End of year	355,000	220,000

   The amount of net income for the year was:

   a. $5,000

   b. $25,000

   c. $30,000

   d. $40,000

9. If revenue was $70,000, expenses were $59,000, and the dividends were $25,000, the amount of net income or net loss was:

   a. net income of $11,000

   b. net income of $36,000

   c. net loss of $59,000

   d. net income of $70,000

10. Which of the following is not one of the major sections of the statement of cash flows?

    a. cash flows from marketing activities

    b. cash flows from investing activities

    c. cash flows from financing activities

    d. cash flows from operating activities

TRUE/FALSE

Instructions: Indicate whether each of the following statements is true or false by placing a check mark in the appropriate column.

	True	**False**
1. Accounting is often characterized as the "language of business."	____	____
2. Accountants who render accounting services on a fee basis and staff accountants employed by them are said to be engaged in private accounting.	____	____
3. Managerial accounting uses estimated data instead of financial accounting data to run day-to-day operations.	____	____
4. The concept that expenses incurred in generating revenue should be matched against the revenue in determining net income or net loss is called the cost concept.	____	____
5. The financing activities section of the statement of cash flows includes cash transactions that enter into the determination of net income.	____	____
6. The debts of a business are called its accounts receivable.	____	____
7. A partnership is owned by not less than four individuals.	____	____
8. A business transaction is the occurrence of an event or of a condition that must be recorded.	____	____
9. A summary of the changes in the earnings retained in the business that have occurred during a specific period of time, such as a month or a year, is called a statement of cash flows.	____	____
10. A claim against a customer for sales made on credit is an account payable.	____	____

EXERCISE 1-1

Instructions: Some typical transactions of Clem's Laundry Service are presented below. For each transaction, indicate the increase (+), the decrease (–), or no change (0) in the assets (A), liabilities (L), and owner's equity (OE) by placing the appropriate sign(s) in the appropriate column(s). More than one sign may have to be placed in the A, L, or OE column for a given transaction.

	A	L	OE
1. Received cash from owner by issuing capital stock	___	___	___
2. Purchased supplies on account	___	___	___
3. Charged customers for services sold on account	___	___	___
4. Received cash from cash customers	___	___	___
5. Paid cash for rent on building	___	___	___
6. Collected an account receivable in full	___	___	___
7. Paid cash for supplies	___	___	___
8. Returned supplies purchased on account and not yet paid for	___	___	___
9. Paid cash to creditors on account	___	___	___
10. Paid cash to stockholder as a dividend	___	___	___

PROBLEM 1-1

Instructions: The assets, liabilities, and owner's equity of Casey Corp., a small repair shop, are expressed in equation form below. Following the equation are ten transactions completed by Casey Corp. On each of the numbered lines, show by addition or subtraction the effect of each of the transactions on the equation. For each transaction, identify the changes in owner's equity by placing the letter R (revenue), E (expense), D (dividend), or I (investment) at the right of each increase or decrease in owner's equity. On the lines labeled "Bal.," show the new equation resulting from the transaction.

	Assets			=	Liabilities	+	Owner's Equity	
Cash	+	Supplies	+ Land =	Accounts Payable	+	Capital Stock	+	Retained Earnings

1. Al Casey invested $40,000 cash in the business in exchange for capital stock. .... **(1)** _____

2. Purchased $2,000 of supplies on account. .... **(2)** _____

   Bal. _____

3. Purchased land for a future building site for $14,000 cash. .... **(3)** _____

   Bal. _____

4. Paid creditors $1,800 on account. .... **(4)** _____

   Bal. _____

5. Received $5,000 for various service calls............... **(5)** _____

   Bal. _____

6. During the month, another $900 of expenses were incurred on account. .... **(6)** _____

   Bal. _____

7. During the month, Al Casey invested another $10,000 cash in the business in exchange for capital stock. .... **(7)** _____

   Bal. _____

8. Casey paid $2,800 for building and equipment rent for the month............................ **(8)** _____

   Bal. _____

9. Paid dividends to Al Casey, $200.................................... **(9)** _____

   Bal. _____

10. Used $600 worth of supplies................................ **(10)** _____

   Bal. _____

PROBLEM 1-2

The amounts of the assets and liabilities of Tom's Painting Service Inc. at December 31 of the current year, and the revenues and expenses for the year are as follows:

Cash	$10,050
Accounts receivable	8,950
Supplies	4,000
Accounts payable	4,450
Sales	27,450
Supplies expense	5,450
Advertising expense	4,825
Truck rental expense	1,525
Utilities expense	700
Miscellaneous expense	1,400

The capital stock of Tom's Painting Service Inc. was $4,000 at the beginning of the current year. During the year, dividends of $1,000 were paid, and additional capital stock of $2,000 was issued.

Instructions: Using the forms provided, prepare the following:

(1) An income statement for the year ended December 31, 20--.

(2) A retained earnings statement for the year ended December 31, 20--.

(3) A balance sheet as of December 31, 20--.

(1)
Tom's Painting Service Inc.

Income Statement

For Year Ended December 31, 20--

(2)
Tom's Painting Service Inc.

Retained Earnings Statement

For Year Ended December 31, 20--

(3)

Tom's Painting Service Inc.

Balance Sheet

December 31, 20--

2 Analyzing Transactions

QUIZ AND TEST HINTS

The following hints may be helpful to you in preparing for a quiz or a test over the material covered in Chapter 2.

1. Terminology is important in this chapter. Do the Matching exercises included in this Study Guide. Pay special attention to major account classifications discussed on pages 48–49 of the text.

2. Memorize the "Rules of Debit and Credit" and the "Normal Balances of Accounts." All instructors will ask questions to test your knowledge of these items.

3. Be able to prepare general journal entries for the types of transactions presented in this chapter. Review the illustration beginning on page 51 and be sure you understand each entry. Be especially careful not to confuse debits and credits. Remember that a credit is indented slightly to the right when preparing a general journal entry. A good review is to rework the Illustrative Problem.

4. You should be familiar with the process of posting accounts for working assigned problems. However, you will probably not be required to post accounts on an examination.

5. You may be required to prepare a trial balance from a list of accounts with normal balances.

6. You might expect one or two questions on how to correct errors. These types of questions may require you to prepare a correcting journal entry. Review the section of the chapter and illustration containing this information.

MATCHING

Instructions: Match each of the statements below with its proper term. Some terms may not be used.

A.	account	O.	liabilities
B.	assets	P.	materiality concept
C.	balance of the account	Q.	objectivity concept
D.	chart of accounts	R.	owner's equity
E.	credits	S.	posting
F.	debits	T.	revenues
G.	dividends	U.	slide
H.	double-entry accounting	V.	T account
I.	expenses	W.	transposition
J.	horizontal analysis	X.	trial balance
K.	journal	Y.	two-column journal
L.	journal entry	Z.	unearned revenue
M.	journalizing	AA.	vertical analysis
N.	ledger		

_____ **1.** An accounting form that is used to record the increases and decreases in each financial statement item.

_____ **2.** A group of accounts for a business.

_____ **3.** A list of the accounts in the ledger.

_____ **4.** Resources that are owned by the business.

_____ **5.** Debts owed to outsiders (creditors).

_____ **6.** The owner's right to the assets of the business.

_____ **7.** Increases in owner's equity as a result of selling services or products to customers.

_____ **8.** Assets used up or services consumed in the process of generating revenues.

_____ **9.** The simplest form of an account.

_____ **10.** Amounts entered on the left side of an account.

_____ **11.** Amounts entered on the right side of an account.

_____ **12.** The amount of the difference between the debits and the credits that have been entered into an account.

_____ **13.** The initial record in which the effects of a transaction are recorded.

_____ **14.** The process of recording a transaction in the journal.

_____ **15.** The form of recording a transaction in a journal.

_____ **16.** A system of accounting for recording transactions, based on recording increases and decreases in accounts so that debits equal credits.

___ 17. The account used to record distributions of earnings to stockholders.

___ 18. The process of transferring the debits and credits from the journal entries to the accounts.

___ 19. An all-purpose journal.

___ 20. The liability created by receiving revenue in advance.

___ 21. A summary listing of the titles and balances of accounts in the ledger.

___ 22. A concept of accounting that implies that an error may be treated in the easiest possible way.

___ 23. An error in which the order of the digits is changed, such as writing $542 as $452 or $524.

___ 24. An error in which the entire number is moved one or more spaces to the right or the left, such as writing $542.00 as $54.20 or $5,420.00.

___ 25. Financial analysis that compares an item in a current statement with the same item in prior statements.

FILL IN THE BLANK—PART A

Instructions: Answer the following questions or complete the statements by writing the appropriate words or amounts in the answer blanks.

1. An accounting form that is used to record the increases and decreases in each financial statement item is the _____.

2. A list of the accounts in the ledger is called the _____ _____ _____.

3. Increases in owner's equity as a result of selling services or products to customers is called _____.

4. The simplest form of an account is the _____.

5. Amounts entered on the left side of an account are _____.

6. An increase in Accounts Receivable is recorded by a _____ entry in the account.

7. An increase in Retained Earnings is recorded by a _____ entry in the account.

8. A decrease in Accounts Payable is recorded by a _____ entry in the account.

9. A decrease in Salaries Expense is recorded by a _____ entry in the account.

10. Unearned Revenue is a(n) _____ account.

11. A decrease in Cash is recorded by a _____ entry in the account.

12. The normal balance of the supplies account is a _____ balance.

13. The normal balance of Retained Earnings is a _____ balance.

14. The initial record in which the effects of a transaction are recorded is the _____.

15. The process of recording a transaction in the journal is called _____.

16. The _____-_____ _____ is a system of accounting for recording transactions, based on recording increases and decreases in accounts so that debits equal credits.

17. The process of transferring the debits and credits from the journal entries to the accounts is called _____.

18. An all-purpose journal is the _____-_____ _____.

19. The _____ concept of accounting implies that the error may be treated in the easiest possible way.

20. An error in which the order of the digits is changed mistakenly, such as writing $542 as $452 or $524, is called a(n) _____.

FILL IN THE BLANK—PART B

Instructions: Answer the following questions or complete the statements by writing the appropriate words or amounts in the answer blanks.

1. A group of accounts for a business is called a(n) _____.

2. Resources that are owned by the business are called _____.

3. Debts owed to outsiders (creditors) are _____ of the business.

4. The owner's right to the assets of the business is the _____ _____.

5. Assets used up or services consumed in the process of generating revenues are reported as _____.

6. Amounts entered on the right side of an account are _____.

7. The amount of the difference between the debits and the credits that have been entered into an account is the _____ of the account.

8. The recording of a transaction in a journal is called _____.

9. The _____ account is used to record amounts distributed to stockholders from earnings of a corporation.

10. _____ _____ is the liability created by receiving the revenue in advance.

11. A decrease in Notes Payable is recorded by a _____ entry in the account.

12. An increase in Dividends is recorded by a _____ entry in the account.

13. A decrease in Accounts Receivable is recorded by a _____ entry in the account.

14. _____ analysis compares an item in a current statement with the same item in prior statements.

15. Wages Payable is a(n) _____ account.

16. Patent Rights is a(n) _____ account.

17. The normal balance of the prepaid insurance account is a _____ balance.

18. The normal balance of the fees earned account is a _____ balance.

19. A summary listing the titles and balances of accounts in the general ledger is called a(n) _____ _____.

20. An error in which the entire number is mistakenly moved one or more spaces to the right or the left, such as writing $542.00 as $54.20 or $5,420.00, is called a(n) _____.

MULTIPLE CHOICE

Instructions: Circle the best answer for each of the following questions.

1. The receipt of cash from customers in payment of their accounts would be recorded by a:
   a. debit to Cash and a credit to Accounts Payable
   b. debit to Cash and a credit to Accounts Receivable
   c. debit to Accounts Receivable and a credit to Retained Earnings
   d. debit to Accounts Payable and a credit to Cash

2. The first step in recording a transaction in a two-column journal is to:
   a. list the account to be credited
   b. list the amount to be credited
   c. list the amount to be debited
   d. list the account to be debited

3. The dividends account of a corporation is debited when:
   a. the stockholders invest cash
   b. cash is paid to stockholders from earnings retained in the business
   c. a liability is paid
   d. an expense is paid

4. The equality of debits and credits in the ledger should be verified at the end of each accounting period by preparing a(n):

   a. accounting statement

   b. balance report

   c. trial balance

   d. account verification report

5. Of the following errors, the one that will cause an inequality in the trial balance totals is:

   a. incorrectly computing an account balance

   b. failure to record a transaction

   c. recording the same transaction more than once

   d. posting a transaction to the wrong account

6. Credits to cash result in:

   a. an increase in owner's equity

   b. a decrease in assets

   c. an increase in liabilities

   d. an increase in revenue

7. Debits to expense accounts signify:

   a. increases in owner's equity

   b. decreases in owner's equity

   c. increases in assets

   d. decreases in liabilities

8. When rent is prepaid for several months in advance, the debit is to:

   a. an expense account

   b. an owner's equity account

   c. a liability account

   d. an asset account

9. When an asset is purchased on account, the credit is to:

   a. an owner's equity account

   b. a revenue account

   c. a liability account

   d. an expense account

10. When a payment is made to a supplier for goods previously purchased on account, the debit is to:

    a. an asset account

    b. a liability account

    c. an owner's equity account

    d. an expense account

TRUE/FALSE

Instructions: Indicate whether each of the following statements is true or false by placing a check mark in the appropriate column.

		True	False
1.	Amounts entered on the left side of an account, regardless of the account title, are called credits or charges to the account.	____	____
2.	The difference between the total debits and the total credits posted to an account yields a figure called the balance of the account.	____	____
3.	Accounting systems provide information on business transactions for use by management in directing operations and preparing financial statements.	____	____
4.	Accounts receivable are reported as liabilities on the balance sheet.	____	____
5.	The residual claim against the assets of a business after the total liabilities are deducted is called stockholders' equity.	____	____
6.	Every business transaction affects a minimum of one account.	____	____
7.	The process of recording a transaction in a journal is called posting.	____	____
8.	A group of accounts for a business entity is called a journal.	____	____
9.	A listing of the accounts in a ledger is called a chart of accounts.	____	____
10.	A recording error caused by the erroneous rearrangement of digits, such as writing $627 as $672, is called a slide.	____	____

EXERCISE 2-1

Eight transactions are recorded in the following T accounts:

Cash			
(1)	20,000	(5)	2,500
(7)	2,000	(8)	3,500

Machinery	
(2)	6,300

Dividends	
(8)	3,500

Accounts Receivable			
(4)	5,000	(7)	2,000

Accounts Payable			
(5)	2,500	(2)	6,300
		(3)	820
		(6)	1,600

Service Revenue	
(4)	5,000

Supplies	
(3)	820

Capital Stock	
(1)	20,000

Operating Expenses	
(6)	1,600

Instructions: For each debit and each credit, indicate in the following form the type of account affected (asset, liability, owner's equity, revenue, or expense) and whether the account was increased (+) or decreased (−).

	Account Debited		Account Credited	
Transaction	Type	Effect	Type	Effect
(1)				
(2)				
(3)				
(4)				
(5)				
(6)				
(7)				
(8)				

PROBLEM 2-1

During June of the current year, Joan Star started Star Service Corporation.

Instructions:

(1) Record the following transactions in the two-column journal given below.

June 1. Joan invested $5,000 in cash, equipment valued at $14,500, and a van worth $21,000, in exchange for capital stock in Star Service Corporation.

16. Purchased additional equipment on account, $5,500.

28. Purchased supplies on account, $500.

30. Paid $2,100 to creditors on account.

(2) Post to the appropriate ledger accounts on the following pages.

(3) Prepare a trial balance of the ledger accounts of Star Service Corporation as of June 30 of the current year, using the form that follows the ledger accounts.

(1) JOURNAL PAGE *1*

	DATE	DESCRIPTION	POST. REF.	DEBIT	CREDIT	
1						1
2						2
3						3
4						4
5						5
6						6
7						7
8						8
9						9
10						10
11						11
12						12
13						13
14						14
15						15
16						16
17						17
18						18
19						19
20						20
21						21

(2)   **LEDGER ACCOUNTS**

ACCOUNT   *Cash*   ACCOUNT NO.   *11*

DATE		ITEM	POST. REF.	DEBIT	CREDIT	BALANCE	
						DEBIT	CREDIT

ACCOUNT   *Supplies*   ACCOUNT NO.   *12*

DATE		ITEM	POST. REF.	DEBIT	CREDIT	BALANCE	
						DEBIT	CREDIT

ACCOUNT   *Equipment*   ACCOUNT NO.   *18*

DATE		ITEM	POST. REF.	DEBIT	CREDIT	BALANCE	
						DEBIT	CREDIT

ACCOUNT   *Vehicles*   ACCOUNT NO.   *19*

DATE		ITEM	POST. REF.	DEBIT	CREDIT	BALANCE	
						DEBIT	CREDIT

ACCOUNT   *Accounts Payable*   ACCOUNT NO.   *21*

DATE		ITEM	POST. REF.	DEBIT	CREDIT	BALANCE	
						DEBIT	CREDIT

ACCOUNT   *Capital Stock*   ACCOUNT NO.   *31*

DATE	ITEM	POST. REF.	DEBIT	CREDIT	BALANCE	
					DEBIT	CREDIT

(3)

PROBLEM 2-2

On January 2, 20--, Judy Turner, an attorney, opened a law office as Turner Law Services, P.C., a professional services corporation. The following transactions were completed during the month.

a. Judy invested $20,000 cash and $13,200 worth of office equipment in the business in exchange for capital stock.

b. Paid a month's rent of $2,500.

c. Paid $1,000 for office supplies.

d. Collected legal fees of $19,600.

e. Paid secretary a salary of $1,100.

f. Purchased $200 worth of office supplies on account.

g. Bought an auto for business use. It cost $13,000. Paid $2,600 down and charged the balance.

h. Paid $5,000 of dividends.

i. Paid $800 for auto repairs and maintenance.

j. Received a $240 telephone bill.

k. Paid the $240 telephone bill.

l. Paid premiums of $1,700 on property insurance.

m. Paid $2,000 on accounts payable.

n. Paid $5,000 cash for books for the law library.

o. Paid $500 cash for janitor service.

Instructions:

(1) Record the transactions in the T accounts that follow.

(2) Prepare a trial balance using the form on the following page.

Cash	Office Supplies	Office Equipment
	Prepaid Insurance	Auto
	Library	Accounts Payable

Capital Stock	Rent Expense	Auto Repairs & Maintenance Expense

Dividends	Salary Expense	Janitor Expense

Legal Fees	Telephone Expense	

(2)

PROBLEM 2-3

The following errors were made in journalizing and posting transactions:

a. A $1,000 premium paid for insurance was debited to Prepaid Rent and credited to Cash.

b. A $200 purchase of supplies on account was recorded as a debit to Supplies and a credit to Accounts Receivable.

c. A dividend of $1,500 was debited to Cash and credited to the dividends account.

Instructions: Prepare entries in the two-column journal provided below to correct these errors.

JOURNAL   PAGE

	DATE	DESCRIPTION	POST. REF.	DEBIT	CREDIT	
1						1
2						2
3						3
4						4
5						5
6						6
7						7
8						8
9						9
10						10
11						11
12						12
13						13
14						14
15						15
16						16
17						17
18						18
19						19
20						20
21						21
22						22
23						23
24						24
25						25

3

The Matching Concept and the Adjusting Process

QUIZ AND TEST HINTS

The following hints may be helpful to you in preparing for a quiz or a test over the material covered in Chapter 3.

1. Terminology is important in this chapter. Do the Matching exercises included in this Study Guide.

2. The major focus of this chapter is the adjusting process. You should be able to prepare adjusting entries for each of the four types of adjustments: deferred expenses, deferred revenues, accrued expenses, and accrued revenues. You should also be able to prepare the adjusting entry for depreciation. Review the illustrations in the chapter, especially Exhibit 5, and the adjusting entries required in the Illustrative Problem.

3. Some instructors may give you an unadjusted trial balance and adjusted trial balance and require you to figure out what the adjusting entries must have been. This would be similar to Exercises 3-27 and 3-28 and Problems 3-3A and 3-4B. To review for this type of problem, cover up the "Effect of Adjusting Entry" column in Exhibit 8 and see if you can figure out what the adjusting entries must have been.

MATCHING

Instructions: Match each of the statements below with its proper term. Some terms may not be used.

A.	accounting period concept	**M.**	deferred expenses
B.	accrual basis	**N.**	deferred revenues
C.	accrued expenses	**O.**	depreciation
D.	accrued revenues	**P.**	depreciation expense
E.	accumulated depreciation	**Q.**	final trial balance
F.	adjusted trial balance	**R.**	fixed assets
G.	adjusting entries	**S.**	horizontal analysis
H.	adjusting process	**T.**	matching concept
I.	book value of the asset	**U.**	objectivity concept
J.	cash basis	**V.**	post-closing trial balance
K.	closing entries	**W.**	revenue recognition concept
L.	contra account	**X.**	vertical analysis

_____ **1.** The accounting concept that assumes that the economic life of the business can be divided into time periods.

_____ **2.** Under this basis of accounting, revenues and expenses are reported in the income statement in the period in which cash is received or paid.

_____ **3.** Under this basis of accounting, revenues are reported in the income statement in the period in which they are earned.

_____ **4.** The accounting concept that supports reporting revenues when the services are provided to customers.

_____ **5.** The accounting concept that supports reporting revenues and the related expenses in the same period.

_____ **6.** An analysis and updating of the accounts when financial statements are prepared.

_____ **7.** The journal entries that bring the accounts up to date at the end of the accounting period.

_____ **8.** Items that have been initially recorded as assets but are expected to become expenses over time or through the normal operations of the business.

_____ **9.** Items that have been initially recorded as liabilities but are expected to become revenues over time or through the normal operations of the business.

_____ **10.** Expenses that have been incurred *but not recorded* in the accounts.

_____ **11.** Revenues that have been earned *but not recorded* in the accounts.

_____ **12.** Physical resources that are owned and used by a business and are permanent or have a long life.

_____ **13.** The decrease in the ability of a fixed asset to provide useful services.

____ **14.** The portion of the cost of a fixed asset that is recorded as an expense each year of its useful life.

____ **15.** The asset account credited when recording the depreciation of a fixed asset.

____ **16.** The difference between the cost of a fixed asset and its accumulated depreciation.

____ **17.** The trial balance prepared after all the adjusting entries have been posted.

____ **18.** An analysis that compares each item in a current statement with a total amount within the same statement.

____ **19.** An account offset against another account.

FILL IN THE BLANK—PART A

Instructions: Answer the following questions or complete the statements by writing the appropriate words or amounts in the answer blanks.

1. The _____ _____ concept assumes that the economic life of the business can be divided into time periods.

2. Under the _____ basis of accounting, revenues and expenses are reported in the income statement in the period in which cash is received or paid.

3. The _____ _____ concept supports reporting revenues when the services are provided to customers.

4. _____ journal entries bring the accounts up to date at the end of the accounting period.

5. Items that have been initially recorded as assets but are expected to become expenses over time or through the normal operations of the business are called _____ _____.

6. Expenses that have been incurred *but have not been recorded* in the accounts are called _____ _____.

7. The _____ _____ account is debited for the amount of prepaid advertising expense expired during the period.

8. The _____ _____—_____ account is credited for the amount of depreciation of equipment during the period.

9. The _____ _____ account is debited for the amount of unearned fees that have been earned during the period.

10. The _____ _____ account is credited for taxes accrued at the end of the period.

11. If the adjusting entry to record depreciation expense on equipment is omitted, the net income for the period will be _____.

12. If the adjusting entry to record accrued fees earned at the end of the period is omitted, the retained earnings will be _____ on the balance sheet.

13. If the adjusting entry to record accrued wages expense at the end of the period is omitted, the liabilities will be _____ on the balance sheet.

14. If the balance of the supplies account on January 1 is $2,500, supplies purchased during the year were $10,000, and the supplies on hand at December 31 were $1,800, the amount for the appropriate adjusting entry at December 31 is _____.

15. The prepaid insurance account has a debit balance of $1,200 at the end of the year. If unexpired insurance at the end of the year is $800, the amount of prepaid insurance that should be reported on the end-of-year balance sheet is _____.

16. Physical resources that are owned and used by a business and are permanent or have a long life are called _____ _____.

17. The portion of the cost of a fixed asset that is recorded as an expense each year of its useful life is called _____.

18. The difference between the cost of a fixed asset and its accumulated depreciation is called the _____ _____ of the asset.

19. The net income reported on the income statement is $90,000. However, adjusting entries have not been made at the end of the period for insurance expense of $550 and accrued salaries of $750. The correct net income should have been _____.

20. The _____ trial balance is prepared after all the adjusting entries have been posted.

FILL IN THE BLANK—PART B

Instructions: Answer the following questions or complete the statements by writing the appropriate words or amounts in the answer blanks.

1. Under the _____ basis of accounting, revenues are reported in the income statement in the period in which they are earned.

2. The _____ concept supports the reporting of revenues and the related expenses in the same period.

3. An analysis and updating of the accounts when financial statements are prepared is called the _____ process.

4. Items that have been initially recorded as liabilities but are expected to become revenues over time or through the normal operations of the business are called _____ _____.

5. Revenues that have been earned *but have not been recorded* in the accounts are called _____ _____.

6. The decrease in the ability of a fixed asset to provide useful services is called _____.

7. The _____ _____ account is credited when recording depreciation of a fixed asset.

8. If the adjusting entry to record accrued interest revenue is omitted, the total assets will be _____ on the balance sheet.

9. If the adjusting entry to record the amount of prepaid insurance that has expired during the period is omitted, the stockholders' equity will be _____ on the balance sheet.

10. The _____ _____ account is debited for the amount of accrued interest expense at the end of the period.

11. The _____ _____ account is credited for the amount of prepaid rent that has expired during the period.

12. The _____ _____ account is debited for the amount of depreciation on equipment during the period.

13. The _____ _____ account is credited for the amount of accrued fees at the end of the period.

14. _____ analysis compares each item in a current statement with a total amount within the same statement.

15. If the debit amount of an adjusting entry adjusts an income statement account, the credit amount of the adjusting entry must adjust a(n) _____ _____ account.

16. If the credit amount of an adjusting entry adjusts an asset account, the debit amount of the adjusting entry must adjust a(n) _____ account.

17. If the adjusting entry to record the amount of prepaid insurance that has expired during the period is omitted, the net income for the period will be _____.

18. If the adjusting entry to record depreciation on equipment for the period is omitted, total assets will be _____ on the balance sheet.

19. If the balance of the supplies account on January 1 was $500, supplies purchased during the year were $1,750, and the supplies on hand at December 31 were $300, the amount for the appropriate adjusting entry at December 31 is _____.

20. The prepaid insurance account has a debit balance of $3,600 at the beginning of the year. If unexpired insurance at the end of the year is $2,800, the amount of insurance expense that should be reported on the income statement is _____.

MULTIPLE CHOICE

Instructions: Circle the best answer for each of the following questions.

1. Entries required at the end of an accounting period to bring the accounts up to date and to assure the proper matching of revenues and expenses are called:

    a. matching entries

    b. adjusting entries

    c. contra entries

    d. correcting entries

2. The amount of accrued but unpaid expenses at the end of the fiscal period is both an expense and a(n):

    a. liability

    b. asset

    c. deferral

    d. revenue

3. If the effect of the debit portion of an adjusting entry is to increase the balance of an expense account, which of the following describes the effect of the credit portion of the entry?

    a. decreases the balance of a contra asset account

    b. increases the balance of an asset account

    c. decreases the balance of an asset account

    d. increases the balance of an expense account

4. If the effect of the credit portion of an adjusting entry is to increase the balance of a liability account, which of the following describes the effect of the debit portion of the entry?

    a. increases the balance of a contra asset account

    b. increases the balance of an asset account

    c. decreases the balance of an asset account

    d. increases the balance of an expense account

5. The balance in the prepaid rent account before adjustment at the end of the year is $12,000, which represents three months' rent paid on December 1. The adjusting entry required on December 31 is:

    a. debit Prepaid Rent, $4,000; credit Rent Expense, $4,000

    b. debit Rent Expense, $4,000; credit Prepaid Rent, $4,000

    c. debit Prepaid Rent, $8,000; credit Rent Expense, $8,000

    d. debit Rent Expense, $8,000; credit Prepaid Rent, $8,000

6. At the end of the preceding fiscal year, the usual adjusting entry for accrued salaries owed to employees was omitted. The error was not corrected, but the accrued salaries were included in the first salary payment in the current fiscal year. Which of the following statements is true?

    a. Salary Expense was overstated and net income was understated for the current year.

    b. Salaries Payable is understated at the end of the current fiscal year.

    c. Salary Expense was overstated and net income was understated for the preceding year.

    d. Salary Expense and Salaries Payable were overstated for the preceding year.

7. The decrease in usefulness of fixed assets as time passes is called:

    a. consumption

    b. deterioration

    c. depreciation

    d. contra asset

8. The difference between the fixed asset account and the related accumulated depreciation account is called the:

    a. book value of the asset

    b. fair market value of the asset

    c. net cost of the asset

    d. contra account balance of the asset

9. If a $250 adjustment for depreciation is not recorded, which of the following financial statement errors will occur?

    a. Expenses will be overstated.

    b. Net income will be understated.

    c. Assets will be understated.

    d. Retained earnings will be overstated.

10. The net income reported on the income statement is $50,000. However, adjusting entries have not been made at the end of the period for supplies expense of $500 and accrued salaries of $1,300. Net income, as corrected, is:

    a. $48,200

    b. $48,700

    c. $50,500

    d. $51,800

TRUE/FALSE

Instructions: Indicate whether each of the following statements is true or false by placing a check mark in the appropriate column.

		True	False
1.	Most businesses use the accrual basis of accounting.........	____	____
2.	When the reduction in prepaid expenses is not properly recorded, this causes the asset accounts and expense accounts to be overstated..	____	____
3.	Accumulated depreciation accounts may be referred to as contra asset accounts.	____	____
4.	If the adjusting entry to record accrued wages at the end of the year is omitted, net income, retained earnings, and total assets will be overstated.	____	____
5.	If the debit portion of an adjusting entry debits an expense, the credit portion must credit either a contra asset, an asset, or a liability account...	____	____
6.	The adjusting entry to record depreciation of fixed assets consists of a debit to a depreciation expense account and a credit to an accumulated depreciation account.	____	____
7.	When expenses, such as employee wages, are not paid for until after they have been performed, the accrued expense is recorded in the accounts by an adjusting entry at the end of the accounting period......................................	____	____
8.	A deferral is an expense that has not been paid or a revenue that has not been received..	____	____
9.	Accrued expenses may be described on the balance sheet as accrued liabilities..	____	____
10.	The amount of accrued revenue is recorded by debiting a liability account and crediting a revenue account.	____	____

EXERCISE 3-1

Don Taylor closes the books of Taylor Inc. at the end of each year (December 31). On May 1 of the current year, Don insured the business assets for three years at a premium of $5,400.

Instructions:

(1) Using the T accounts below, enter the adjusting entry that should be made by Taylor Inc. as of December 31 to record the amount of insurance expired as of that date. The May 1 premium payment is recorded in the T accounts.

Cash	Prepaid Insurance	Insurance Expense
May 1 5,400	May 1 5,400	

(2) Taylor Inc.'s balance sheet as of December 31 should show the asset value of the unexpired insurance as .... $ _____

(3) Taylor Inc.'s income statement for the year ended December 31 should show insurance expense of .... $ _____

EXERCISE 3-2

Jan Olin closes the books of Olin Corp. at the end of each month. Olin Corp. has only one employee, who is paid at the rate of $50 per day. The employee is paid every Friday at the end of the day. Each workweek is composed of five days, starting on Monday. Assume that the Fridays of this month (October) fall on the 7th, 14th, 21st, and 28th.

Instructions:

(1) Using the T accounts below, enter the four weekly wage payments for October. Then enter the adjusting entry that should be made by Olin Corp. as of October 31 to record the salary owed the employee but unpaid as of that date.

Cash	Salary Expense	Salaries Payable

(2) Olin Corp.'s income statement for October should show total salary expense of .... $ _____

(3) Olin Corp.'s balance sheet as of October 31 should show a liability for salaries payable of .... $ _____

EXERCISE 3-3

Keller Inc.'s unearned rent account has an unadjusted balance of $6,000 as of December 31 of the current year. This amount represents the rental of an apartment for a period of one year. The lease began on December 1 of the current year.

Instructions: Using the T accounts below, record the adjusting entry as of December 31 to recognize the rent income for the appropriate portion of the year. Then journalize the entry.

Unearned Rent	Rent Revenue
Dec. 1 6,000	

JOURNAL   PAGE

	DATE		DESCRIPTION	POST. REF.	DEBIT	CREDIT	
1							1
2							2
3							3
4							4
5							5
6							6
7							7
8							8
9							9
10							10
11							11
12							12
13							13
14							14

EXERCISE 3-4

Garret Corp. has accrued but uncollected interest of $320 as of December 31 on a note receivable.

Instructions: Using the T accounts below, record the adjusting entry for accrued interest income as of December 31. Then journalize the entry.

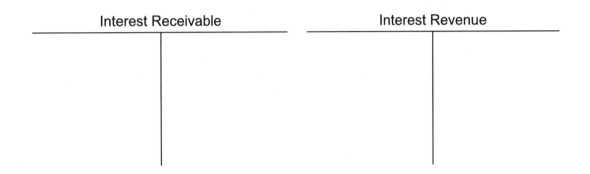

Interest Receivable

Interest Revenue

JOURNAL   PAGE

	DATE	DESCRIPTION	POST. REF.	DEBIT	CREDIT	
1						1
2						2
3						3
4						4
5						5
6						6
7						7
8						8
9						9
10						10
11						11
12						12
13						13
14						14

PROBLEM 3-1

An unadjusted trial balance for Bob's Service Inc. as of July 31, 20-- is shown below.

Bob's Service Inc.
Unadjusted Trial Balance
July 31, 20--

Cash	9,218	
Accounts Receivable	7,277	
Supplies	2,750	
Prepaid Rent	8,712	
Tools & Equipment	21,829	
Accumulated Depreciation		1,535
Accounts Payable		7,117
Capital Stock		10,000
Retained Earnings		27,417
Dividends	3,234	
Service Fees		28,699
Salary Expense	15,929	
Miscellaneous Expense	5,819	
	74,768	74,768

The data needed to determine end-of-month adjustments are as follows:

(a) Salaries accrued but not paid at the end of the month amount to $2,000.

(b) The $8,712 debit in the prepaid rent account is the payment of one year's rent on July 1.

(c) The supplies on hand as of July 31 cost $1,000.

(d) Depreciation of the tools and equipment for July is estimated at $400.

(e) Unrecorded fees for service rendered in July but collected in August amount to $2,100.

Instructions:

(1) Journalize the adjusting entries. Add additional accounts as needed.

(2) Determine the balances of the accounts affected by the adjusting entries and prepare an adjusted trial balance.

(1)   **JOURNAL**   PAGE

	DATE		DESCRIPTION	POST. REF.	DEBIT	CREDIT	
1							1
2							2
3							3
4							4
5							5
6							6
7							7
8							8
9							9
10							10
11							11
12							12
13							13
14							14
15							15
16							16
17							17
18							18
19							19
20							20
21							21
22							22
23							23
24							24
25							25
26							26
27							27
28							28
29							29
30							30
31							31
32							32
33							33
34							34
35							35
36							36

(2)

Completing the Accounting Cycle

QUIZ AND TEST HINTS

The following hints may be helpful to you in preparing for a quiz or a test over the material covered in Chapter 4.

1. Terminology is important in this chapter. Do the Matching exercises included in this Study Guide.

2. The preparation of the work sheet is an important part of this chapter. Although most instructors will not require you to prepare a work sheet from scratch, a test question might include a partially completed work sheet that you would be asked to complete.

3. Be thoroughly familiar with the financial statements presented in Exhibit 6 in the text. Know the financial statement captions and how the statements tie together. In a test situation, you may be provided with partially completed financial statements that you would be asked to complete.

4. You should be able to prepare the formal adjusting entries and closing entries in general journal form. You may have to prepare these entries from a completed work sheet.

5. The accounting cycle is an essential part of accounting. Expect multiple-choice or other types of short answer questions related to the accounting cycle.

6. Your instructor may or may not have discussed the material in the end-of-chapter appendix on reversing entries. If your instructor covered the appendix, you should know what adjusting entries normally require reversing entries and be able to prepare reversing entries.

MATCHING

Instructions: Match each of the statements below with its proper term. Some terms may not be used.

A.	accounting cycle	**L.**	note receivable
B.	adjusted trial balance	**M.**	owner's equity
C.	adjusting entries	**N.**	permanent assets
D.	closing entries	**O.**	post-closing trial balance
E.	current assets	**P.**	property, plant, and equipment
F.	current liabilities	**Q.**	real accounts
G.	current ratio	**R.**	solvency
H.	fiscal year	**S.**	temporary accounts
I.	Income Summary	**T.**	work sheet
J.	long-term liabilities	**U.**	working capital
K.	natural business year		

_____ **1.** A working paper that accountants may use to summarize adjusting entries and the account balances for the financial statements.

_____ **2.** Cash and other assets that are expected to be converted to cash or sold or used up, usually within one year or less, through the normal operations of the business.

_____ **3.** A customer's written promise to pay an amount and possibly interest at an agreed-upon rate.

_____ **4.** Liabilities that will be due within a short time (usually one year or less) and that are to be paid out of current assets.

_____ **5.** Liabilities that usually will not be due for more than one year.

_____ **6.** An account to which the revenue and expense account balances are transferred at the end of a period.

_____ **7.** The trial balance prepared after the closing entries have been posted.

_____ **8.** The annual accounting period adopted by a business.

_____ **9.** A fiscal year that ends when business activities have reached the lowest point in an annual operating cycle.

_____ **10.** The process that begins with analyzing and journalizing transactions and ends with the post-closing trial balance.

_____ **11.** The ability of a business to pay its debts.

_____ **12.** The excess of the current assets of a business over its current liabilities.

_____ **13.** A financial ratio that is computed by dividing current assets by current liabilities.

_____ **14.** The entries that transfer the balances of the revenue, expense, and dividends accounts to the retained earnings account.

___ **15.** The section of the balance sheet that includes equipment, machinery, buildings, and land.

___ **16.** Accounts that report amounts for only one period.

FILL IN THE BLANK—PART A

Instructions: Answer the following questions or complete the statements by writing the appropriate words or amounts in the answer blanks.

1. A(n) _____ _____ is a working paper that accountants may use to summarize adjusting entries and the account balances for the financial statements.

2. A(n) _____ _____ is a customer's written promise to pay an amount and possibly interest at an agreed rate.

3. Liabilities that will be due within a short time (usually one year or less) and that are to be paid out of current assets are called _____ _____.

4. In completing the work sheet, the adjusted trial balance amount for office equipment is extended to the _____ _____ Debit column.

5. In completing the work sheet, the adjusted trial balance amount for the dividends account is extended to the _____ _____ Debit column.

6. After all of the account balances have been extended to the Income Statement columns of the work sheet, the totals of the Debit and Credit columns are $89,900 and $99,500, respectively. The difference of $9,600 is the _____ _____ for the period.

7. After all of the account balances have been extended to the Balance Sheet columns of the work sheet, the totals of the Debit and Credit columns are $94,300 and $110,500, respectively. The difference of $16,200 is the _____ _____ for the period.

8. Revenue and expense account balances are transferred to the _____ _____ account at the end of a period.

9. The dividends account is closed at the end of the period by crediting it for its balance and debiting the _____ _____ account.

10. The fees earned account is closed at the end of the period by debiting it for its balance and crediting the _____ _____ account.

11. The income summary account (net income) is closed at the end of the period by debiting it for its balance and crediting the _____ _____ account.

12. The trial balance prepared after the closing entries have been posted is called the _____-_____ trial balance.

13. A fiscal year that ends when business activities have reached the lowest point in the annual operating cycle is called the _____ _____ _____.

14. The _____ _____ begins with analyzing and journalizing transactions and ends with the post-closing trial balance.

15. The excess of the current assets over current liabilities is called the _____ _____ of a business.

FILL IN THE BLANK—PART B

Instructions: Answer the following questions or complete the statements by writing the appropriate words or amounts in the answer blanks.

1. Cash and other assets that are expected to be converted to cash or sold or used up within one year or less through the normal operations of the business are classified on the balance sheet as _____ _____.

2. The _____, _____, and _____, section of the balance sheet includes equipment, machinery, buildings, and land.

3. Liabilities that will not be due for usually more than one year are classified on the balance sheet as _____-_____ _____.

4. In completing the work sheet, the adjusted trial balance amount for depreciation expense is extended to the _____ _____ Debit column.

5. In completing the work sheet, the adjusted trial balance amount for the fees earned account is extended to the _____ _____ Credit column.

6. After all of the account balances have been extended to the Income Statement columns of the work sheet, the totals of the Debit and Credit columns are $120,000 and $115,000, respectively. The difference of $5,000 is the _____ _____ for the period.

7. After all of the account balances have been extended to the Balance Sheet columns of the work sheet, the totals of the Debit and Credit columns are $280,000 and $240,000, respectively. The difference of $40,000 is the _____ _____ for the period.

8. The _____ _____ transfer the balances of the revenue, expense, and dividends accounts to the retained earnings account.

9. Revenue and expense account balances are transferred to the _____ _____ account at the end of a period.

10. The dividends account is closed at the end of the period by crediting it and debiting the _____ _____ account.

11. The office salaries expense account is closed at the end of the period by crediting it and debiting the _____ _____ account.

12. The income summary account (net loss) is closed at the end of the period by crediting it and debiting the _____ _____ account.

13. The _____ _____ is the annual accounting period adopted by a business.

14. _____ refers to the ability of a business to pays its debts.

15. The _____ ratio is computed by dividing current assets by current liabilities.

MULTIPLE CHOICE

Instructions: Circle the best answer for each of the following questions.

1. Notes receivable are written claims against:
   a. creditors
   b. owner's equity
   c. customers
   d. assets

2. A work sheet is completed by:
   a. extending the adjusted trial balance amounts to the Income Statement and Balance Sheet columns
   b. totaling the Adjustment columns
   c. extending the work sheet adjustments to the Adjusted Trial Balance columns
   d. all the above

3. If the Income Statement Credit column is greater than the Income Statement Debit column:
   a. a net income exists
   b. a net loss exists
   c. an asset account is debited
   d. a liability account is credited

4. After all of the account balances have been extended to the Balance Sheet columns of the work sheet, the totals of the Debit and Credit columns are $377,750 and $387,750, respectively. What is the amount of net income or net loss for the period?

   a. $10,000 net income

   b. $10,000 net loss

   c. $377,750 net income

   d. $388,750 net income

5. After all of the account balances have been extended to the Income Statement columns of the work sheet, the totals of the Debit and Credit columns are $62,300 and $67,600, respectively. What is the amount of the net income or net loss for the period?

   a. $5,300 net income

   b. $5,300 net loss

   c. $119,300 net income

   d. $119,300 net loss

6. Which of the following accounts should be closed to Income Summary at the end of the fiscal year?

   a. Dividends

   b. Accumulated Depreciation—Equipment

   c. Sales

   d. Accounts Payable

7. Which of the following accounts will be closed at the end of the fiscal year by debiting Retained Earnings?

   a. Salaries Expense

   b. Sales

   c. Dividends

   d. Accounts Receivable

8. Which of the following accounts will ordinarily appear in the post-closing trial balance?

   a. Salaries Expense

   b. Dividends

   c. Sales

   d. Capital Stock

9. The maximum length of an accounting period is normally:

   a. 6 months

   b. 1 year

   c. 2 years

   d. 3 years

10. The complete sequence of accounting procedures for a fiscal period is frequently called the:

   a. work sheet process

   b. opening and closing cycle

   c. accounting cycle

   d. fiscal cycle

TRUE/FALSE

Instructions: Indicate whether each of the following statements is true or false by placing a check mark in the appropriate column.

	True	False

1. The balance of Accumulated Depreciation—Equipment is extended to the Income Statement columns of the work sheet. .... ____ ____

2. The difference between the Debit and Credit columns of the Income Statement section of the work sheet is normally larger than the difference between the Debit and Credit columns of the Balance Sheet section. .... ____ ____

3. The first item normally presented in the retained earnings statement is the balance of the retained earnings account at the beginning of the period. .... ____ ____

4. The balance that is transferred from the income summary account to the retained earnings account is the net income or net loss for the period. .... ____ ____

5. The balances of the accounts reported in the balance sheet are carried from year to year and are called temporary accounts. .... ____ ____

6. An account titled Income Summary is normally used for transferring the revenue and expense account balances to the retained earnings account at the end of the period. ...... ____ ____

7. If the Income Statement Debit column is greater than the Income Statement Credit column, the difference is net income. .... ____ ____

8. A type of working paper frequently used by accountants prior to the preparation of financial statements is called a post-closing trial balance. .... ____ ____

9. At the end of the period, the balances are removed from the temporary accounts and the net effect is recorded in the permanent account by means of closing entries. .... ____ ____

10. The annual accounting period adopted by a business is known as its fiscal year. .... ____ ____

EXERCISE 4-1

The account titles and Adjustments columns of the work sheet for Sally's Small Engine Repair Corp. are listed below.

Sally's Small Engine Repair Corp.
Work Sheet
For Month Ended August 31, 20--

	Adjustments			
	Debit		Credit	
Cash				
Accounts Receivable	(e)	3,200		
Supplies			(c)	700
Prepaid Rent			(b)	560
Tools/Equipment				
Accumulated Depreciation			(d)	1,000
Accounts Payable				
Capital Stock				
Retained Earnings				
Dividends				
Repair Fees			(e)	3,200
Salary Expense	(a)	1,500		
Miscellaneous Expense				
Salaries Payable			(a)	1,500
Rent Expense	(b)	560		
Supplies Expense	(c)	700		
Depreciation Expense	(d)	1,000		

Instructions: Prepare journal entries for the adjustments indicated for Sally's Small Engine Repair Corp.

JOURNAL

PAGE

	DATE		DESCRIPTION	POST. REF.	DEBIT	CREDIT	
1							1
2							2
3							3
4							4
5							5
6							6
7							7
8							8
9							9
10							10
11							11
12							12
13							13
14							14

EXERCISE 4-2

Instructions: The journal, the income summary account, the service fees account, the salary expense account, and the supplies expense account of Brown Inc. as of March 31, the first month of the current fiscal year, follow. In the journal, prepare the entries to close Brown Inc.'s revenue and expense accounts into the income summary account. Then post to the ledger.

JOURNAL   PAGE 7

	DATE	DESCRIPTION	POST. REF.	DEBIT	CREDIT	
1						1
2						2
3						3
4						4
5						5
6						6
7						7
8						8
9						9
10						10
11						11
12						12
13						13
14						14
15						15

ACCOUNT   *Income Summary*   ACCOUNT NO.   *45*

DATE	ITEM	POST. REF.	DEBIT	CREDIT	BALANCE DEBIT	BALANCE CREDIT

ACCOUNT   *Service Fees*   ACCOUNT NO.   *50*

DATE		ITEM	POST. REF.	DEBIT	CREDIT	BALANCE	
						DEBIT	CREDIT
20-- Mar.	15		5		4 8 5 0		4 8 5 0
	31		6		14 3 7 5		19 2 2 5

ACCOUNT   *Salary Expense*   ACCOUNT NO.   *58*

DATE		ITEM	POST. REF.	DEBIT	CREDIT	BALANCE	
						DEBIT	CREDIT
20-- Mar.	31		5	8 5 5 0		8 5 5 0	

ACCOUNT   *Supplies Expense*   ACCOUNT NO.   *67*

DATE		ITEM	POST. REF.	DEBIT	CREDIT	BALANCE	
						DEBIT	CREDIT
20-- Mar.	15		5	2 4 3 0		2 4 3 0	
	25		6	1 7 2 0		4 1 5 0	
	31		6	1 2 8 0		5 4 3 0	

PROBLEM 4-1

The partially completed ten-column work sheet of Castle Shop Inc. for the fiscal year ended April 30, 20--, appears on the following pages. The following adjustment data have been entered in the Adjustments columns of the work sheet:

(a) Supplies on hand as of April 30, 20--, $1,800.

(b) Rent prepaid for 12 months on April 1, $9,504.

(c) Depreciation on tools and equipment during the year, $1,000.

(d) Wages accrued but not paid as of April 30, 20--, $2,000.

(e) Accrued fees earned but not recorded as of April 30, 20--, $3,000.

(f) Unearned fees as of April 30, 20--, $1,500.

Instructions:

(1) Complete the ten-column work sheet contained on the next two pages.

(2) Prepare an income statement, retained earnings statement, and a balance sheet using the forms on the following pages.

(1) *Castle*

Work

For the Year

	ACCOUNT TITLE	TRIAL BALANCE		ADJUSTMENTS		
		DEBIT	CREDIT	DEBIT	CREDIT	
1	Cash	10056				1
2	Accounts Receivable	7938		(e) 3000		2
3	Supplies	3000			(a) 1200	3
4	Prepaid Rent	9504			(b) 792	4
5	Tools & Equipment	23814				5
6	Accumulated Depreciation		1674		(c) 1000	6
7	Accounts Payable		7764			7
8	Unearned Fees		2000	(f) 500		8
9	Capital Stock		10000			9
10	Retained Earnings		28818			10
11	Dividends	3528				11
12	Service Fees		31308		(e) 3000	12
13					(f) 500	13
14	Wages Expense	17376		(d) 2000		14
15	Miscellaneous Expense	6348				15
16		81564	81564			16
17						17
18	Wages Payable				(d) 2000	18
19	Rent Expense			(b) 792		19
20	Supplies Expense			(a) 1200		20
21	Depreciation Expense			(c) 1000		21
22				8492	8492	22
23						23
24						24
25						25
26						26
27						27
28						28
29						29
30						30
31						31
32						32
33						33
34						34

Shop Inc.

Sheet

Ended April 30, 20--

	ADJUSTED TRIAL BALANCE		INCOME STATEMENT		BALANCE SHEET		
	DEBIT	CREDIT	DEBIT	CREDIT	DEBIT	CREDIT	
1							1
2							2
3							3
4							4
5							5
6							6
7							7
8							8
9							9
10							10
11							11
12							12
13							13
14							14
15							15
16							16
17							17
18							18
19							19
20							20
21							21
22							22
23							23
24							24
25							25
26							26
27							27
28							28
29							29
30							30
31							31
32							32
33							33
34							34

(2)

Income Statement

Retained Earnings Statement

Balance Sheet

PROBLEM 4-2

Instructions:

(1) On the basis of the data in the Adjustments columns of the work sheet in Problem 4-1, journalize the adjusting entries.

(2) On the basis of the data in the Income Statement and Balance Sheet columns of the work sheet in Problem 4-1, journalize the closing entries.

JOURNAL

PAGE

	DATE	DESCRIPTION	POST. REF.	DEBIT	CREDIT	
1						1
2						2
3						3
4						4
5						5
6						6
7						7
8						8
9						9
10						10
11						11
12						12
13						13
14						14
15						15
16						16
17						17
18						18
19						19
20						20
21						21
22						22
23						23
24						24
25						25
26						26
27						27
28						28
29						29

JOURNAL

	DATE		DESCRIPTION	POST. REF.	DEBIT	CREDIT	
1							1
2							2
3							3
4							4
5							5
6							6
7							7
8							8
9							9
10							10
11							11
12							12
13							13
14							14
15							15
16							16
17							17
18							18
19							19
20							20
21							21
22							22
23							23
24							24
25							25
26							26
27							27
28							28
29							29
30							30
31							31
32							32
33							33
34							34
35							35
36							36

5 Accounting for Merchandising Businesses

QUIZ AND TEST HINTS

The following hints may be helpful to you in preparing for a quiz or a test over the material covered in Chapter 5.

1. This chapter introduces merchandising business terminology that you should know. Do the Matching exercises included in this Study Guide.

2. A major portion of this chapter describes the preparation of financial statements for a merchandising business. Particular emphasis may be placed on determining the cost of merchandise sold and preparing the income statement. Practice preparing the financial statements for NetSolutions. Your instructor may provide partially completed financial statements, and you will be required to complete the statements.

3. You should be able to prepare general journal entries for the types of transactions illustrated in the chapter. Be sure you can compute purchases discounts and sales discounts. Review the chapter illustrations. The Illustrative Problem in the Chapter Review is an excellent review of the types of entries you might have to prepare.

4. The accounting for transportation costs can be confusing, but you will probably be required to prepare one or more journal entries, or answer one or more multiple-choice questions, involving such costs. Review the chapter discussion and illustration related to such costs.

5. The illustration of the journal entries for both the buyer and seller of merchandise on pages 196–202 of the chapter provides an excellent review. Often, instructors will require students to prepare journal entries based upon the same data for both the buyer and the seller.

6. Review the chart of accounts for a merchandising business as a basis for distinguishing the types of accounts used by merchandising businesses.

7. You should be able to prepare the adjusting and closing entries for a merchandising business. These entries are similar to those you prepared in earlier chapters.

8. If your instructor lectures on preparing a merchandising work sheet from the appendix to the chapter, you may expect some questions related to the work sheet. Oftentimes instructors provide a partially completed work sheet and

require students to complete it. You may find it a helpful exercise to cover up portions of Exhibit 12 and see if you know how to complete the covered sections. Except for the merchandising-related accounts, a merchandising business work sheet is similar to others you have prepared.

9. If your instructor lectures on the periodic inventory system using the appendix at the end of the text, you may have to prepare journal entries, a work sheet, and financial statements using this system.

MATCHING

Instructions: Match each of the statements below with its proper term. Some terms may not be used.

A. account form
B. administrative expenses (general expenses)
C. controlling account
D. cost of merchandise sold
E. credit memorandum
F. debit memorandum
G. FOB (free on board) destination
H. FOB (free on board) shipping point
I. general ledger
J. gross profit
K. income from operations (operating income)
L. inventory shrinkage
M. invoice
N. loss from operations

O. merchandise inventory
P. multiple-step income statement
Q. other expense
R. other income
S. periodic inventory system
T. perpetual inventory system
U. physical inventory
V. purchases discounts
W. purchases return or allowance
X. report form
Y. sales discounts
Z. sales return or allowance
AA. selling expenses
BB. single-step income statement
CC. subsidiary ledger
DD. trade discounts

____ 1. The cost that is reported as an expense when merchandise is sold.

____ 2. Sales minus the cost of merchandise sold.

____ 3. Merchandise on hand (not sold) at the end of an accounting period.

____ 4. The account in the general ledger that summarizes the balances of the accounts in a subsidiary ledger.

____ 5. The primary ledger, when used in conjunction with subsidiary ledgers, that contains all of the balance sheet and income statement accounts.

____ 6. A ledger containing individual accounts with a common characteristic.

____ 7. The inventory system in which each purchase and sale of merchandise is recorded in an inventory account.

____ 8. The inventory system in which the inventory records do not show the amount available for sale or sold during the period.

____ 9. A detailed listing of the merchandise for sale at the end of an accounting period.

____ 10. The bill that the seller sends to the buyer.

____ 11. Discounts taken by the buyer for early payment of an invoice.

____ 12. From the buyer's perspective, returned merchandise or an adjustment for defective merchandise.

_____ **13.** A form used by a buyer to inform the seller of the amount the buyer proposes to debit to the account payable due the seller.

_____ **14.** From the seller's perspective, discounts that a seller may offer the buyer for early payment.

_____ **15.** From the seller's perspective, returned merchandise or an adjustment for defective merchandise.

_____ **16.** A form used by a seller to inform the buyer of the amount the seller proposes to credit to the account receivable due from the buyer.

_____ **17.** Discounts from the list prices in published catalogs or special discounts offered to certain classes of buyers.

_____ **18.** Freight terms in which the buyer pays the transportation costs from the shipping point to the final destination.

_____ **19.** Freight terms in which the seller pays the transportation costs from the shipping point to the final destination.

_____ **20.** A form of income statement that contains several sections, subsections, and subtotals.

_____ **21.** Expenses that are incurred directly in the selling of merchandise.

_____ **22.** Expenses incurred in the administration or general operations of the business.

_____ **23.** The excess of gross profit over total operating expenses.

_____ **24.** The excess of operating expenses over gross profit.

_____ **25.** Revenue from sources other than the primary operating activity of a business.

_____ **26.** Expenses that cannot be traced directly to operations.

_____ **27.** A form of income statement in which the total of all expenses is deducted from the total of all revenues.

_____ **28.** The amount by which the merchandise for sale, as indicated by the balance of the merchandise inventory account, is larger than the total amount of merchandise counted during the physical inventory.

_____ **29.** The form of balance sheet in which assets are reported on the left-hand side and the liabilities and stockholders' equity on the right-hand side.

_____ **30.** The form of balance sheet in which assets, liabilities, and stockholders' equity are reported in a downward sequence.

FILL IN THE BLANK—PART A

Instructions: Answer the following questions or complete the statements by writing the appropriate words or amounts in the answer blanks.

1. The cost that is reported as an expense when merchandise is sold is called

   _____ _____ _____ _____.

2. _____ _____ is merchandise on hand (not sold) at the end of an accounting period.

3. The _____ account in the general ledger summarizes the balances of the accounts in a subsidiary ledger.

4. The _____ ledger, when used in conjunction with subsidiary ledgers, contains all of the income statement and balance sheet accounts.

5. The _____ inventory system does not show the amount available for sale or sold during the period.

6. Beginning merchandise inventory plus cost of merchandise purchased equals

   _____ _____ _____

   _____.

7. A buyer refers to returned merchandise or an adjustment for defective merchandise as a(n) _____ _____ _____

   _____.

8. A seller refers to discounts offered to the buyer for early payment as

   _____ _____.

9. A seller informs the buyer of the amount that they propose to credit to the buyer's account receivable by issuing a _____ memorandum.

10. If the buyer pays the transportation costs from the shipping point to the final destination, the freight terms are referred to as _____

    _____ _____.

11. A sales invoice for $5,000, terms 1/10, n/30, FOB shipping point, is paid within the discount period. Transportation costs of $75 are paid and added to the invoice. The amount of the discount is _____.

12. A return of $300 has been recorded against a purchase invoice of $3,300, terms 2/10, n/30. The invoice is paid within the discount period. The amount of the discount is _____.

13. Merchandise with a list price of $1,000 is sold with a trade discount of 30%, terms 2/10, n/30. The amount to be recorded in the sales account is

    _____.

14. The _____-_____ form of income statement contains several sections, subsections, and subtotals.

15. Expenses incurred in the administration or general operations of the business are reported on the income statement as _____ expenses.

16. The excess of operating expenses over gross profit is _____ _____ _____.

17. Expenses that cannot be traced directly to operations are reported on the income statement as _____ expenses.

18. The amount by which the merchandise for sale, as indicated by the balance of the merchandise inventory account, is larger than the total amount of merchandise counted during the physical inventory is referred to as _____ _____.

19. Balances of selected accounts at the end of the year, before adjustments, are as follows: Sales, $900,000; Sales Returns and Allowances, $50,000; Sales Discounts, $10,000; Cost of Merchandise Sold, $600,000; Selling Expenses, $80,000; Administrative Expenses, $25,500; Interest Revenue, $5,000; Interest Expense, $2,000. The gross profit is _____.

20. The _____ form of balance sheet reports assets, liabilities, and owner's equity in a downward sequence.

FILL IN THE BLANK—PART B

Instructions: Answer the following questions or complete the statements by writing the appropriate words or amounts in the answer blanks.

1. Sales minus cost of merchandise sold is called _____ _____.

2. A _____ ledger contains individual accounts with a common characteristic.

3. In the _____ inventory system each purchase and sale of merchandise is recorded in an inventory account when the transactions occur.

4. A(n) _____ _____ is a detailed listing of the merchandise for sale at the end of the accounting period.

5. A buyer refers to discounts taken for early payment of an invoice as _____ _____.

6. A buyer informs the seller of the amount the buyer proposes to debit to the seller's account payable by issuing a _____ memorandum.

7. A seller refers to returned merchandise or an adjustment for defective merchandise as a(n) _____ _____ _____ _____.

8. Discounts from the list prices in published catalogs or special discounts offered to certain classes of buyers are called _____ _____.

9. If the seller pays the transportation costs from the shipping point to the final destination, the freight terms are referred to as _____ _____.

10. A sales invoice for $8,000, terms 2/10, n/30, FOB shipping point, is paid within the discount period. Transportation costs of $125 are paid and added to the invoice. The amount of the discount is _____.

11. A sales invoice for $15,000, terms 1/10, n/30, FOB shipping point, is paid within the discount period. Transportation costs of $250 are paid and added to the invoice. The total amount paid by the buyer is _____.

12. A return of $500 has been recorded against a purchase invoice of $3,800, terms 1/10, n/30. The invoice is paid within the discount period. The amount of the discount is _____.

13. A buyer purchased merchandise for $10,000, terms 1/10, n/30, FOB destination. The seller pays transportation costs of $500. If the buyer pays the invoice within the discount period, the amount paid by the buyer is _____.

14. Merchandise with a list price of $12,000 is sold with a trade discount of 45%, terms 2/10, n/30. The amount to be recorded in the sales account is _____.

15. Expenses that are incurred directly in the selling of merchandise are reported on the income statement as _____ expenses.

16. The excess of gross profit over total operating expenses is _____ _____ _____.

17. Revenue from sources other than the primary operating activity of a business is reported on the income statement as _____ _____.

18. The _____-_____ form of income statement deducts the total of all expenses from the total of all revenues.

19. Balances of selected accounts at the end of the year, before adjustments, are as follows: Sales, $750,000; Sales Returns and Allowances, $25,000; Sales Discounts, $10,000; Cost of Merchandise Sold, $500,000; Selling Expenses, $80,000; Administrative Expenses, $20,000; Interest Revenue, $5,000; Interest Expense, $2,000. The gross profit is _____.

20. The _____ form of balance sheet reports assets on the left-hand side and the liabilities and owner's equity on the right-hand side.

MULTIPLE CHOICE

Instructions: Circle the best answer for each of the following questions.

1. The basic differences between the financial statements of a merchandising business and a service business include reporting cost of merchandise sold on the income statement and the:

    a. stockholders' equity section of the balance sheet

    b. other income section of the income statement

    c. inclusion of merchandise inventory on the balance sheet as a current asset

    d. inclusion of a retained earnings statement

2. A buyer receives an invoice for $60 dated June 10. If the terms are 2/10, n/30, and the buyer pays the invoice within the discount period, what amount will the seller receive?

    a. $60

    b. $58.80

    c. $48

    d. $1.20

3. When a seller of merchandise allows a customer a reduction from the original price for defective goods, the seller usually issues to the customer a(n):

    a. debit memorandum

    b. credit memorandum

    c. sales invoice

    d. inventory slip

4. When the seller prepays the transportation costs and the terms of sale are FOB shipping point, the seller records the payment of the transportation costs by debiting:

    a. Accounts Receivable

    b. Sales

    c. Transportation In

    d. Accounts Payable

5. If the seller collects sales tax at the time of sale, the seller credits the tax to:

    a. Sales

    b. Accounts Receivable

    c. Sales Tax Payable

    d. Sales Tax Receivable

6. The account that appears in the chart of accounts for a merchandising business but not for a service business is:

   a. Accounts Receivable

   b. Advertising Expense

   c. Sales Returns and Allowances

   d. Accumulated Depreciation

7. The excess of net revenue from sales over the cost of merchandise sold is called:

   a. gross profit

   b. operating profit

   c. net profit from operations

   d. merchandising income

8. Income from operations is computed by subtracting from gross profit the:

   a. selling expenses

   b. general expenses

   c. total administrative expenses

   d. total operating expenses

9. After all adjusting entries are posted, the balances of all asset, liability, revenue, and expense accounts correspond exactly to the amounts in the:

   a. work sheet trial balance

   b. general journal

   c. post-closing trial balance

   d. financial statements

10. In a multiple-step income statement of a merchandising business, which of the following would appear as "other income"?

    a. sales

    b. interest revenue

    c. sales discounts

    d. sales returns and allowances

TRUE/FALSE

Instructions: Indicate whether each of the following statements is true or false by placing a check mark in the appropriate column.

	True	False
1. The two main systems for accounting for merchandise held for sale are called periodic and perpetual.	____	____
2. In a perpetual inventory system, purchases of merchandise are recorded in the purchases account.	____	____
3. In a periodic inventory system, no attempt is made to record the cost of merchandise sold at the date of the sale.	____	____
4. A discount offered the purchaser of goods as a means of encouraging payment before the end of the credit period is known as a bank discount.	____	____
5. Credit terms of "2/10, n/30" mean that the buyer may deduct 2% of the amount of the invoice if payment is made within 10 days of the invoice date.	____	____
6. If the seller is to absorb the cost of delivering the goods, the terms are stated FOB (free on board) shipping point. ...	____	____
7. The liability for the sales tax is incurred at the time the seller receives payment from the buyer.	____	____
8. The purchases returns and allowances are credited to Merchandise Inventory.	____	____
9. The chart of accounts for a merchandising business will differ from that of a service business.	____	____
10. The work sheet procedures for a merchandising business are significantly different from those of a service business.	____	____
11. The physical inventory taken at the end of the period is normally larger than the amount of the balance of the merchandise inventory account.	____	____
12. Any merchandise inventory shrinkage is normally debited to the merchandise inventory account.	____	____
13. Expenses incurred directly and entirely in connection with the sale of merchandise are called administrative expenses.	____	____
14. Revenue from sources such as income from interest, rent, dividends, and gains resulting from the sale of fixed assets is classified as income from operations.	____	____

	True	False

15. The single-step form of income statement has the advantage of being simple, and it emphasizes total revenues and total expenses as the factors that determine net income. .... _____ _____

16. Gross profit is not calculated in the single-step form of income statement. .... _____ _____

17. The excess of gross profit over total operating expenses is called income from operations.. _____ _____

18. The traditional balance sheet arrangement of assets on the left-hand side with the liabilities and owner's equity on the right-hand side is called the report form. .... _____ _____

19. After the adjusting and closing entries have been recorded and posted, the general ledger accounts that appear on the balance sheet have no balances. .... _____ _____

20. The closing entries are recorded in the journal immediately following the adjusting entries. .... _____ _____

EXERCISE 5-1

The following information was taken from the records of Dawkins Co. for the year ended June 30, 2006.

Merchandise inventory, July 1, 2005	$130,000
Merchandise inventory, June 30, 2006	125,000
Purchases	600,000
Purchases returns and allowances	45,000
Purchases discounts	10,000
Sales	875,000
Transportation in	7,500

Instructions: Prepare a partial income statement for Dawkins Co. through the reporting of gross profit.

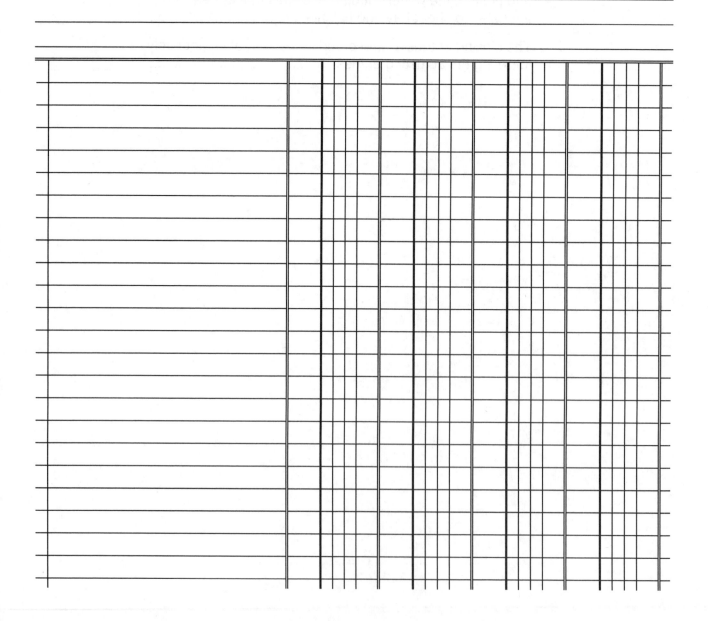

EXERCISE 5-2

Instructions: Prepare entries for each of the following related transactions of Foley Co. in the journal given below.

(1) Purchased $5,000 of merchandise from Phillips Co. on account, terms 2/10, n/30.

(2) Paid Phillips Co. on account for purchases, less discount.

(3) Purchased $3,500 of merchandise from Farris Co. on account, terms FOB shipping point, n/30, with prepaid shipping costs of $80 added to the invoice.

(4) Returned merchandise from Farris Co., $900.

(5) Paid Farris Co. on account for purchases, less return.

JOURNAL

PAGE

	DATE	DESCRIPTION	POST. REF.	DEBIT	CREDIT	
1						1
2						2
3						3
4						4
5						5
6						6
7						7
8						8
9						9
10						10
11						11
12						12
13						13
14						14
15						15
16						16
17						17
18						18
19						19
20						20
21						21
22						22
23						23
24						24

Exercise 5-3

Instructions: Prepare entries for each of the following related transactions of Wilson Co. in the journal given below.

(1) Sold merchandise on nonbank credit cards and reported accounts to the card company, $3,150. The cost of the merchandise sold was $2,000.

(2) Sold merchandise for cash, $2,850. The cost of the merchandise sold was $1,380.

(3) Received cash from card company for nonbank credit card sales, less $100 service fee.

(4) Sold merchandise on account to Rask Co., $4,500, terms 2/10, n/30, FOB shipping point. Prepaid transportation costs of $150 at the customer's request. The cost of the merchandise sold was $3,100.

(5) Received merchandise returned by Rask Co., $400. The cost of the merchandise returned was $275.

(6) Received cash on account from Rask Co. for sale and transportation costs, less returns and discount.

JOURNAL

PAGE

	DATE	DESCRIPTION	POST. REF.	DEBIT	CREDIT	
1						1
2						2
3						3
4						4
5						5
6						6
7						7
8						8
9						9
10						10
11						11
12						12
13						13
14						14
15						15
16						16
17						17
18						18
19						19

JOURNAL

	DATE		DESCRIPTION	POST. REF.	DEBIT	CREDIT	
1							1
2							2
3							3
4							4
5							5
6							6
7							7
8							8
9							9
10							10
11							11
12							12
13							13
14							14
15							15
16							16
17							17
18							18
19							19
20							20
21							21
22							22
23							23
24							24
25							25
26							26
27							27
28							28
29							29
30							30
31							31
32							32
33							33
34							34
35							35
36							36

EXERCISE 5-4

Baker Co. had the following purchases and sales transactions during the month of January.

Jan. 3. Purchased $25,000 of merchandise on account from Zeff Co., terms 2/10, n/30.

  5. Returned merchandise purchased on account from Zeff Co. on January 3, $5,000.

  12. Sold merchandise on account to Smith Co., $50,000, terms 1/10, n/30. The cost of the merchandise sold was $35,000.

  13. Paid Zeff Co. for purchase on January 3, on account, less return and discount.

  15. Received merchandise return on account from Smith Co., $8,000. The cost of the merchandise returned was $5,600.

  22. Received payment in full on account from Smith Co., less return and discount.

Instructions: Prepare journal entries for the preceding transactions.

JOURNAL   PAGE

	DATE	DESCRIPTION	POST. REF.	DEBIT	CREDIT	
1						1
2						2
3						3
4						4
5						5
6						6
7						7
8						8
9						9
10						10
11						11
12						12
13						13
14						14
15						15
16						16
17						17
18						18
19						19
20						20

JOURNAL

PAGE

	DATE		DESCRIPTION	POST. REF.	DEBIT	CREDIT	
1							1
2							2
3							3
4							4
5							5
6							6
7							7
8							8
9							9
10							10
11							11
12							12
13							13
14							14
15							15
16							16
17							17
18							18
19							19
20							20
21							21
22							22
23							23
24							24
25							25
26							26
27							27
28							28
29							29
30							30
31							31
32							32
33							33
34							34
35							35
36							36

PROBLEM 5-1

The following transactions were selected from among those completed by the Bowman Company during September of the current year:

Sept. 3. Purchased merchandise on account from Axel Co., list price $10,000, trade discount 15%, terms FOB destination, 1/10, n/30.

 4. Purchased office supplies for cash, $800.

 6. Sold merchandise on account to Hart Co., list price $5,000, trade discount 20%, terms 2/10, n/30. The cost of merchandise sold was $3,000.

 7. Returned $2,000 of the merchandise purchased on September 3 from Axel Co.

 10. Purchased merchandise for cash, $5,000.

 12. Sold merchandise on nonbank credit cards and reported accounts to the card company, $5,500. The cost of merchandise sold was $3,200.

 13. Paid Axel Co. on account for purchase of September 3, less return of September 7 and discount.

 16. Received cash on account from sale of September 6 to Hart Co., less discount.

 20. Received cash from card company for nonbank credit sales of September 12, less $300 service fee.

 24. Sold merchandise to Wilcox Co., $3,000, terms 1/10, n/30. The cost of merchandise sold was $1,750.

 26. Sold merchandise for cash, $2,200. The cost of merchandise sold was $1,400.

 30. Received merchandise returned by Wilcox Co. from sale on September 24, $1,000. The cost of the merchandise returned was $600.

Instructions: Journalize the transactions for the Bowman Co., using the journal forms provided below and on the following pages.

JOURNAL

PAGE

	DATE		DESCRIPTION	POST. REF.	DEBIT	CREDIT	
1							1
2							2
3							3
4							4
5							5
6							6
7							7
8							8
9							9

JOURNAL

PAGE

	DATE		DESCRIPTION	POST. REF.	DEBIT	CREDIT	
1							1
2							2
3							3
4							4
5							5
6							6
7							7
8							8
9							9
10							10
11							11
12							12
13							13
14							14
15							15
16							16
17							17
18							18
19							19
20							20
21							21
22							22
23							23
24							24
25							25
26							26
27							27
28							28
29							29
30							30
31							31
32							32
33							33
34							34
35							35
36							36

JOURNAL

PAGE

	DATE	DESCRIPTION	POST. REF.	DEBIT	CREDIT	
1						1
2						2
3						3
4						4
5						5
6						6
7						7
8						8
9						9
10						10
11						11

PROBLEM 5-2

The following accounts and their normal balances were taken from the general ledger of Miller Inc. after the adjusting entries have been posted for the fiscal year ending March 31.

Cash	49,620
Accounts Receivable	107,780
Merchandise Inventory	115,800
Office Supplies	1,250
Prepaid Insurance	8,740
Delivery Equipment	60,150
Accumulated Depreciation—Delivery Equipment	22,950
Accounts Payable	75,300
Salaries Payable	2,000
Capital Stock	50,000
Retained Earnings	143,650
Dividends	30,000
Sales	1,016,700
Sales Returns and Allowances	13,010
Cost of Merchandise Sold	681,060
Sales Salaries Expense	78,250
Advertising Expense	13,090
Delivery Expense	42,100
Depreciation Expense—Delivery Equipment	9,050
Miscellaneous Selling Expense	13,950
Office Salaries Expense	55,800
Office Supplies Expense	9,100
Insurance Expense	16,000
Miscellaneous Administrative Expenses	6,870
Interest Revenue	1,020

Instructions:

(a) Prepare a multiple-step income statement for Miller Inc.

(b) Prepare a single-step income statement for Miller Inc.

(c) Assume that the inventory shrinkage for Miller Inc. for the period ending March 31 was $4,200. Prepare the adjusting entry to record the inventory shrinkage.

(a)

Multiple-Step Income Statement

(b)

Single-Step Income Statement

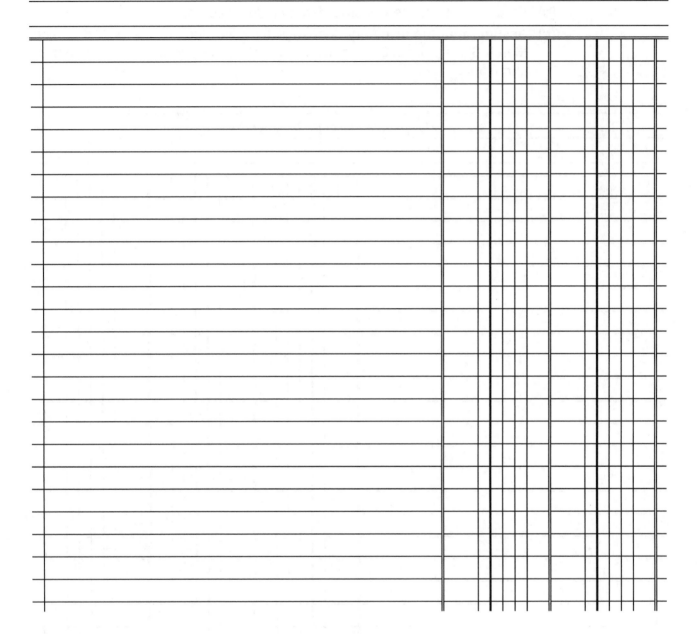

(c) **JOURNAL**

	DATE		DESCRIPTION	POST. REF.	DEBIT	CREDIT	
1							1
2							2
3							3
4							4
5							5
6							6

PROBLEM 5-3

Using the information in Problem 5-2, prepare a retained earnings statement for Miller Inc.

PROBLEM 5-4

Using the information in Problem 5-2, prepare a balance sheet in report form for Miller Inc. as of March 31, 20--.

6 Accounting Systems, Internal Controls, and Cash

Quiz and Test Hints

The following hints may be helpful to you in preparing for a quiz or a test over the material covered in Chapter 6.

1. You may expect some general terminology questions (usually true/false or multiple-choice) related to accounting systems and internal controls. Pay close attention to terms related to a business's internal control of cash receipts and cash payments. Do the Matching exercises included in this Study Guide.

2. You should be able to prepare a bank reconciliation of the type illustrated in the chapter. Instructors often include short bank reconciliations of the type shown in the Illustrative Problem of the text and in Problem 6-1 of this Study Guide. Attempt to work the Illustrative Problem and the Study Guide Problem 6-1 without looking at the solution.

3. Be able to identify in which section of the bank reconciliation different types of reconciling items would be included. The form of the reconciliation illustrated on page 253 may be a helpful study aid. Have a friend read off the reconciling items from the chapter illustration of the bank reconciliation on page 254, and identify whether the item would appear in the section of the reconciliation beginning with "Cash balance according to bank statement" or the section beginning with "Cash balance according to depositor's records."

   Note that sometimes instructors may refer to the "Cash balance according to bank statement" as the "Balance per bank" and "Cash balance according to depositor's records" as "Balance per books."

4. You should be able to prepare journal entries to establish and replenish petty cash funds.

5. Finally, you should read over and be generally familiar with the presentation of cash on the balance sheet.

MATCHING

Instructions: Match each of the statements below with its proper term. Some terms may not be used.

A.	accounting system	I.	elements of internal control
B.	bank reconciliation	J.	employee fraud
C.	bank statement	K.	internal controls
D.	cash	L.	notes receivable
E.	cash equivalents	M.	petty cash fund
F.	cash short and over	N.	voucher
G.	doomsday ratio	O.	voucher system
H.	electronic funds transfer (EFT)	P.	working capital ratio

_____ 1. Coins, currency (paper money), checks, money orders, and money on deposit that is available for unrestricted withdrawal from banks and other financial institutions.

_____ 2. A set of procedures for authorizing and recording liabilities and cash payments.

_____ 3. A special form for recording relevant data about a liability and the details of its payment.

_____ 4. A system in which computers rather than paper (money, checks, etc.) are used to effect cash transactions.

_____ 5. A special cash fund to pay relatively small amounts.

_____ 6. The analysis that details the items responsible for the difference between the cash balance reported in the bank statement and the balance of the cash account in the ledger.

_____ 7. Highly liquid investments that are usually reported with cash on the balance sheet.

_____ 8. The ratio of cash and cash equivalents to current liabilities.

_____ 9. The intentional act of deceiving an employer for personal gain.

_____ 10. The methods and procedures used by a business to collect, classify, summarize, and report financial data for use by management and external users.

_____ 11. The policies and procedures used to safeguard assets, ensure accurate business information, and ensure compliance with laws and regulations.

_____ 12. The control environment, risk assessment, control activities, information and communication, and monitoring.

FILL IN THE BLANK—PART A

Instructions: Answer the following questions or complete the statements by writing the appropriate words or amounts in the answer blanks.

1. The methods and procedures used by a business to collect, classify, summarize, and report financial data for use by management and external users is called the _____ system.

2. Coins, currency (paper money), checks, money orders, and money on deposit that are available for unrestricted withdrawal from banks and other financial institutions are reported in the financial statements as _____.

3. A(n) _____ system is a set of procedures for authorizing and recording liabilities and cash payments.

4. Vouchers are ordinarily filed in the unpaid voucher file in order of _____ date.

5. A(n) _____ _____ _____ system uses computers rather than paper (money, checks, etc.) to effect cash transactions.

6. A(n) _____ _____ details the items responsible for the difference between the cash balance reported in the bank statement and the balance of the cash account in the ledger.

7. In a bank reconciliation, a bank debit memorandum for a customer's check returned because of insufficient funds is _____ _____ the cash balance according to the depositor's records.

8. In a bank reconciliation, checks outstanding are _____ _____ the cash balance according to the bank statement.

9. A company erroneously recorded a check issued for $180 as $810. On the bank reconciliation, the difference of $630 would be added to the cash balance according to the _____ _____.

10. Highly liquid investments that are usually reported with cash on the balance sheet are called _____ _____.

FILL IN THE BLANK—PART B

Instructions: Answer the following questions or complete the statements by writing the appropriate words or amounts in the answer blanks.

1. The policies and procedures used to safeguard assets, ensure accurate business information, and ensure compliance with laws and regulations are called _____ _____.

2. The control environment, risk assessment, control activities, information and communication, and monitoring are all _____ of internal control.

3. _____ _____ is the intentional act of deceiving an employer for personal gain.

4. If Cash Short and Over has a credit balance at the end of the period, the balance would be reported on the income statement in the section entitled _____ _____.

5. A(n) _____ is a special form for recording relevant data about a liability and the details of its payment.

6. A(n) _____ _____ fund is used to pay relatively small amounts.

7. In a bank reconciliation, a bank credit memorandum for a note receivable collected by the bank is _____ _____ the cash balance according to the depositor's records.

8. In a bank reconciliation, deposits in transit are _____ _____ the cash balance according to the bank statement.

9. In a bank reconciliation, a bank debit memorandum for service charges is _____ _____ the cash balance according to the depositor's records.

10. The ratio of cash and cash equivalents to current liabilities is called the _____ ratio.

MULTIPLE CHOICE

Instructions: Circle the best answer for each of the following questions.

1. The job of installing or changing an accounting system is made up of three phases: (1) analysis, (2) design, and (3):
   a. installation
   b. verification
   c. management
   d. implementation

2. Which of the following is not an element of the internal control framework?
   a. risk assessment
   b. control environment
   c. management
   d. monitoring

3. Which of the following is not considered a control procedure?
   a. rotating duties among employees
   b. separating responsibilities for custody of assets and accounting for assets
   c. management's operating style
   d. proofs and security measures

4. Internal control policies and procedures provide reasonable assurance that:
   a. all liabilities will be paid
   b. a net income will be earned
   c. they are being effectively applied
   d. business information is accurate

5. For good internal control over cash receipts, remittance advices should be separated from cash received by mail and sent directly to the:
   a. treasurer
   b. cashier's department
   c. accounting department
   d. voucher clerk

6. An important characteristic of the voucher system is the requirement that:
   a. vouchers be prepared by the treasurer
   b. vouchers be paid immediately after they are prepared
   c. the face of the voucher show the account distribution
   d. a voucher be prepared for each expenditure

7. The bank on which a check is drawn is known as the:
   a. drawer
   b. drawee
   c. payee
   d. creditor

8. In a bank reconciliation, deposits not recorded by the bank are:
   a. added to the balance according to the bank statement
   b. deducted from the balance according to the bank statement
   c. added to the balance according to the depositor's records
   d. deducted from the balance according to the depositor's records

9. The amount of the outstanding checks is included on the bank reconciliation as:
   a. an addition to the balance per bank statement
   b. a deduction from the balance per bank statement
   c. an addition to the balance per depositor's records
   d. a deduction from the balance per depositor's records

10. Receipts from cash sales of $7,500 were recorded incorrectly as $5,700. What entry is required in the depositor's accounts?
    a. debit Cash; credit Accounts Receivable
    b. debit Cash; credit Sales
    c. debit Accounts Receivable; credit Cash
    d. debit Sales; credit Cash

11. Accompanying the bank statement was a credit memorandum for a short-term, non-interest-bearing note collected by the bank. What entry is required in the depositor's accounts?
    a. debit Cash; credit Miscellaneous Income
    b. debit Cash; credit Notes Receivable
    c. debit Accounts Receivable; credit Cash
    d. debit Notes Receivable; credit Cash

12. What entry is required in the depositor's accounts to record outstanding checks?
    a. debit Cash; credit Accounts Payable
    b. debit Accounts Receivable; credit Cash
    c. debit Accounts Payable; credit Cash
    d. No entry is required.

13. Journal entries based on the bank reconciliation are required on the depositor's books for:

   a. additions to the balance according to the depositor's records

   b. deductions from the balance according to the depositor's records

   c. both a and b

   d. both additions to and deductions from the balance according to the bank's records

14. In a bank reconciliation, a note receivable collected by the bank is:

   a. added to the balance according to the bank statement

   b. added to the balance according to the depositor's records

   c. deducted from the balance according to the bank statement

   d. deducted from the balance according to the depositor's records

15. The entry to record the replenishment of the petty cash fund includes a debit to various expense and asset accounts and a credit to:

   a. Cash

   b. Petty Cash

   c. Accounts Receivable

   d. various liability accounts

TRUE/FALSE

Instructions: Indicate whether each of the following statements is true or false by placing a check mark in the appropriate column.

		True	False
1.	The goal of systems design is to determine information needs, the sources of such information, and the deficiencies in procedures and data processing methods presently used.	____	____
2.	Responsibility for maintaining the accounting records should be separated from the responsibility for custody of the firm's assets.	____	____
3.	The drawer is the one to whose order the check is drawn. .	____	____
4.	In a bank reconciliation, checks issued that have not been paid by the bank are added to the balance according to the bank statement..	____	____
5.	Bank memorandums not recorded by the depositor require entries in the depositor's accounts......................................	____	____
6.	For a greater degree of internal control, the bank reconciliation should be prepared by an employee who does not engage in or record cash transactions with the bank...........	____	____
7.	If there is a debit balance in the cash short and over account at the end of the fiscal period, this represents income to be included in "Miscellaneous general income" in the income statement.	____	____
8.	After vouchers are paid, it is customary to file them in numerical sequence in the paid voucher file.......................	____	____
9.	Petty Cash should be debited when the petty cash fund is replenished..	____	____
10.	A voucher system is a set of methods and procedures for authorizing and recording liabilities and cash payments.	____	____

EXERCISE 6-1

A comparison of the bank statement and the accompanying canceled checks and memorandums with the records of Pearl Co. for the month of September of the current year revealed the following reconciling items:

(1) A check drawn for $25 had been erroneously charged by the bank for $250.

(2) The bank collected $1,920 on a note left for collection. The face of the note was $1,800.

(3) Bank service charges for September totaled $28.

(4) Check No. 231, written to Stanley Optical Warehouse for $2,500, and Check No. 236, written to Stella's Janitorial Service for $100, were outstanding.

(5) A deposit of $5,250 made on September 30 was not recorded on the bank statement.

(6) A canceled check for $1,100, returned with the bank statement, had been recorded erroneously in the check register as $1,000. The check was a payment on account to Charlie's Optical Supply.

Instructions: In the following general journal, prepare any necessary entries that Pearl Co. should make as a result of these reconciling items. The accounts have not been closed.

JOURNAL   PAGE

	DATE	DESCRIPTION	POST. REF.	DEBIT	CREDIT	
1						1
2						2
3						3
4						4
5						5
6						6
7						7
8						8
9						9
10						10
11						11
12						12
13						13
14						14
15						15
16						16
17						17
18						18

EXERCISE 6-2

Instructions: In the general journal provided below, prepare the entries to record the following transactions:

(1) Established a petty cash fund of $400.

(2) Replenished the fund, based on the following summary of petty cash receipts. (The amount of cash in the fund is now $128.34.)

Office supplies, $80.25

Miscellaneous selling expense, $115.33

Miscellaneous administrative expense, $78.05

JOURNAL   PAGE

	DATE	DESCRIPTION	POST. REF.	DEBIT	CREDIT	
1						1
2						2
3						3
4						4
5						5
6						6
7						7
8						8
9						9
10						10
11						11
12						12
13						13
14						14
15						15
16						16
17						17
18						18
19						19
20						20
21						21
22						22
23						23
24						24
25						25
26						26
27						27

PROBLEM 6-1

On September 30 of the current year, Dumont Co.'s checkbook showed a balance of $7,540, and the bank statement showed a balance of $8,510. A comparison of the bank statement and Dumont's records as of September 30 revealed the following:

(a) A deposit of $1,900, mailed to the bank by Dumont on September 29, was not included in the bank statement of September 30.

(b) The following checks were outstanding: Check No. 255 for $325, Check No. 280 for $100, Check No. 295 for $700.

(c) Check No. 289 in payment of a voucher had been written for $140 and had been recorded at that amount by the bank. However, Dumont had recorded it in the check register as $410.

(d) A check for $910 received from a customer was deposited in the bank. The bank recorded it at the correct amount, but Dumont recorded it at $190.

(e) Included with the bank statement was a credit memorandum for $780, representing the proceeds of a $700 note receivable left at the bank for collection. This had not been recorded on Dumont's books.

(f) Included with the bank statement was a debit memorandum for $25 for service charges that had not been recorded on Dumont's books.

Instructions:

(1) Complete the bank reconciliation below.

(2) In the general journal, prepare the entry or entries that Dumont should make as a result of the bank reconciliation.

Dumont Co.
Bank Reconciliation
September 30, 20--

Balance according to bank statement .... $

Add:

Deduct:

Adjusted balance .... $_____

Balance according to depositor's records .... $

Add:

Deduct:

Adjusted balance .... $_____

(2)   **JOURNAL**   PAGE

	DATE		DESCRIPTION	POST. REF.	DEBIT	CREDIT	
1							1
2							2
3							3
4							4
5							5
6							6
7							7
8							8
9							9
10							10
11							11
12							12
13							13
14							14
15							15
16							16
17							17
18							18
19							19
20							20
21							21
22							22
23							23
24							24
25							25
26							26
27							27
28							28
29							29
30							30
31							31
32							32
33							33
34							34
35							35
36							36

7

Receivables

QUIZ AND TEST HINTS

The following hints may be helpful to you in preparing for a quiz or a test over the material covered in Chapter 7.

1. You should be able to determine the amount of the adjusting entry for uncollectible receivables (the allowance method) for both estimation methods presented in the chapter (percentage of sales and aging of receivables). Note that the percentage of sales method is the easiest to use since the amount of the entry is the same as the estimate of the uncollectible sales. The aging method requires the entry to be made for an amount that will result in the estimated balance of the allowance account.

2. You should be able to determine the due date, interest, and maturity value of a note receivable.

3. You may be tested on a problem requiring a series of general journal entries that encompass both uncollectible accounts receivable and notes receivable. The materials presented in this Study Guide and the Illustrative Problem in the text provide an excellent review.

4. Finally, study the new terminology introduced in this chapter for possible multiple-choice, matching, or true/false questions. Do the Matching exercises included in this Study Guide.

MATCHING

Instructions: Match each of the statements below with its proper term. Some terms may not be used.

A.	accounts receivable	**H.**	maturity value
B.	accounts receivable turnover	**I.**	notes receivable
C.	aging the receivables	**J.**	number of days' sales in
D.	allowance method		receivables
E.	contra asset	**K.**	promissory note
F.	direct write-off method	**L.**	receivables
G.	dishonored note receivable	**M.**	uncollectible accounts expense

_____ **1.** All money claims against other entities, including people, business firms, and other organizations.

_____ **2.** A receivable created by selling merchandise or services on credit.

_____ **3.** Amounts customers owe, for which a formal, written instrument of credit has been issued.

_____ **4.** The operating expense incurred because of the failure to collect receivables.

_____ **5.** The method of accounting for uncollectible accounts that provides an expense for uncollectible receivables in advance of their write-off.

_____ **6.** The method of accounting for uncollectible accounts that recognizes the expense only when accounts are judged to be worthless.

_____ **7.** The process of analyzing the accounts receivable and classifying them according to various age groupings, with the due date being the base point for determining age.

_____ **8.** The amount that is due at the maturity or due date of a note.

_____ **9.** A note that the maker fails to pay on the due date.

_____ **10.** An estimate of the length of time the accounts receivable have been outstanding.

_____ **11.** Measures how frequently during the year the accounts receivable are being converted to cash.

_____ **12.** A written promise to pay a sum of money on demand or at a definite time.

FILL IN THE BLANK—PART A

Instructions: Answer the following questions or complete the statements by writing the appropriate words or amounts in the answer blanks.

1. All money claims against other entities, including people, business firms, and other organizations are called _____.

2. A(n) _____ _____ is a formal, written instrument of credit that has been received for the amount a customer owes.

3. The _____ method of accounting for uncollectible accounts provides an expense for uncollectible receivables in advance of their write-off.

4. The _____ _____ _____ is a process of analyzing the accounts receivable and classifying them according to various age groupings, with the due date being the base point for determining age.

5. Allowance for Doubtful Accounts has a debit balance of $1,500 at the end of the year, before adjustments. Sales for the year amounted to $740,000, and sales returns and allowances amounted to $25,000. If uncollectible accounts expense is estimated at 1% of net sales, the amount of the appropriate adjusting entry will be _____.

6. Allowance for Doubtful Accounts has a debit balance of $2,500 at the end of the year, before adjustments. Sales for the year amounted to $950,000, and sales returns and allowances amounted to $20,000. If the analysis of the accounts in the customers' ledger indicates doubtful accounts of $30,000, the amount of the appropriate adjusting entry will be _____.

7. The maturity value of a $300,000, 90-day, 12% note receivable is _____.

8. The due date of a 90-day note receivable dated July 12 is _____.

9. A note that the maker fails to pay on the due date is referred to as a(n) _____ note.

10. _____ _____ _____

    measures how frequently during the year the accounts receivable are being converted to cash.

FILL IN THE BLANK—PART B

Instructions: Answer the following questions or complete the statements by writing the appropriate words or amounts in the answer blanks.

1. A(n) _____ receivable is created by selling merchandise or services on credit.

2. The operating expense incurred because of the failure to collect receivables is recorded as _____ _____ expense.

3. The _____ _____-_____ method of accounting for uncollectible accounts recognizes an expense only when accounts are judged to be worthless.

4. At the end of the fiscal year, after the accounts are closed, Accounts Receivable has a balance of $350,000 and Allowance for Doubtful Accounts has a credit balance of $40,000. The expected realizable value of the receivables is _____.

5. Allowance for Doubtful Accounts has a credit balance of $800 at the end of the year, before adjustments. If an analysis of receivables indicates doubtful accounts of $11,200, the amount of the appropriate adjusting entry is _____.

6. The amount that is due at the maturity or due date of a note is called the _____ _____.

7. The maturity value of a $150,000, 60-day, 15% note receivable is _____.

8. The due date of a 120-day note receivable dated on August 18 is _____.

9. The _____ _____ _____ _____ _____ _____ is an estimate of the length of time the accounts receivable have been outstanding, expressed in days.

10. A written promise to pay a sum of money on demand or at a definite time is called a(n) _____ note.

MULTIPLE CHOICE

Instructions: Circle the best answer for each of the following questions.

1. When the allowance method is used in accounting for uncollectible accounts, any uncollectible account is written off against the:

   a. allowance account

   b. sales account

   c. accounts receivable account

   d. uncollectible accounts expense account

2. When the direct write-off method is used in accounting for uncollectible accounts, any uncollectible account is written off against the:

   a. allowance account

   b. sales account

   c. accounts receivable account

   d. uncollectible accounts expense account

3. What is the type of account and normal balance of Allowance for Doubtful Accounts?

   a. asset, debit

   b. asset, credit

   c. contra asset, debit

   d. contra asset, credit

4. Assume that the allowance account has a credit balance of $170 at the end of the year, before adjustments. If the estimate of uncollectible accounts based on aging the receivables is $3,010, the amount of the adjusting entry for uncollectible accounts would be:

   a. $170

   b. $2,840

   c. $3,010

   d. $3,180

5. Assume that the allowance account has a debit balance of $250 at the end of the year, before adjustments. If the estimate of uncollectible accounts based on sales for the period is $2,200, the amount of the adjusting entry for uncollectible accounts would be:

   a. $250

   b. $1,950

   c. $2,200

   d. $2,450

6. After the accounts are adjusted and closed at the end of the fiscal year, Accounts Receivable has a balance of $430,000 and Allowance for Doubtful Accounts has a balance of $25,000. What is the expected realizable value of the accounts receivable?

   a. $25,000

   b. $405,000

   c. $430,000

   d. $455,000

7. On a promissory note, the one making the promise to pay is called the:

   a. payee

   b. creditor

   c. maker

   d. noter

8. The amount that is due on a note at the maturity or due date is called the:

   a. terminal value

   b. face value

   c. book value

   d. maturity value

9. The due date of a 90-day note dated July 1 is:

   a. September 28

   b. September 29

   c. September 30

   d. October 1

10. A 60-day, 12% note for $15,000, dated May 1, is received from a customer on account. The maturity value of the note is:

   a. $14,700

   b. $15,000

   c. $15,300

   d. $16,200

TRUE/FALSE

Instructions: Indicate whether each of the following statements is true or false by placing a check mark in the appropriate column.

	True	False

1. The method of accounting which provides in advance for receivables deemed uncollectible is called the allowance method. .... ____ ____

2. The process of analyzing the receivable accounts in order to estimate the uncollectibles is sometimes called aging the receivables. .... ____ ____

3. The direct write-off method of accounting for uncollectible receivables provides for uncollectible accounts in the year of sale. .... ____ ____

4. Estimation of uncollectible accounts based on the analysis of receivables emphasizes the current net realizable value of the receivables. .... ____ ____

5. The allowance method of accounting for uncollectible receivables emphasizes the matching of uncollectible expense with the related sales. .... ____ ____

6. The term *notes* includes all money claims against people, organizations, or other debtors. .... ____ ____

7. Accounts and notes receivable originating from sales transactions are sometimes called trade receivables. .... ____ ____

8. For good internal control, an employee who handles the accounting for notes and accounts receivable should not be involved with credit approvals or collections of receivables. .... ____ ____

9. When a note is received from a customer from a previous sale on account, it is recorded by debiting Notes Receivable and crediting Sales. .... ____ ____

10. Jacob Co. issues a 90-day, 12% note on May 13; the due date of the note is August 11. .... ____ ____

EXERCISE 7-1

Star Co. uses the allowance method of accounting for uncollectibles. On March 31, 20--, Star deemed that an amount of $3,150 due from Jane Eades was uncollectible and wrote it off. On May 8, 20--, Eades paid the $3,150.

Instructions:

(1) Prepare the entry to write off the account on March 31.

(2) Prepare the entry to reinstate the account on May 8, and to record the cash received.

JOURNAL   PAGE

	DATE	DESCRIPTION	POST. REF.	DEBIT	CREDIT	
1						1
2						2
3						3
4						4
5						5
6						6
7						7
8						8
9						9
10						10
11						11
12						12
13						13
14						14
15						15
16						16
17						17
18						18
19						19
20						20

EXERCISE 7-2

Coco Co. uses the direct write-off method of accounting for uncollectibles. On August 31, 20--, Coco deemed that an amount of $550 due from Don Shore was uncollectible and wrote it off. On October 8, 20--, Shore paid the $550.

Instructions:

(1) Prepare the entry to write off the account on August 31.

(2) Prepare the entry to reinstate the account on October 8, and to record the cash received.

JOURNAL   PAGE

	DATE		DESCRIPTION	POST. REF.	DEBIT	CREDIT	
1							1
2							2
3							3
4							4
5							5
6							6
7							7
8							8
9							9
10							10
11							11
12							12
13							13
14							14
15							15
16							16
17							17
18							18
19							19
20							20

EXERCISE 7-3

Instructions: Using the basic formula for interest and assuming a 360-day year, compute the interest on the following notes.

1. $8,000 at 12% for 30 days .... $ _____
2. $3,500 at 6% for 60 days .... $ _____
3. $2,000 at 12% for 90 days .... $ _____
4. $8,000 at 9% for 30 days .... $ _____
5. $7,500 at 6% for 60 days .... $ _____
6. $12,000 for 90 days at 9% .... $ _____
7. $5,250 for 120 days at 12% .... $ _____

EXERCISE 7-4

The following data regarding the current assets of Walton Company were selected from the accounting records after adjustment at the end of the current fiscal year:

Accounts Receivable	$35,000
Allowance for Doubtful Accounts	1,200
Cash	37,500
Interest Receivable	9,900
Notes Receivable	20,000

Instructions: Prepare the Current Assets section of the balance sheet for Walton Company.

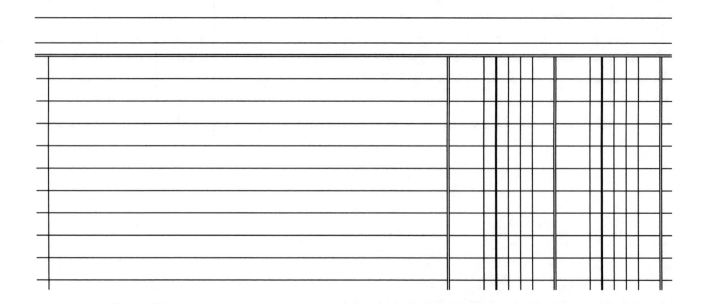

PROBLEM 7-1

Instructions: Prepare the appropriate general journal entries for each of the following situations.

(1) Net sales for the year are $800,000, uncollectible accounts expense is estimated at 3% of net sales, and the allowance account has a $425 credit balance before adjustment. Prepare the adjusting entry at year end for the uncollectibles.

(2) Based on an analysis of accounts in the customers' ledger, estimated uncollectible accounts total $6,280, and the allowance account has a $325 credit balance before adjustment. Prepare the adjusting entry at year end for the uncollectibles.

(3) A $3,500 account receivable from Bentley Co. is written off as uncollectible. The allowance method is used.

(4) A $1,235 account receivable from Apple Co., which was written off three months earlier, is collected in full. The allowance method is used.

JOURNAL
PAGE ____

	DATE	DESCRIPTION	POST. REF.	DEBIT	CREDIT	
1						1
2						2
3						3
4						4
5						5
6						6
7						7
8						8
9						9
10						10
11						11
12						12
13						13
14						14
15						15
16						16
17						17
18						18
19						19
20						20
21						21

PROBLEM 7-2

Instructions: Prepare the general journal entries to record the following transactions. (Omit explanations.)

(1) Pequot Co. received a 60-day, 12% note for $8,000 from a customer, Dave Davidson, in settlement of Davidson's account.

(2) Davidson failed to pay the note in (1) at maturity.

(3) Ten days after the maturity of the note in (1), Davidson paid Pequot in full, including interest at 11% for this 10-day period.

(4) Pequot received a 90-day, 10% note for $3,000 from a customer, Sue Smith, in settlement of Smith's account.

(5) The note in (4) was dishonored at maturity.

JOURNAL

PAGE

	DATE	DESCRIPTION	POST. REF.	DEBIT	CREDIT	
1						1
2						2
3						3
4						4
5						5
6						6
7						7
8						8
9						9
10						10
11						11
12						12
13						13
14						14
15						15
16						16
17						17
18						18
19						19
20						20
21						21
22						22
23						23
24						24

Inventories

QUIZ AND TEST HINTS

The following hints may be helpful to you in preparing for a quiz or a test over the material covered in Chapter 8.

1. You should carefully review the new terminology introduced in this chapter. Do the Matching exercises included in this Study Guide.

2. The chapter emphasizes determining the cost of inventory using the first-in, first-out (fifo), last-in, first-out (lifo), and average cost methods. Most instructors ask questions related to these cost flow assumptions using the perpetual and periodic inventory systems. The Illustrative Problem in the Chapter Review is an excellent study aid for this type of question.

3. The retail method and gross profit method of estimating inventory are also popular subjects for quiz and test questions with instructors. Be prepared to work each method.

MATCHING

Instructions: Match each of the statements below with its proper term. Some terms may not be used.

A. average cost method
B. first-in, first-out (fifo) method
C. gross profit method
D. inventory turnover
E. last-in, first-out (lifo) method
F. lower-of-cost-or-market (LCM) method

G. net realizable value
H. number of days' sales in inventory
I. physical inventory
J. retail inventory method

_____ 1. A detailed listing of merchandise on hand.

_____ 2. A method of inventory costing that is based on the assumption that the costs of merchandise sold should be charged against revenue in the order in which the costs were incurred.

_____ 3. A method of inventory costing that is based on the assumption that the most recent merchandise inventory costs should be charged against revenue.

_____ 4. The method of inventory costing that is based on the assumption that costs should be charged against revenue by using the weighted average unit cost of the items sold.

_____ 5. A method of valuing inventory that reports the inventory at the lower of its cost or current market value (replacement cost).

_____ 6. The estimated selling price of an item of inventory less any direct costs of disposal, such as sales commissions.

_____ 7. A method of estimating inventory cost that is based on the relationship of the cost of merchandise available for sale to the retail price of the same merchandise.

_____ 8. A method of estimating inventory cost that is based on the relationship of gross profit to sales.

_____ 9. A ratio that measures the relationship between the volume of goods (merchandise) sold and the amount of inventory carried during the period.

_____ 10. A measure of the length of time it takes to acquire, sell, and replace the inventory.

FILL IN THE BLANK—PART A

Instructions: Answer the following questions or complete the statements by writing the appropriate words or amounts in the answer blanks.

1. A detailed listing of merchandise on hand is called a(n) _____

    _____.

2. At the end of the year, the physical inventory is overstated. As a result, the cost of merchandise sold will be _____.

3. At the end of the year, the physical inventory is understated. As a result, the owner's capital reported on the balance sheet will be

    _____.

4. The _____-_____, _____-_____ method of costing inventory is based on the assumption that the most recent merchandise inventory costs should be charged against revenue.

5. On June 1, there was beginning inventory of 5 units at $100 per unit. During June, the following three purchases were made: June 7, 10 units at $110 per unit; June 17, 15 units at $115 per unit; and June 23, 8 units at $116 per unit. If 12 units are on hand on June 30, the total cost of the ending inventory using the periodic method and the last-in, first-out cost flow is

    _____.

6. During a period of consistently falling prices, the _____ (fifo or lifo) method will result in reporting the greater amount of gross profit.

7. The _____-_____-_____-_____-_____ method reports inventory at the lower of its cost or current market value (replacement cost).

8. During July, merchandise available for sale at cost and retail is $240,000 and $400,000, respectively. If $25,000 of merchandise at retail is on hand on July 31, the estimated cost of the merchandise on hand on July 31 is

    _____.

9. The _____ _____ method estimates inventory cost based on the relationship of gross profit to sales.

10. The _____ _____ ratio measures the relationship between the volume of goods (merchandise) sold and the amount of inventory carried during the period.

FILL IN THE BLANK—PART B

Instructions: Answer the following questions or complete the statements by writing the appropriate words or amounts in the answer blanks.

1. At the end of the year, the physical inventory is overstated. As a result, net income will be _____ .

2. At the end of the year, the physical inventory is understated. As a result, gross profit will be _____ .

3. The _____-_____, _____-_____ method of costing inventory is based on the assumption that the costs of merchandise sold should be charged against revenue in the order in which the costs were incurred.

4. The _____ _____ method costs inventory based upon the assumption that costs should be charged against revenue in accordance with the weighted average unit costs of the items sold.

5. On June 1, there was beginning inventory of 5 units at $100 per unit. During June, the following three purchases were made: June 7, 10 units at $110 per unit; June 17, 15 units at $115 per unit; and June 23, 8 units at $116 per unit. If 12 units are on hand on June 30, the total cost of the ending inventory using the first-in, first-out method is _____ .

6. The estimated selling price of an item of inventory less any direct costs of disposal, such as sales commissions, is called _____ _____ _____ .

7. If the cost of an item of inventory is $50, the current replacement cost is $45, and the selling price is $80, the amount included in inventory according to the lower-of-cost-or-market concept is _____ .

8. The _____ _____ method estimates inventory cost based on the relationship of the cost of merchandise available for sale to the retail price of the same merchandise.

9. During November, the cost of merchandise available for sale was $750,000. Sales of $900,000 were made during November at an average gross profit of 30% of sales. Using the gross profit method, the estimated cost of the inventory on hand on November 30 is _____ .

10. The _____ _____ _____ _____ _____ _____ is a measure of the length of time it takes to acquire, sell, and replace the inventory.

MULTIPLE CHOICE

Instructions: Circle the best answer for each of the following questions.

1. If merchandise inventory at the end of the period is understated:
    a. gross profit will be overstated
    b. owner's equity will be overstated
    c. net income will be understated
    d. cost of merchandise sold will be understated

2. If merchandise inventory at the end of period 1 is overstated and at the end of period 2 is correct:
    a. gross profit in period 2 will be understated
    b. assets at the end of period 2 will be overstated
    c. owner's equity at the end of period 2 will be understated
    d. cost of merchandise sold in period 2 will be understated

3. The following units of a particular item were purchased and sold during the period:

    Beginning inventory .... 10 units at $5
    First purchase .... 15 units at $6
    Sale .... 10 units
    Second purchase .... 10 units at $7
    Sale .... 8 units
    Third purchase .... 15 units at $8
    Sale .... 17 units

    What is the total cost of the 15 units on hand at the end of the period, as determined under the perpetual inventory system by the lifo costing method?
    a. $80
    b. $90
    c. $100
    d. $120

4. Assuming the data given in No. 3, determine the total cost of the 15 units on hand at the end of the period assuming a perpetual inventory system and the fifo costing method.
    a. $80
    b. $90
    c. $100
    d. $120

5. Assuming the data given in No. 3, determine the total cost of the 15 units on hand at the end of the period assuming a periodic inventory system and the lifo costing method.

a. $80

b. $90

c. $100

d. $120

6. Assuming the data given in No. 3, determine the total cost of the 15 units on hand at the end of the period assuming a periodic inventory system and the fifo costing method.

a. $80

b. $90

c. $99

d. $120

7. Assuming the data given in No. 3, determine the total cost of the 15 units on hand at the end of the period assuming a periodic inventory system and the average costing method.

a. $80

b. $90

c. $99

d. $120

8. During a period of rising prices, the inventory costing method that will result in the lowest amount of net income is:

a. fifo

b. lifo

c. average cost

d. perpetual

9. If the replacement price of an item of inventory is lower than its cost, the use of the lower of cost or market method:

a. is not permitted unless a perpetual inventory system is maintained

b. is recommended in order to maximize the reported net income

c. tends to overstate the gross profit

d. reduces gross profit for the period in which the decline occurred

10. When lifo is strictly applied to a perpetual inventory system, the unit cost prices assigned to the ending inventory will not necessarily be those associated with the earliest unit costs of the period if:

     a. a physical inventory is taken at the end of the period

     b. physical inventory records are maintained throughout the period in terms of quantities only

     c. at any time during a period the number of units of a commodity sold exceeds the number previously purchased during the same period

     d. moving average inventory cost is maintained

TRUE/FALSE

Instructions: Indicate whether each of the following statements is true or false by placing a check mark in the appropriate column.

	True	**False**
1. If merchandise inventory at the end of the period is understated, gross profit will be overstated.	____	____
2. The two principal systems of inventory accounting are periodic and physical.	____	____
3. When terms of a sale are FOB destination, title usually does not pass to the buyer until the commodities are delivered.	____	____
4. If merchandise inventory at the end of the period is overstated, owner's equity at the end of the period will be understated.	____	____
5. During a period of rising prices, the inventory costing method that will result in the highest amount of net income is lifo.	____	____
6. If the cost of units purchased and the prices at which they were sold remained stable, all three inventory methods would yield the same results.	____	____
7. When the rate of inflation is high, the larger gross profits that result from using the fifo method are frequently called inventory profits.	____	____
8. As used in the phrase "lower of cost or market," *market* means selling price.	____	____
9. When the retail inventory method is used, inventory at retail is converted to cost on the basis of the ratio of cost to replacement cost of the merchandise available for sale......	____	____
10. Merchandise inventory is usually presented on the balance sheet immediately following receivables.	____	____

EXERCISE 8-1

At the fiscal year end of October 31, 2006, the merchandise inventory was understated by $5,000. The error was discovered in 2007.

Instructions: In the spaces provided below, indicate the effect of the error on the sales, cost of merchandise sold, gross profit, net income, merchandise inventory (October 31, 2006), current assets, total assets, liabilities, and owner's equity for the year ending October 31, 2006. For each item, indicate (1) whether it is understated, overstated, or correct; and (2) the dollar amount of the error, if any.

Sales

(1) _____

(2) _____

Cost of Merchandise Sold

(1) _____

(2) _____

Gross Profit

(1) _____

(2) _____

Net Income

(1) _____

(2) _____

Merchandise Inventory (October 31, 2006)

(1) _____

(2) _____

Current Assets

(1) _____

(2) _____

Total Assets

(1) _____

(2) _____

Liabilities

(1) _____

(2) _____

Owner's Equity

(1) _____

(2) _____

EXERCISE 8-2

Instructions: Complete the following summary, which illustrates the application of the lower-of-cost-or-market rule to individual inventory items of Unks Co.

	Quantity	Unit Cost Price	Unit Market Price	Total Cost	Total Lower of Cost or Market
Commodity A	750	$5.00	$4.80	$	$
Commodity B	460	6.00	7.00		
Commodity C	200	7.25	6.00		
Commodity D	300	4.80	4.30		
Total				$	$

PROBLEM 8-1

Hawkins Co. is a small wholesaler of hiking shoes. The accounting records show the following purchases and sales of the Mountain model during the first year of business.

A physical count of the Mountain model at the end of the year reveals that 12 are still on hand.

Purchases				Sales	
Date	Units	Price	Total Cost	Date	Units
Jan. 10	10	$48	$ 480	Feb. 10	8
Feb. 15	100	54	5,400	Apr. 1	95
July 3	65	55	3,575	Aug. 10	65
Nov. 1	35	58	2,030	Nov. 15	30
Total	210		$11,485		198

Instructions:

(1) Determine the cost of the Mountain model inventory as of December 31 by means of the first-in, first-out (fifo) method with a perpetual inventory system.

INVENTORY (Fifo Perpetual)

Date Purchased	Units	Price	Total Cost

(2) Determine the cost of the Mountain Model inventory as of December 31 by means of the last-in, first-out (lifo) method with a perpetual inventory system.

INVENTORY (Lifo Perpetual)

Date Purchased	Units	Price	Total Cost

(3) Determine the cost of the Mountain model inventory as of December 31 by means of the first-in, first-out (fifo) method with a periodic inventory system.

INVENTORY (Fifo Periodic)

Date Purchased	Units	Price	Total Cost

(4) Determine the cost of the Mountain model inventory as of December 31 by means of the last-in, first-out (lifo) method with a periodic inventory system.

INVENTORY (Lifo Periodic)

Date Purchased	Units	Price	Total Cost

(5) Determine the cost of the Mountain model inventory as of December 31 by means of the average cost method with a periodic system. (Round unit cost to two decimal places.)

INVENTORY (Average Cost)

Average unit cost = $_____ = $_____

_____ units in the inventory @ $_____ = $_____

PROBLEM 8-2

Bartle Co. began operating on January 1 of the current year. During the year, Bartle sold 28,000 units at an average price of $80 each, and made the following purchases:

Date of Purchase	Units	Unit Price	Total Cost
January 1	5,400	$50	$ 270,000
March 1	4,100	54	221,400
June 1	4,800	56	268,800
September 1	8,400	61	512,400
November 1	5,400	69	372,600
December 1	1,900	73	138,700
	30,000		$1,783,900

Instructions: Using the periodic inventory system, determine the ending inventory, the cost of merchandise sold, and the gross profit for Bartle, using each of the following methods of inventory costing: **(1)** fifo, **(2)** lifo, and **(3)** average cost. (Round unit cost to two decimal places.)

	(1) Fifo	**(2)** Lifo	**(3)** Average Cost
Sales	$	$	$
Purchases	$ 1,783,900	$ 1,783,900	$ 1,783,900
Less ending inventory	$	$	$
Cost of merchandise sold ...	$	$	$
Gross profit	$	$	$

PROBLEM 8-3

Knish Co. operates a department store and takes a physical inventory at the end of each calendar year. However, Knish likes to have a balance sheet and an income statement available at the end of each month in order to study financial position and operating trends. Knish estimates inventory at the end of each month for accounting statement preparation purposes. The following information is available as of August 31 of the current year:

	Cost	Retail
Merchandise inventory, August 1	$118,500	$170,000
Purchases in August	307,125	481,400
Purchases returns and allowances—August ...	8,000	8,900
Sales in August		493,200
Sales returns and allowances—August		14,200

Instructions:

(1) Determine the estimated cost of the inventory on August 31, using the retail method.

	Cost	Retail
Merchandise inventory, August 1	$	$
Purchases in August (net)		
Merchandise available for sale	$	$

Ratio of cost to retail:

$$\frac{\$_____}{\$_____} = _____ \%$$

Sales in August (net)	
Merchandise inventory, August 31, at retail	$
Merchandise inventory, August 31, at estimated cost ($_____ × _____%)	$

(2) Determine the estimated cost of inventory on August 31, using the gross profit method. On the basis of past experience, Knish estimates a rate of gross profit of 30% of net sales.

Merchandise inventory, August 1	$
Purchases in August (net)	
Merchandise available for sale	$
Sales in August (net)	$
Less estimated gross profit ($_____ × _____%)	
Estimated cost of merchandise sold	$
Estimated merchandise inventory, August 31	$

CHAPTER

9 Fixed Assets and Intangible Assets

QUIZ AND TEST HINTS

The following hints may be helpful to you in preparing for a quiz or a test over the material covered in Chapter 9.

1. The chapter emphasizes the computation of depreciation. You should be able to compute depreciation using each of the three methods: straight-line, units-of-production, and declining-balance. If your instructor lectures on the sum-of-the-years-digits method of depreciation in the appendix to the chapter, you should also be prepared to compute depreciation under this method.

2. A common question on quizzes and tests involves the recording of fixed asset disposals. You should be able to prepare general journal entries for disposals, including the exchange of similar assets. Exhibit 9 may be useful for reviewing the journal entries of exchanges of similar assets.

3. The chapter introduces a significant amount of new terminology. These terms lend themselves to numerous multiple-choice and matching questions. Do the Matching exercises included in this Study Guide.

4. You should expect some questions related to intangible assets. The computation of amortization is relatively simple, and it is similar to the units-of-production depreciation method. This section of the chapter lends itself to multiple-choice questions.

MATCHING

Instructions: Match each of the statements below with its proper term. Some terms may not be used.

A.	accelerated depreciation method	**M.**	intangible assets
B.	amortization	**N.**	operating leases
C.	book value	**O.**	patents
D.	boot	**P.**	ratio of fixed assets to long-term liabilities
E.	capital expenditures	**Q.**	ratio of fixed assets to total assets
F.	capital leases		
G.	copyright	**R.**	residual value
H.	declining-balance method	**S.**	revenue expenditures
I.	depletion	**T.**	straight-line method
J.	depreciation	**U.**	trade-in allowance
K.	fixed assets	**V.**	trademark
L.	goodwill	**W.**	units-of-production method

_____ **1.** Long-term or relatively permanent tangible assets that are used in the normal business operations.

_____ **2.** The systematic periodic transfer of the cost of a fixed asset to an expense account during its expected useful life.

_____ **3.** The estimated value of a fixed asset at the end of its useful life.

_____ **4.** A method of depreciation that provides for equal periodic depreciation expense over the estimated life of a fixed asset.

_____ **5.** A method of depreciation that provides for depreciation expense based on the expected productive capacity of a fixed asset.

_____ **6.** A method of depreciation that provides periodic depreciation expense based on the declining book value of a fixed asset over its estimated life.

_____ **7.** The cost of a fixed asset minus accumulated depreciation on the asset.

_____ **8.** A depreciation method that provides for a higher depreciation amount in the first year of the asset's use, followed by a gradually declining amount of depreciation.

_____ **9.** The costs of acquiring fixed assets, adding to a fixed asset, improving a fixed asset, or extending a fixed asset's useful life.

_____ **10.** Costs that benefit only the current period or costs incurred for normal maintenance and repairs of fixed assets.

_____ **11.** The amount a seller allows a buyer for a fixed asset that is traded in for a similar asset.

_____ **12.** The amount a buyer owes a seller when a fixed asset is traded in on a similar asset.

_____ **13.** Leases that include one or more provisions that result in treating the leased assets as purchased assets in the accounts.

_____ **14.** Leases that do not meet the criteria for capital leases and thus are accounted for as operating expenses.

_____ **15.** The process of transferring the cost of natural resources to an expense account.

_____ **16.** Long-term assets that are useful in the operations of a business, are not held for sale, and are without physical qualities.

_____ **17.** The periodic transfer of the cost of an intangible asset to expense.

_____ **18.** An intangible asset that is created from such favorable factors as location, product quality, reputation, and managerial skill.

_____ **19.** Exclusive rights to produce and sell goods with one or more unique features.

_____ **20.** An exclusive right to publish and sell a literary, artistic, or musical composition.

_____ **21.** A name, term, or symbol used to identify a business and its products.

_____ **22.** A financial ratio that provides a measure indicating the margin of safety to creditors.

FILL IN THE BLANK—PART A

Instructions: Answer the following questions or complete the statements by writing the appropriate words or amounts in the answer blanks.

1. Long-term or relatively permanent tangible assets that are used in the normal business operation are called _____ assets.

2. Surveying fees incurred in connection with securing title of land for use by a business is debited to the _____ account.

3. The cost of a special foundation incurred in connection with the acquisition of a secondhand machine would be debited to the _____ account.

4. The estimated value of a fixed asset at the end of its useful life is called _____ value.

5. The _____-_____-_____ method is a method of depreciation that provides for depreciation expense based on the expected productive capacity of a fixed asset.

6. The cost of a fixed asset minus accumulated depreciation on the asset is called the _____ value.

7. A useful life of 4 years is equivalent to a straight-line depreciation rate of _____.

8. Equipment acquired on the first day of the current fiscal year for $50,000 has an estimated life of 4 years or 25,000 hours and a residual value of $5,000. Depreciation for the current year using the straight-line method is _____.

9. Equipment acquired on the first day of the current fiscal year for $50,000 has an estimated life of 4 years or 25,000 hours and a residual value of $5,000. Depreciation for the current year using the declining-balance method (using twice the straight-line rate) is _____.

10. Equipment acquired on the first day of the current fiscal year for $50,000 has an estimated life of 4 years or 25,000 hours and a residual value of $5,000. The equipment was used for 7,000 hours during the current year. Depreciation for the current year using the units-of-production method is _____.

11. The costs of acquiring fixed assets, adding to a fixed asset, improving a fixed asset, or extending a fixed asset's useful life are called _____ expenditures.

12. Costs that benefit only the current period or costs incurred for normal maintenance and repairs are called _____ _____.

13. The amount a seller allows a buyer for a fixed asset that is traded in for a similar asset is called a(n) _____-_____ _____.

14. Old equipment with a book value of $25,000 is traded in on similar equipment priced at $70,000. A trade-in allowance of $30,000 is allowed on the old equipment, and the balance is paid in cash. The new equipment should be recorded at a cost of _____.

15. _____ leases treat the leased assets as purchased assets for the accounts.

16. The process of transferring the cost of natural resources to an expense account is called _____.

17. _____ is the periodic transfer of a cost of an intangible asset to expense.

18. _____ are exclusive rights to produce and sell goods with one or more unique features.

19. The cost of a patent is amortized by debiting Amortization Expense—Patents and crediting _____.

20. A name, term, or symbol used to identify a business and its products is called a(n) _____.

FILL IN THE BLANK—PART B

Instructions: Answer the following questions or complete the statements by writing the appropriate words or amounts in the answer blanks.

1. The cost of razing an unwanted building on land purchased for use by a business is debited to the _____ account.

2. The systematic, periodic transfer of the cost of a fixed asset to expense during its expected useful life is called _____.

3. The _____-_____ method is a method of depreciation that provides for equal periodic depreciation expense over the estimated life of a fixed asset.

4. The _____-_____ method is a method of depreciation that provides declining periodic depreciation expense over the estimated life of a fixed asset.

5. A useful life of 5 years is equivalent to a straight-line depreciation rate of _____.

6. Equipment acquired on the first day of the current fiscal year for $80,000 has an estimated life of 5 years or 25,000 hours and a residual value of $10,000. Depreciation for the current year using the straight-line method is _____.

7. Equipment acquired on the first day of the current fiscal year for $80,000 has an estimated life of 5 years or 25,000 hours and a residual value of $10,000. Depreciation for the current year using the declining-balance method (using twice the straight-line rate) is _____.

8. Equipment acquired on the first day of the current fiscal year for $80,000 has an estimated life of 5 years or 25,000 hours and a residual value of $10,000. The equipment was used for 6,000 hours during the current year. Depreciation for the current year using the units-of-production method is _____.

9. Depreciation methods that provide for a higher depreciation amount in the first year of the asset's use, followed by a gradually declining amount of depreciation, are referred to as _____ depreciation methods.

10. Costs that benefit only the current period or costs incurred for normal maintenance and repairs of fixed assets are called _____ expenditures.

11. The costs of acquiring fixed assets, adding to a fixed asset, improving a fixed asset, or extending a fixed asset's useful life are called _____ _____.

12. _____ is the amount a buyer owes a seller when a fixed asset is traded in on a similar asset.

13. Old equipment with a book value of $25,000 is traded in on similar equipment priced at $70,000. A trade-in allowance of $18,000 is allowed on the old equipment, and the balance is paid in cash. The new equipment should be recorded at a cost of _____.

14. _____ leases do not meet the criteria for capital leases and thus are accounted for as operating expenses.

15. Long-term assets that are useful in the operations of a business, are not held for sale, and are without physical qualities are called _____ assets.

16. _____ is an intangible asset of a business that is created from such favorable factors as location, product quality, reputation, and managerial skill.

17. A(n) _____ is an exclusive right to publish and sell a literary, artistic, or musical composition.

18. Depletion expense related to a mineral ore deposit is recorded by debiting Depletion Expense and crediting _____ _____.

19. Research and development costs are normally accounted for as _____ _____ _____ in the period in which they are incurred.

20. The ratio of _____ _____ _____ _____-_____ _____ provides a measure of the margin of safety to creditors.

MULTIPLE CHOICE

Instructions: Circle the best answer for each of the following questions.

1. If unwanted buildings are located on land acquired for a plant site, the cost of their removal, less any salvage recovered, should be charged to the:
    a. expense accounts
    b. building account
    c. land account
    d. accumulated depreciation account

2. The depreciation method used most often in the financial statements is the:
    a. straight-line method
    b. declining-balance method
    c. units-of-production method
    d. MACRS method

3. The depreciation method that would provide the highest reported net income in the early years of an asset's life would be:

 a. straight-line

 b. declining-balance

 c. 150% straight-line

 d. accelerated

4. Equipment with an estimated useful life of 5 years and an estimated residual value of $1,000 is acquired at a cost of $15,000. Using the declining-balance method (at twice the straight-line rate), what is the amount of depreciation for the first year of use of the equipment?

 a. $2,600

 b. $3,000

 c. $5,600

 d. $6,000

5. Equipment that cost $20,000 was originally estimated to have a useful life of 5 years and a residual value of $2,000. The equipment has been depreciated for 2 years using straight-line depreciation. During the third year it is estimated that the remaining useful life is 2 years (instead of 3) and that the residual value is $1,000 (instead of $2,000). The depreciation expense on the equipment in Year 3 using the straight-line method would be:

 a. $5,500

 b. $5,900

 c. $6,000

 d. $7,500

6. Assume that a drill press is rebuilt during its sixth year of use so that its useful life is extended 5 years beyond the original estimate of 10 years. In this case, the cost of rebuilding the drill press is a(n):

 a. revenue expenditure

 b. replacement component

 c. additional component

 d. expense

7. Old equipment which cost $11,000 and has accumulated depreciation of $6,300 is given, along with $9,000 in cash, for the same type of new equipment with a price of $15,600. At what amount should the new equipment be recorded?

 a. $15,600

 b. $15,300

 c. $13,700

 d. $9,000

8. Assume the same facts as in No. 7, except that the old equipment and $11,500 in cash is given for the new equipment. At what amount should the new equipment be recorded for financial accounting purposes?

    a. $16,200

    b. $15,600

    c. $11,500

    d. $10,900

9. In a lease contract, the party who legally owns the asset is the:

    a. contractor

    b. operator

    c. lessee

    d. lessor

10. Which of the following items would not be considered an intangible asset?

    a. mineral ore deposits

    b. patent

    c. copyright

    d. goodwill

TRUE/FALSE

Instructions: Indicate whether each of the following statements is true or false by placing a check mark in the appropriate column.

	True	False
1. The declining-balance method provides for a higher depreciation charge in the first year of use of the asset, followed by a gradually declining periodic charge...............	____	____
2. The method of depreciation which yields a depreciation charge that varies with the amount of asset usage is known as the units-of-production method.	____	____
3. In using the declining-balance method, the asset should not be depreciated below the net book value.	____	____
4. Accelerated depreciation methods are most appropriate for situations in which the decline in productivity or earning power of the asset is proportionately greater in the early years of its use than in later years.	____	____
5. MACRS depreciation methods permit the use of asset lives that are often much shorter than the actual useful life.	____	____

	True	**False**

6. When an old fixed asset is traded in for a new fixed asset having a similar use, proper accounting treatment prohibits recognition of a gain. .... ____ ____

7. A lease that transfers ownership of the leased asset to the lessee at the end of the lease term should be classified as an operating lease. .... ____ ____

8. Long-lived assets that are without physical characteristics but useful in the operations of a business are classified as fixed assets. .... ____ ____

9. Fully depreciated assets should be retained in the accounting records until disposal has been authorized and they are removed from service. .... ____ ____

10. Intangible assets are usually reported on the balance sheet in the current asset section. .... ____ ____

EXERCISE 9-1

A fixed asset acquired on January 2 at a cost of $420,000 has an estimated useful life of 8 years. Assuming that it will have a residual value of $20,000, determine the depreciation for each of the first two years (a) by the straight-line method and (b) by the declining-balance method, using twice the straight-line rate.

(a) Straight-line method   Depreciation

         Year 1 .... _____

         Year 2 .... _____

(b) Declining-balance method   Depreciation

         Year 1 .... _____

         Year 2 .... _____

EXERCISE 9-2

Bidwell Co. uses the units-of-production method for computing the depreciation on its machines. One machine, which cost $88,000, is estimated to have a useful life of 22,000 hours and no residual value. During the first year of operation, this machine was used a total of 5,200 hours. Record the depreciation of this machine on December 31, the end of the first year. (Omit explanation.)

JOURNAL   PAGE

	DATE	DESCRIPTION	POST. REF.	DEBIT	CREDIT	
1						1
2						2
3						3
4						4
5						5
6						6
7						7
8						8
9						9
10						10

EXERCISE 9-3

On March 8, Tilly's Wholesale decides to sell for $2,000 cash some fixtures for which it paid $4,000 and on which it has taken total depreciation of $2,500 to date of sale. Record this sale. (Omit explanation.)

JOURNAL   PAGE

	DATE	DESCRIPTION	POST. REF.	DEBIT	CREDIT	
1						1
2						2
3						3
4						4
5						5
6						6
7						7
8						8
9						9
10						10

EXERCISE 9-4

Mine-It Co. paid $2,400,000 for some mineral rights in Idaho. The deposit is estimated to contain 800,000 tons of ore of uniform grade. Record the depletion of this deposit on December 31, the end of the first year, assuming that 80,000 tons are mined during the year. (Omit explanation.)

JOURNAL   PAGE

	DATE		DESCRIPTION	POST. REF.	DEBIT	CREDIT	
1							1
2							2
3							3
4							4
5							5
6							6
7							7
8							8
9							9
10							10

EXERCISE 9-5

Stables Co. acquires a patent at the beginning of its calendar (fiscal) year for $100,000. Although the patent will not expire for another ten years, it is expected to be of value for only five years. Record the amortization of this patent at the end of the fiscal year. (Omit explanation.)

JOURNAL   PAGE

	DATE		DESCRIPTION	POST. REF.	DEBIT	CREDIT	
1							1
2							2
3							3
4							4
5							5
6							6
7							7
8							8
9							9
10							10

PROBLEM 9-1

Bishop Company purchased equipment on January 1, 20XA, for $80,000. The equipment is expected to have a useful life of 4 years or 15,000 operating hours and a residual value of $5,000. The equipment was used 3,400 hours in 20XA, 4,000 hours in 20XB, 6,000 hours in 20XC, and 1,600 hours in 20XD.

Instructions: Determine the amount of depreciation expense for the years ended December 31, 20XA, 20XB, 20XC, and 20XD, for each method of depreciation in the table below.

Year	Straight-Line	Declining-Balance	Units-of-Production
20XA			
20XB			
20XC			
20XD			
Total			

PROBLEM 9-2

Getco Co. has a sales representative who must travel a substantial amount. A car for this purpose was acquired January 2 four years ago at a cost of $20,000. It is estimated to have a total useful life of 4 years or 100,000 miles.

Instructions:

(1) Record the annual depreciation on Getco's car at the end of the first and third years of ownership using the straight-line method, assuming no residual value, and using a December 31 year end. (Omit explanation.)

(2) Record the annual depreciation on Getco's car at the end of the first and third years of ownership using the declining-balance method at twice the straight-line rate and a December 31 year end. (Omit explanation.)

(3) Record the annual depreciation on Getco's car at the end of the first and third years of ownership using the units-of-production method, assuming no residual value, and using a December 31 year end. The car was driven 35,000 miles in the first year and 28,000 miles in the third year. (Omit explanation.)

(1)–(3)   **JOURNAL**   PAGE

	DATE		DESCRIPTION	POST. REF.	DEBIT	CREDIT	
1							1
2							2
3							3
4							4
5							5
6							6
7							7
8							8
9							9
10							10
11							11
12							12
13							13
14							14
15							15
16							16
17							17
18							18
19							19
20							20
21							21
22							22
23							23
24							24
25							25
26							26
27							27
28							28
29							29
30							30
31							31
32							32
33							33
34							34
35							35
36							36

PROBLEM 9-3

(a) Braso Co. is planning to trade in its present truck for a new model on April 30 of the current year. The existing truck was purchased May 1 three years ago at a cost of $15,000, and accumulated depreciation is $12,000 through April 30 of the current year. The new truck has a list price of $20,700. Ralston Motors agrees to allow Braso $3,500 for the present truck, and Braso agrees to pay the balance of $17,200 in cash.

Instructions: Record the exchange in general journal form according to acceptable methods of accounting for exchanges. (Omit explanation.)

JOURNAL   PAGE

	DATE	DESCRIPTION	POST. REF.	DEBIT	CREDIT	
1						1
2						2
3						3
4						4
5						5
6						6
7						7
8						8
9						9

(b) Assume the same facts as in (a), except that the allowance on the present truck is $1,000 and Braso agrees to pay the balance of $19,700 in cash.

Instructions: Record the exchange according to acceptable methods of accounting for exchanges.

JOURNAL   PAGE

	DATE	DESCRIPTION	POST. REF.	DEBIT	CREDIT	
1						1
2						2
3						3
4						4
5						5
6						6
7						7
8						8
9						9

10 Current Liabilities

QUIZ AND TEST HINTS

The following hints may be helpful to you in preparing for a quiz or a test over the material covered in Chapter 10.

1. A major focus of this chapter is on the computation of payroll. You should be able to compute total earnings, social security and Medicare tax, state and federal unemployment tax, and net pay and prepare the necessary journal entries. Review the chapter illustrations related to these computations.

2. The journal entries for vacation pay, pensions, and warranty expense are fairly easy to do. Spend a few minutes reviewing these entries.

3. Most instructors will ask some questions related to notes payable. You should be able to compute interest and prepare the necessary journal entries, including an adjusting entry for accrued interest. Also, carefully review the discounting of notes.

4. The Illustrative Problem is a good overall review of the types of journal entries you might have to prepare on a test or a quiz. Try to work the problem without looking at the solution. Check your answer. If you made any errors, review those sections of the chapter. If you still don't understand the answer, ask your instructor for help.

5. Do the Matching exercises included in this Study Guide.

MATCHING

Instructions: Match each of the statements below with its proper term. Some terms may not be used.

A.	defined benefit plan	**H.**	gross pay
B.	defined contribution plan	**I.**	net pay
C.	discount	**J.**	payroll
D.	discount rate	**K.**	payroll register
E.	employee's earnings record	**L.**	postretirement benefits
F.	FICA tax	**M.**	proceeds
G.	fringe benefits	**N.**	quick ratio

_____ **1.** A detailed record of each employee's earnings.

_____ **2.** A multicolumn form used to assemble and summarize payroll data at the end of each payroll period.

_____ **3.** A pension plan that promises employees a fixed annual pension benefit at retirement, based on years of service and compensation levels.

_____ **4.** Gross pay less payroll deductions; the amount the employer is obligated to pay the employee.

_____ **5.** The net amount available from discounting a note payable.

_____ **6.** A pension plan that requires a fixed amount of money to be invested for the employee's behalf during the employee's working years.

_____ **7.** Benefits provided to employees in addition to wages and salaries.

_____ **8.** The rate used in computing the interest to be deducted from the maturity value of a note.

_____ **9.** The total earnings of an employee for a payroll period.

_____ **10.** Rights to benefits that employees earn during their term of employment, for themselves and their dependents, after they retire.

_____ **11.** The total amount paid to employees for a certain period.

_____ **12.** Federal Insurance Contributions Act tax used to finance federal programs for old-age and disability benefits (social security) and health insurance for the aged (Medicare).

_____ **13.** A financial ratio that measures the ability to pay current liabilities within a short period of time.

_____ **14.** The interest deducted from the maturity value of a note.

FILL IN THE BLANK—PART A

Instructions: Answer the following questions or complete the statements by writing the appropriate words or amounts in the answer blanks.

1. The maturity value of a 90-day, 12%, $30,000 note payable is

   _____.

2. In buying equipment, a business issues a $90,000, 180-day note dated January 17, which the seller discounts at 12%. The cost of the equipment would be recorded at _____.

3. The total earnings of an employee for a payroll period is called _____ pay.

4. _____ _____ is the amount the employer is obligated to pay the employee after payroll deductions.

5. _____ _____ _____ _____ tax is used to finance federal programs for old-age and disability benefits (social security) and health insurance for the aged (Medicare).

6. A(n) _____ _____ _____ is a detailed record of each employee's earnings.

7. Employer's payroll taxes become liabilities when the related employee payroll is _____.

8. A pension plan that promises employees a fixed annual pension benefit based on years of service and compensation levels is called a(n) _____ _____ plan.

9. Rights to benefits that employees earn during their term of employment but take effect after they retire are called _____ benefits.

10. The _____ ratio measures the ability to pay current liabilities within a short period of time.

FILL IN THE BLANK—PART B

Instructions: Answer the following questions or complete the statements by writing the appropriate words or amounts in the answer blanks.

1. The maturity value of a 120-day, 9%, $75,000 note payable is

   _____.

2. In buying a building, a business issues a $240,000, 120-day note dated August 3, which the seller discounts at 10%. The cost of the building would be recorded at _____.

3. The interest deducted from the maturity value of a note is called the
   _____.

4. The _____ rate is used in computing the interest to be deducted from the maturity value of a note.

5. Gross pay less payroll deductions is _____ pay.

6. A(n) _____ _____ is a multicolumn form used to assemble and summarize payroll data at the end of each payroll period.

7. The employer's matching portion of the Federal Insurance Contribution Act (FICA) tax that represents the contribution to health insurance for senior citizens is credited to _____ _____ Payable.

8. _____ refers to the total amount paid to employees for a certain period.

9. Benefits provided to employees in addition to wages and salaries are called _____ benefits.

10. A pension plan that requires a fixed amount of money to be invested for the employee's behalf during the employee's working years is called a(n) _____ _____ plan.

MULTIPLE CHOICE

Instructions: Circle the best answer for each of the following questions.

1. The interest charged by the bank, at the rate of 12%, on a 90-day, non-interest-bearing note payable for $75,000 is:
   a. $1,000
   b. $2,250
   c. $3,000
   d. $9,000

2. The cost of a product warranty should be included as an expense:
   a. in the period of the sale of the product
   b. in the period of the collection of the cash from the sale of the product
   c. in the future period when the product is repaired or replaced
   d. in the future period when the cost of repairing the product is paid

3. An employee's rate of pay is $8 per hour, with time and a half for hours worked in excess of 40 during a week. If the employee works 50 hours during a week and has social security tax withheld at a rate of 6.0%, Medicare tax withheld at a rate of 1.5%, and federal income tax withheld at a rate of 15%, the employee's net pay for the week is:

   a. $440

   b. $374

   c. $341

   d. $310

4. An employee receives an hourly rate of $18, with time and a half for all hours worked in excess of 40 during a week. Payroll data for the current week are as follows: hours worked, 45; federal income tax withheld, $350; cumulative earnings for year prior to current week, $49,700; social security tax rate, 6.0%; Medicare tax rate, 1.5%. What is the gross pay for the employee?

   a. $475

   b. $505

   c. $720

   d. $855

5. Prior to the last weekly payroll period of the calendar year, the cumulative earnings of employees A and B are $79,800 and $21,000, respectively. Their earnings for the last completed payroll period of the year are $1,000 each. The amount of earnings subject to social security tax is $80,000, and the tax rate is 6%. All earnings are subject to Medicare tax at 1.5%. Assuming that the payroll will be paid on December 29, what will be the employer's total FICA tax (social security and Medicare) for this payroll period on the two salary amounts of $1,000 each?

   a. $75

   b. $90

   c. $120

   d. $150

6. Payroll taxes levied against employees become liabilities:

   a. when earned by the employee

   b. at the end of an accounting period

   c. the first of the following month

   d. at the time the liability for the employee's wages is paid

7. Which of the following items would not be considered a fringe benefit?
    a. vacations
    b. employee pension plans
    c. health insurance
    d. FICA benefits

8. For proper matching of revenues and expenses, the estimated cost of fringe benefits must be recognized as an expense of the period the:
    a. employee earns the benefit
    b. employee is paid the benefit
    c. fringe benefit contract is signed
    d. fringe benefit contract becomes effective

9. The inputs into a payroll system may be classified as either constants or variables. All of the following are variables except for:
    a. number of hours worked
    b. vacation credits
    c. number of income tax withholding allowances
    d. number of days sick leave with pay

10. An aid in internal control over payrolls that indicates employee attendance is a(n):
    a. payroll register
    b. employee earnings record
    c. "In and Out" card
    d. payroll check

TRUE/FALSE

Instructions: Indicate whether each of the following statements is true or false by placing a check mark in the appropriate column.

		True	False
1.	The total earnings of an employee for a payroll period are called gross pay.	____	____
2.	Only employers are required to contribute to the Federal Insurance Contributions Act program.	____	____
3.	All states require that unemployment compensation taxes be withheld from employees' pay.	____	____

	True	False

4. Most employers are also subject to federal and state payroll taxes based on the amount earned by their employees, not the amount paid. .... ____ ____

5. The amounts withheld from employees' earnings have an effect on the firm's debits to the salary or wage expense accounts. .... ____ ____

6. All payroll taxes levied against employers become liabilities at the time the related remuneration is paid to employees. .... ____ ____

7. The recording procedures when special payroll checks are used are different from the procedures when the checks are drawn on the regular bank account. .... ____ ____

8. Depending on when it is to be paid, vacation liability may be classified in the balance sheet as either a current liability or a long-term liability. .... ____ ____

9. To properly match revenues and expense, employees' vacation pay should be accrued as a liability as the vacation rights are earned. .... ____ ____

10. In order for revenues and expenses to be matched properly, a liability to cover the cost of a product warranty must be recorded in the period when the product is repaired. ...... ____ ____

11. Potential liabilities that may arise in the future because of past transactions are called contingent liabilities. .... ____ ____

12. All changes in the constants of the payroll system, such as changes in pay rates, should be properly authorized in writing. .... ____ ____

13. The net periodic pension cost of a defined benefit plan is debited to Pension Expense, the amount funded is credited to Cash, and any unfunded amount is credited to Unfunded Pension Revenue. .... ____ ____

14. Examples of postretirement benefits from an employer may include dental care, eye care, medical care, life insurance, tuition assistance, or tax services. .... ____ ____

15. The rate used by a bank in discounting a note is called the prime rate. .... ____ ____

EXERCISE 10-1

Instructions: In each of the following situations, determine the correct amount.

(1) An employee of a firm operating under the Federal Wage and Hour Law worked 50 hours last week. If the hourly rate of pay is $14, what is the employee's gross earnings for the week?

(2) During the current pay period, an employee earned $2,000. Prior to the current period, the employee earned (in the current year) $79,500. If the social security tax is 6.0% on the first $80,000 of annual earnings and the Medicare tax rate is 1.5% on all earnings, what is the total amount to be withheld from the employee's pay this period?

(3) During the current pay period, an employee earned $3,000. Prior to the current period, the employee earned (in the current year) $137,800. Using the social security and Medicare tax rates and bases in (2), compute the total amount to be withheld from the employee's pay this period.

(4) Using the rates and maximum bases in (2), compute the total amount of social security and Medicare tax withheld from the pay of an employee who has earned $10,000 during the year but has actually received only $9,700, with the remaining $300 to be paid in the next year.

EXERCISE 10-2

Instructions: Prepare the general journal entries to record each of the following items for Wiler Co. for the year ended December 31. (Omit explanations.)

(1) Accrued employee vacation pay at the end of the year is $3,225.

(2) The estimated product warranty liability at the end of the year is 3% of sales of $150,000.

(3) A partially funded pension plan is maintained for employees at an annual cost of $40,000. At the end of the year, $27,500 is paid to the fund trustee and the remaining accrued pension liability is recognized.

JOURNAL   PAGE

	DATE	DESCRIPTION	POST. REF.	DEBIT	CREDIT	
1						1
2						2
3						3
4						4
5						5
6						6
7						7
8						8
9						9
10						10
11						11
12						12
13						13
14						14
15						15
16						16
17						17
18						18
19						19
20						20
21						21
22						22
23						23
24						24
25						25
26						26

PROBLEM 10-1

The weekly gross payroll of O'Brien Co. on December 7 amounts to $50,000, distributed as follows: sales salaries, $34,000; office salaries, $16,000. The following amounts are to be withheld: social security tax, $3,000; Medicare tax, $750; employees' income tax, $7,500; union dues, $900; and United Way, $450.

Instructions: Omitting explanations, prepare general journal entries to:

(1) Record the payroll.

(2) Record the payment of the payroll.

(3) Record the employer's payroll taxes. Assume that the entire payroll is subject to social security tax at 6.0%, Medicare tax at 1.5%, federal unemployment tax at 0.8%, and state unemployment tax at 5.4%.

(4) Disregarding (3), record the employer's payroll taxes. Assume that $40,000 of payroll is subject to social security tax at 6.0% and $50,000 is subject to Medicare tax at 1.5%. Assume that none of the payroll is subject to federal or state unemployment tax.

JOURNAL

PAGE

	DATE		DESCRIPTION	POST. REF.	DEBIT	CREDIT	
1							1
2							2
3							3
4							4
5							5
6							6
7							7
8							8
9							9
10							10
11							11
12							12
13							13
14							14
15							15
16							16
17							17
18							18
19							19
20							20

JOURNAL

PAGE

	DATE		DESCRIPTION	POST. REF.	DEBIT	CREDIT	
1							1
2							2
3							3
4							4
5							5
6							6
7							7
8							8
9							9
10							10
11							11
12							12
13							13
14							14
15							15
16							16
17							17
18							18
19							19
20							20
21							21
22							22
23							23
24							24
25							25
26							26
27							27
28							28
29							29
30							30
31							31
32							32
33							33
34							34
35							35
36							36

PROBLEM 10-2

Instructions: For the employees listed below, compute the individual taxes indicated as well as total taxes by type and by employee. Assume the social security tax rate is 6.0% on the first $80,000 of annual earnings, the Medicare tax rate is 1.5% on all earnings, the state unemployment tax rate is 5.4% on a maximum of $7,000, and the federal unemployment tax rate is 0.8% on a maximum of $7,000.

| Employee | Annual Earnings | Employer's Taxes | | | | |
		Social Security Tax	Medicare Tax	State Unemploy-ment	Federal Unemploy-ment	Total
Avery	$ 12,000					
Johnson	5,000					
Jones	59,000					
Smith	73,000					
Wilson	141,000					
Total	$290,000					

PROBLEM 10-3

Instructions: Prepare the general journal entries to record the following transactions. (Omit explanations.)

(1) Audrey Newman issued a 90-day, 12% note for $2,000 to Mayday Co. for a $2,000 overdue account.

(2) Newman paid the note in (1) at maturity.

(3) Paula Wheat borrowed $8,000 from the bank and gave the bank a 90-day, 11% note.

(4) Wheat paid the note in (3) at maturity.

(5) Randy Lucky borrowed $6,000 from the bank, giving a 60-day, non-interest-bearing note that was discounted at 9%.

(6) Lucky paid the note recorded in (5) at maturity.

JOURNAL   PAGE

	DATE	DESCRIPTION	POST. REF.	DEBIT	CREDIT	
1						1
2						2
3						3
4						4
5						5
6						6
7						7
8						8
9						9
10						10
11						11
12						12
13						13
14						14
15						15
16						16
17						17
18						18
19						19
20						20
21						21
22						22
23						23

11 Corporations: Organization, Capital Stock Transactions, and Dividends

QUIZ AND TEST HINTS

The following hints may be helpful to you in preparing for a quiz or a test over the material covered in Chapter 11.

1. Many new terms related to the corporate form of organization are introduced in this chapter that may be tested using true/false or multiple-choice questions. Do the Matching exercises included in this Study Guide.

2. You should be able to compute the amount of dividends allocated between nonparticipating cumulative preferred stock and common stock.

3. You should be able to prepare journal entries for the issuance of par and no-par stock, treasury stock transactions, and cash and stock dividends. Expect at least one problem requiring such entries.

4. It is unlikely that you will be required to prepare a journal entry for organization expenses. However, you may be asked a multiple-choice question related to organization expenses.

MATCHING

Instructions: Match each of the statements below with its proper term. Some terms may not be used.

A. cash dividend
B. common stock
C. cumulative preferred stock
D. discount
E. dividend yield
F. nonparticipating preferred stock
G. outstanding stock
H. par
I. preferred stock

J. premium
K. stated value
L. statement of stockholders' equity
M. stock
N. stock dividend
O. stock split
P. stockholders
Q. treasury stock

_____ 1. Shares of ownership of a corporation.

_____ 2. The owners of a corporation.

_____ 3. The stock in the hands of stockholders.

_____ 4. A value, similar to par value, approved by the board of directors of a corporation for no-par stock.

_____ 5. The stock outstanding when a corporation has issued only one class of stock.

_____ 6. A class of stock with preferential rights over common stock.

_____ 7. A class of preferred stock whose dividend rights are usually limited to a certain amount.

_____ 8. A class of preferred stock that has a right to receive regular dividends that have been passed (not declared) before any common stock dividends are paid.

_____ 9. The excess of the issue price of a stock over its par value.

_____ 10. The excess of the par value of a stock over its issue price.

_____ 11. Stock that a corporation has once issued and then reacquires.

_____ 12. A reduction in the par or stated value of a common stock and the issuance of a proportionate number of additional shares.

_____ 13. A cash distribution of earnings by a corporation to its shareholders.

_____ 14. A distribution of shares of stock to its stockholders.

_____ 15. A ratio, computed by dividing the annual dividends paid per share of common stock by the market price per share at a specific date, that indicates the rate of return to stockholders in terms of cash dividend distributions.

_____ 16. The monetary amount printed on a stock certificate.

_____ 17. A statement summarizing significant changes in stockholders' equity that have occurred during a period.

FILL IN THE BLANK—PART A

Instructions: Answer the following questions or complete the statements by writing the appropriate words or amounts in the answer blanks.

1. Shares of ownership of a corporation are called _____.

2. Corporations whose shares of stock are traded in public markets are called _____ corporations.

3. Stockholders of corporations have _____ liability.

4. The stockholders' equity section of a balance sheet is composed of preferred $7 stock, $250,000; discount on preferred stock, $25,000; common stock, $750,000; premium on common stock, $100,000; retained earnings, $190,000; treasury stock, $80,000. The total paid-in capital is _____.

5. Stock in the hands of stockholders is called _____ stock.

6. When a corporation has issued only one class of stock, it is called _____ stock.

7. A class of preferred stock whose dividend rights are usually limited to a certain amount is referred to as _____ preferred stock.

8. A company has outstanding stock that is composed of 10,000 shares of $5 cumulative, nonparticipating, $50 par preferred stock and 150,000 shares of $10 par common stock. Preferred dividends were passed last year, and no dividends have been paid thus far in the current year. A total of $280,000 in dividends is to be distributed. The total amount of dividends to be paid on the preferred stock is _____.

9. When the issuance price of a stock exceeds its par value, the stock is said to have been issued at a(n) _____.

10. Land is acquired by issuing 5,000 shares of $20 par common stock with a current market price of $32 per share. The land should be recorded at a cost of _____.

11. If a corporation issues stock and then reacquires the stock, the stock reacquired is referred to as _____ stock.

12. A company purchases 500 shares of its $50 par common stock for $32,500 cash. The effect (increase, decrease, or none) of this purchase on the company's retained earnings is _____ (indicate amount and effect).

13. A(n) _____ is a cash distribution of earnings by a corporation to its shareholders.

14. A balance sheet indicated 20,000 shares of common stock authorized, 8,000 shares issued, and 1,500 shares of treasury stock. If a cash dividend of $5 per share is declared on the common stock, the total amount of the dividend is _____.

15. The effect of a stock dividend on the stockholders' equity of a corporation's balance sheet is to increase paid-in capital and decrease _____ _____.

FILL IN THE BLANK—PART B

Instructions: Answer the following questions or complete the statements by writing the appropriate words or amounts in the answer blanks.

1. The owners of a corporation are the _____.

2. After the application of incorporation has been approved, a state grants the corporation a charter or _____ _____ _____.

3. Costs incurred in organizing a corporation are recorded by debiting the _____ _____ account.

4. A value, similar to par value, approved by the board of directors of a corporation for no-par stock is called _____ value.

5. A class of stock with preferential rights over common stock is called _____ stock.

6. _____ preferred stock has a right to receive regular dividends that have been passed (not declared) before any common stock dividends are paid.

7. A company has outstanding stock that is composed of 25,000 shares of $3 cumulative, nonparticipating, $100 par preferred stock and 150,000 shares of $10 par common stock. Preferred dividends were passed last year, and no dividends have been paid thus far in the current year. A total of $140,000 in dividends is to be distributed. The total amount of dividends to be paid on the preferred stock is _____.

8. When the par value of a stock exceeds its issuance price, the stock is said to have been issued at a(n) _____.

9. A company purchases 500 shares of its $50 par common stock for $32,500 cash. The effect (increase, decrease, or none) of this purchase on the company's paid-in capital is _____ (indicate amount and effect).

10. The stockholders' equity section of a balance sheet is composed of preferred $7 stock, $250,000; discount on preferred stock, $25,000; common stock, $750,000; premium on common stock, $100,000; retained earnings, $100,000 deficit; treasury stock, $80,000. The total stockholders' equity is _____.

11. A(n) _____ _____ is the reduction in the par or stated value of common stock and the issuance of a proportionate number of additional shares.

12. A corporation announced a 5-for-1 stock split of its $100 par value stock, which is currently trading for $180. The estimated market value of the stock after the split is _____.

13. A(n) _____ _____ is a distribution of shares of stock to its stockholders.

14. The _____ value is the monetary amount printed on a stock certificate.

15. The _____ _____ is a ratio computed by dividing the annual dividends paid per share of common stock by the market price per share at a specific date, and it indicates the rate of return to stockholders in terms of cash dividend distributions.

MULTIPLE CHOICE

Instructions: Circle the best answer for each of the following questions.

1. Which of the following is not a characteristic of the corporate form of organization?
   a. ownership represented by shares of stock
   b. separate legal existence
   c. unlimited liability of stockholders
   d. earnings subject to the federal income tax

2. The amount printed on a stock certificate is known as:
   a. stated value
   b. premium
   c. discount
   d. par value

3. Assume that a corporation has outstanding 5,000 shares of $6 cumulative preferred stock of $100 par and dividends have been passed for the preceding four years. What is the amount of preferred dividends that must be declared in the current year before a dividend can be declared on common stock?
   a. $90,000
   b. $120,000
   c. $150,000
   d. $180,000

4. When a corporation purchases its own stock, what account is debited for the cost of the stock?

   a. Common Stock Subscribed

   b. Treasury Stock

   c. Preferred Stock

   d. Common Stock Receivable

5. The excess of the proceeds from selling treasury stock over its cost should be credited to:

   a. Retained Earnings

   b. Premium on Capital Stock

   c. Gain from Sale of Treasury Stock

   d. Paid-In Capital from Sale of Treasury Stock

6. The claims of the _____ must first be satisfied upon liquidation of a corporation.

   a. preferred stockholders

   b. cumulative preferred stockholders

   c. common stockholders

   d. creditors

7. A company with 20,000 authorized shares of $20 par common stock issued 12,000 shares at $50. Subsequently, the company declared a 5% stock dividend on a date when the market price was $60 per share. What is the amount transferred from the retained earnings account to paid-in capital accounts as a result of the stock dividend?

   a. $36,000

   b. $30,000

   c. $12,000

   d. $6,000

8. The charter of a corporation provides for the issuance of 100,000 shares of common stock. Assume that 60,000 shares were originally issued and 5,000 were subsequently reacquired. What is the number of shares outstanding?

   a. 5,000

   b. 55,000

   c. 60,000

   d. 100,000

9. The entry to record the issuance of common stock at a price above par would include a credit to:

   a. Donated Capital

   b. Retained Earnings

   c. Treasury Stock

   d. Paid-In Capital in Excess of Par—Common Stock

10. A corporation purchases 10,000 shares of its own $20 par common stock for $35 per share, recording it at cost. What will be the effect on total stockholders' equity?

   a. increase, $200,000

   b. increase, $350,000

   c. decrease, $200,000

   d. decrease, $350,000

TRUE/FALSE

Instructions: Indicate whether each of the following statements is true or false by placing a check mark in the appropriate column.

	True	False
1. A partnership is similar to a proprietorship except that it has more than one owner.	____	____
2. A corporation may acquire, own, and dispose of property in its corporate name.	____	____
3. The two main sources of stockholders' equity are paid-in capital and long-term debt.	____	____
4. The common stockholders have a greater chance of receiving regular dividends than do preferred stockholders.	____	____
5. The board of directors has the sole authority to distribute earnings to the stockholders in the form of dividends.	____	____
6. The specified minimum stockholders' contribution that a corporation is required by law to retain for protection of its creditors is called legal capital.	____	____
7. Preferred stock for which dividend rights are limited to a certain amount is said to be noncumulative.	____	____
8. When par stock is issued for more than par, the excess of the contract price over par is termed a premium.	____	____
9. Sales of treasury stock result in a net decrease in paid-in capital.	____	____

	True	False

10. Expenditures incurred in organizing a corporation, such as legal fees, taxes, fees paid to the state, and promotional costs, are charged to an intangible asset account entitled Goodwill. .... ____ ____

11. A commonly used method for accounting for the purchase and resale of treasury stock is the derivative method.......... ____ ____

12. A major objective of a stock split is to increase stockholders' equity.. ____ ____

13. Paid-in capital and retained earnings are two major subdivisions of stockholders' equity... ____ ____

14. A liability for a dividend is normally recorded in the accounting records on the date of record. .... ____ ____

15. An accounting entry is required to record a stock dividend. ____ ____

EXERCISE 11-1

Prepare the entries in general journal form to record each of the following unrelated transactions. (Omit explanations.)

(1) Cannuck Corp. issued 20,000 shares of no-par common stock for cash at $35 per share.

JOURNAL   PAGE

	DATE	DESCRIPTION	POST. REF.	DEBIT	CREDIT	
1						1
2						2
3						3
4						4
5						5

(2) Dunlo Corp. issued 20,000 shares of $25 par common stock for cash at $25 per share.

JOURNAL   PAGE

	DATE	DESCRIPTION	POST. REF.	DEBIT	CREDIT	
1						1
2						2
3						3
4						4
5						5

(3) Erickson Corp. issued 20,000 shares of $50 par common stock for cash at $60 per share.

JOURNAL   PAGE

	DATE	DESCRIPTION	POST. REF.	DEBIT	CREDIT	
1						1
2						2
3						3
4						4
5						5
6						6
7						7

(4) Felix Corp. issued 10,000 shares of $10 par common stock in exchange for new manufacturing equipment with a fair market value of $145,000.

JOURNAL   PAGE

	DATE	DESCRIPTION	POST. REF.	DEBIT	CREDIT	
1						1
2						2
3						3
4						4
5						5
6						6
7						7

(5) Huddley Corp. issued 10,000 shares of $25 par preferred stock for cash at $30 per share.

JOURNAL   PAGE

	DATE	DESCRIPTION	POST. REF.	DEBIT	CREDIT	
1						1
2						2
3						3
4						4
5						5
6						6
7						7

EXERCISE 11-2

Prepare the entries in general journal form to record each of the following treasury stock transactions of Pinell Corp. using the cost basis method. (Omit explanations.)

(1) On October 1, Pinell purchased 2,000 shares of treasury stock at $75.

(2) On October 31, Pinell sold 800 shares of the treasury stock it purchased on October 1 at $82.

(3) On November 20, Pinell sold 100 shares of the treasury stock it purchased on October 1 at $70.

JOURNAL   PAGE

	DATE	DESCRIPTION	POST. REF.	DEBIT	CREDIT	
1						1
2						2
3						3
4						4
5						5
6						6
7						7
8						8
9						9
10						10
11						11
12						12
13						13
14						14
15						15
16						16
17						17
18						18
19						19
20						20
21						21
22						22
23						23
24						24
25						25
26						26
27						27

EXERCISE 11-3

Journalize the following transactions of Copper Corp. (Omit explanations.)

(1) On February 20, Copper declared a $60,000 cash dividend.

(2) On March 22, Copper paid the cash dividend declared on February 20.

(3) On December 15, Copper declared a 5% stock dividend on 160,000 shares of $20 par value common stock with a market value of $25 per share.

(4) On January 14, Copper issued the stock certificates for the stock dividend declared on December 15.

(5) On February 20, Copper declared a 2 for 1 stock split, exchanging 380,000 shares of $10 par common stock for 190,000 shares of $20 par common stock.

JOURNAL   PAGE

	DATE	DESCRIPTION	POST. REF.	DEBIT	CREDIT	
1						1
2						2
3						3
4						4
5						5
6						6
7						7
8						8
9						9
10						10
11						11
12						12
13						13
14						14
15						15
16						16
17						17
18						18
19						19
20						20
21						21
22						22
23						23
24						24
25						25

PROBLEM 11-1

Pattering Corp. has 4,000 shares of $10 par common stock outstanding and 1,000 shares of $100 par 8% preferred stock outstanding. Pattering expects to pay annual dividends of $7,000, $9,000, $28,000, and $48,000 respectively for the next four years.

Instructions: By completing the following forms, indicate how the dividends should be distributed in each case if the preferred stock is given the rights or the restrictions indicated.

(1) The preferred stock is cumulative and nonparticipating.

Year	Total Dividends	Preferred Dividends		Common Dividends	
		Total	Per Share	Total	Per Share
1	$ 7,000				
2	9,000				
3	28,000				
4	48,000				

(2) The preferred stock is noncumulative and nonparticipating.

Year	Total Dividends	Preferred Dividends		Common Dividends	
		Total	Per Share	Total	Per Share
1	$ 7,000				
2	9,000				
3	28,000				
4	48,000				

PROBLEM 11-2

The stockholders' equity of Southland Corp. consists of 100,000 shares of $25 par stock, additional paid-in capital of $1,500,000, and retained earnings of $6,440,000. Theodore Rafael owns 1,000 of the outstanding shares.

Instructions:

(1) In Column A below, fill in the blanks with the appropriate figures based on the data given.

(2) In Column B, fill in the blanks with the appropriate figures based on the data given, but after a $1.50 per share cash dividend has been declared and paid.

(3) In Column C, fill in the blanks with the appropriate figures based on the data given, but after a 5% stock dividend has been declared and distributed. The market value of Southland Corp.'s stock is $30. (Ignore the instructions in (2) when making these calculations.)

	A	B	C
	Before Any Dividend	After Cash Dividend	After Stock Dividend
a. Total number of shares outstanding..................................			
b. Total par value of shares outstanding..................................			
c. Total additional paid-in capital.........			
d. Total retained earnings....................			
e. Total stockholders' equity................			
f. Amount required to pay a $1.50 per share cash dividend next year. (Assume no further changes in the capital structure.)..................			
g. Percentage of total stock owned by Rafael			
h. Total number of shares owned by Rafael			
i. Total par value of Rafael's shares...			
j. Total equity of Rafael's shares........			

PROBLEM 11-3

The following accounts and their balances appear in the ledger of Charleston Corporation on December 31, the end of the current fiscal year.

Common Stock, $25 par	$2,500,000
Paid-In Capital in Excess of Par—Common Stock	500,000
Paid-In Capital in Excess of Par—Preferred Stock	375,000
Paid-In Capital in Excess of Par—Treasury Stock	4,000
Preferred $10 Stock, $100 par	750,000
Retained Earnings	1,000,000
Treasury Stock—Common	50,000

Instructions: Prepare the stockholders' equity section of the balance sheet as of December 31, the end of the current year. Ten thousand shares of preferred and 150,000 shares of common stock are authorized. One thousand shares of common stock are held as treasury stock.

12 Income Taxes, Unusual Income Items, and Investments in Stocks

QUIZ AND TEST HINTS

The following hints may be helpful to you in preparing for a quiz or a test over the material covered in Chapter 12.

1. Many new terms are introduced in this chapter. Oftentimes terms are tested using true/false or multiple-choice questions.

2. You should be able to prepare journal entries for deferred taxes. The most common examples involve (1) the difference between depreciation used for financial reporting and tax purposes and (2) the revenue recognition differences between book and tax.

3. The discussion of the reporting of unusual items in the financial statements is an important part of this chapter. You should be able to describe each of the types of unusual items and how they are reported in the financial statements. Be especially careful in studying how discontinued operations, extraordinary items, and changes in accounting principles are reported on the income statement, including the reporting of earnings per common share. Note that these three unusual items are reported *below* the income from continuing operations. Asset impairments and restructuring charges are unusual items that are reported *above* the income from continuing operations. The Illustrative Problem in the text is a good review of the reporting of unusual items. You might also look for several multiple-choice questions related to this topic.

4. You should be able to prepare journal entries for investments in stocks. The accounting for investments depends upon whether the investment is treated as an available-for-sale security or is accounted for under the equity method. The former uses lower-of-cost-or-market valuation with unrealized gains and losses becoming part of other comprehensive income. The equity method is a method used for long-term investments in which there is significant control of the investee.

MATCHING

Instructions: Match each of the statements below with its proper term. Some terms may not be used.

A.	accumulated other comprehensive income	**L.**	investments
B.	available-for-sale securities	**M.**	merger
C.	comprehensive income	**N.**	minority interest
D.	consolidated financial statements	**O.**	other comprehensive income
E.	consolidation	**P.**	parent company
F.	discontinued operations	**Q.**	price-earnings ratio
G.	earnings per common share (EPS)	**R.**	purchase method
H.	equity method	**S.**	restructuring charge
I.	equity securities	**T.**	subsidiary company
J.	extraordinary items	**U.**	taxable income
K.	fixed asset impairments	**V.**	temporary differences
		W.	temporary investments
		X.	trading securities
		Y.	unrealized holding gain or loss

_____ 1. The income according to the tax laws that is used as a base for determining the amount of taxes owed.

_____ 2. Differences between taxable income and income before income taxes, created because items are recognized in one period for tax purposes and in another period for income statement purposes. Such differences reverse or turn around in later years.

_____ 3. Operations of a major line of business for a company, such as a division, a department, or a certain class of customer, that have been disposed of.

_____ 4. Events and transactions that (1) are significantly different (unusual) from the typical or the normal operating activities of a business and (2) occur infrequently.

_____ 5. Net income per share of common stock outstanding during a period.

_____ 6. The cumulative effects of other comprehensive income items reported separately in the stockholders' equity section of the balance sheet.

_____ 7. The costs associated with involuntarily terminating employees, terminating contracts, consolidating facilities, or relocating employees.

_____ 8. All changes in stockholders' equity during a period except those resulting from dividends and stockholders' investments.

_____ 9. The preferred and common stock of a firm.

____ 10. Securities that management intends to actively trade for profit.

____ 11. Securities that management expects to sell in the future but which are not actively traded for profit.

____ 12. The balance sheet caption used to report investments in income-yielding securities that can be quickly sold and converted to cash as needed.

____ 13. The difference between the fair market values of the securities and their cost.

____ 14. The balance sheet caption used to report long-term investments in stocks not intended as a source of cash in the normal operations of the business.

____ 15. A condition when the fair value of a fixed asset falls below its book value and is not expected to recover.

____ 16. A method of accounting for an investment in common stock by which the investment account is adjusted for the investor's share of periodic net income and cash dividends of the investee.

____ 17. The joining of two corporations in which one company acquires all the assets and liabilities of another corporation, which is then dissolved.

____ 18. The creation of a new corporation by the transfer of assets and liabilities of two or more existing corporations, which are then dissolved.

____ 19. The corporation owning all or a majority of the voting stock of the other corporation.

____ 20. The corporation that is controlled by a parent company.

____ 21. The accounting method used when a corporation acquires the controlling share of the voting common stock of another corporation by paying cash, exchanging other assets, issuing debt, or some combination of these methods.

____ 22. Specified items that are reported separately from net income, including foreign currency items, pension liability adjustments, and unrealized gains and losses on investments.

____ 23. Financial statements resulting from combining parent and subsidiary statements.

____ 24. The portion of a subsidiary corporation's stock owned by outsiders.

____ 25. The ratio computed by dividing a corporation's stock market price per share at a specific date by the company's annual earnings per share.

FILL IN THE BLANK—PART A

Instructions: Answer the following questions or complete the statements by writing the appropriate words or amounts in the answer blanks.

1. The _____ income is used as a base for determining the amount of taxes owed.

2. Income before income tax reported on the income statement for the first year of operations is $300,000. Because of timing differences in accounting and tax methods, the taxable income for the same year is $250,000. If the income tax rate is 50%, the amount of income tax expense reported on the income statement should be _____.

3. _____ _____ are associated with involuntarily terminating employees, terminating contracts, consolidating facilities, or relocating employees.

4. When a company disposes of operations of a major line of business for a company (such as a division, a department, or a certain class of customer), the gain or loss is reported on the income statement as a gain or loss from _____ operations.

5. Events and transactions that (1) are significantly different (unusual) from the typical or the normal operating activities of a business and (2) occur infrequently are reported in the income statement as _____ _____.

6. A company which recently decided to stop producing and selling its products in foreign markets would report the resulting loss on its income statement as a(n) _____ _____ _____ _____.

7. Net income per share of common stock outstanding during a period is called _____ _____ _____.

8. If a company has preferred stock, the _____ _____ must first be subtracted from the net income in the numerator when calculating the earnings per share to be reported on the income statement.

9. All changes in stockholders' equity during a period except those resulting from investments by stockholders and dividends should be reported as part of _____ income.

10. Securities that management intends to actively trade for profit are referred to as _____ securities.

11. The balance sheet caption _____ _____ is used to report investments in income-yielding securities that can be quickly sold and converted to cash as needed.

12. The _____ method is used in accounting for an investment in common stock, by which the investment account is adjusted for the investor's share of periodic net income and property dividends of the investee.

13. A(n) _____ is the creation of a new corporation by the transfer of assets and liabilities of two or more existing corporations that are then dissolved.

14. The corporation that is controlled by a parent company is referred to as the _____ company.

15. The portion of a subsidiary corporation's stock owned by outsiders is called _____ _____ .

FILL IN THE BLANK—PART B

Instructions: Answer the following questions or complete the statements by writing the appropriate words or amounts in the answer blanks.

1. Differences between taxable income and income before income tax that reverse or turn around in later years are called _____ differences.

2. Income before income tax reported on the income statement for the first year of operations is $300,000. Because of timing differences in accounting and tax methods, the taxable income for the same year is $250,000. If the income tax rate is 50%, the amount of deferred income tax payable is _____ .

3. A company must record a(n) _____ _____ _____ on the income statement if the carrying amount of an asset exceeds its fair value.

4. A company that has never experienced a loss from a hurricane would report an uninsured hurricane loss on its income statement as a(n) _____ _____ .

5. A statement of _____ _____ summarizes significant changes in stockholders' equity that have occurred during a period.

6. Preferred or common stock are referred to as _____ securities.

7. Securities that management expects to sell in the future, but which are not actively traded for profit, are referred to as _____-_____-_____ securities.

8. The difference between the fair market values of the securities and their cost is a(n) _____ gain or loss.

9. The _____ method is used in accounting for an investment in common stock, by which the investor recognizes as income its share of cash dividends of the investee.

10. A(n) _____ is the joining of two corporations in which the acquiring company acquires all the assets and liabilities of another corporation that is then dissolved.

11. The balance sheet caption _____ is used to report long-term investments in stocks not intended as a source of cash in the normal operations of the business.

12. The corporation owning all or a majority of the voting stock of another corporation is referred to as the _____ company.

13. Other comprehensive income is closed to _____ _____ _____ _____ on the balance sheet.

14. The combining of parent and subsidiary financial statements for reporting purposes results in _____ financial statements.

15. The _____-_____ ratio is computed by dividing a corporation's stock market price per share at a specific date by the company's annual earnings per share.

MULTIPLE CHOICE

Instructions: Circle the best answer for each of the following questions.

1. During its first year of operations, a corporation elected to use the straight-line method of depreciation for financial reporting purposes and the sum-of-the-years-digits method for reporting taxable income. If the income tax is 40% and the amount of depreciation expense is $200,000 under the straight-line method and $300,000 under the sum-of-the-years-digits method, what is the amount of income tax deferred to future years?

   a. $40,000

   b. $80,000

   c. $100,000

   d. $120,000

2. All except which of the following are examples of items that create temporary differences?

   a. A method of recognizing revenue when the sale is made is used for financial statements, and a method of recognizing revenue at the time the cash is collected is used for tax reporting.

   b. Warranty expense is recognized in the year of sale for financial statements and when paid for tax reporting.

   c. An accelerated depreciation method is used for tax reporting, and the straight-line method is used for financial statements.

   d. Interest income on municipal bonds is recognized for financial statements and not for tax reporting.

3. Which of the following would appear as an extraordinary item on the income statement?

   a. correction of an error in the prior year's financial statements

   b. gain resulting from the sale of fixed assets

   c. loss on sale of temporary investments

   d. loss on condemnation of land

4. Earnings per share is required to be presented on the face of the income statement for:

   a. extraordinary items

   b. discontinued operations

   c. income from continuing operations and net income

   d. all of the above

5. All changes in stockholders' equity during a period except those resulting from investments by stockholders and dividends is the definition of:

    a. income from continuing operations

    b. comprehensive income

    c. net income

    d. retained earnings

6. The receipt of cash dividends on a long-term investment in common stock is accounted for as a debit to Cash and a credit to Dividend Revenue. Which of the following methods is being used to account for the investment?

    a. equity method

    b. market method

    c. cost method

    d. revenue method

7. The receipt of cash dividends on a long-term investment in common stock is accounted for as a debit to Cash and a credit to Investment in Spacek Inc. Which of the following methods is being used to account for the investment?

    a. equity method

    b. market method

    c. cost method

    d. revenue method

8. During the year in which Parent Company owned 75% of the outstanding common stock of Subsidiary Company, Subsidiary reported net income of $200,000 and dividends declared and paid of $50,000. What is the amount of net increase in the Investment in Subsidiary account for the year?

    a. $37,500

    b. $112,500

    c. $200,000

    d. $250,000

9. An investor purchased 800 shares of common stock, $50 par, for $96,000. Subsequently, 200 shares were sold for $115 per share. What is the amount of gain or loss on the sale?

    a. $1,000 loss

    b. $1,000 gain

    c. $4,000 loss

    d. $4,000 gain

10. In what section of the parent company's balance sheet would the balance of the account Investment in Subsidiary appear?

    a. current assets

    b. temporary investments

    c. investments

    d. stockholders' equity

11. If the other comprehensive loss is $5,000, what would be the balance of the accumulated other comprehensive income at the end of the period if the beginning balance were $12,000?

    a. $5,000

    b. $7,000

    c. $12,000

    d. $17,000

TRUE/FALSE

Instructions: Indicate whether each of the following statements is true or false by placing a check mark in the appropriate column.

	True	False
1. Income that is exempt from federal taxes, such as interest income on municipal bonds, is an example of a temporary tax difference.	____	____
2. Restructuring charges should have a separate earnings per share disclosure.	____	____
3. The amount reported as a gain or loss from discontinued operations on the income statement should be reported net of related income tax.	____	____
4. Income tax should be allocated to the fiscal year in which the related income is reported and earned..........................	____	____
5. To be classified as an extraordinary item, an item must be unusual in nature and infrequent in occurrence.	____	____
6. Over the life of a business, temporary differences reduce the total amount of tax paid.	____	____
7. All changes in stockholders' equity during a period except those resulting from investments by stockholders and dividends should be reported as part of comprehensive income.	____	____

		True	False

8. The accumulated other comprehensive income should be disclosed in the income statement, in a separate statement of comprehensive income, or in the statement of stockholders' equity. ....   ____   ____

9. Under the cost method of accounting for investments in stocks, the investor records its share of cash dividends as a decrease in the investment account and an increase in the cash account. ....   ____   ____

10. A corporation that is controlled by another corporation is known as a subsidiary. ....   ____   ____

11. The two methods of accounting for investments in stock are the cost method and the equity method. ....   ____   ____

12. When two or more corporations transfer their assets and liabilities to a corporation that has been created for the purpose of the takeover, the combination is called a merger. ....   ____   ____

13. Mergers and consolidations should be accounted for by the purchase method. ....   ____   ____

14. Subsequent to acquisition of a subsidiary, a parent company's investment account should be increased periodically for its share of the subsidiary's income. ....   ____   ____

15. A note representing a loan by a parent corporation to its subsidiary would appear as a note receivable in the parent's balance sheet and a note payable in the subsidiary's balance sheet. ....   ____   ____

EXERCISE 12-1

(1) Jabbs Corp. reported $550,000 income before tax on its income statement for the year. Because of temporary differences in accounting and tax methods, taxable income for the year is $320,000. Assuming an income tax rate of 40%, prepare the journal entry to record the income tax expense, liability, and deferred liability of Jabbs Corp.

JOURNAL   PAGE

	DATE	DESCRIPTION	POST. REF.	DEBIT	CREDIT	
1						1
2						2
3						3
4						4
5						5
6						6
7						7
8						8
9						9
10						10

(2) In the following year, Jabbs Corp. reported $500,000 income before income tax. Because of temporary differences in accounting and tax methods, taxable income for this year is $600,000. Assuming an income tax rate of 40%, prepare the journal entry to record the income tax expense, liability, and reduction of the deferred liability of Jabbs Corp.

JOURNAL   PAGE

	DATE	DESCRIPTION	POST. REF.	DEBIT	CREDIT	
1						1
2						2
3						3
4						4
5						5
6						6
7						7
8						8
9						9
10						10

EXERCISE 12-2

Mills Corp. estimates its income tax expense for the year to be $250,000. At the end of the year, Mills Corp. determines that its actual income tax for the year is $280,000.

(1) Prepare the entry to record one of the four estimated income tax payments.

JOURNAL

PAGE

	DATE	DESCRIPTION	POST. REF.	DEBIT	CREDIT	
1						1
2						2
3						3
4						4
5						5
6						6
7						7
8						8
9						9
10						10

(2) Prepare the entry to record the additional income tax liability for the year.

JOURNAL

PAGE

	DATE	DESCRIPTION	POST. REF.	DEBIT	CREDIT	
1						1
2						2
3						3
4						4
5						5
6						6
7						7
8						8
9						9
10						10

PROBLEM 12-1

During a recent year of operations, the Emory Corporation purchased the following securities as temporary investments:

Security	Shares Purchased	Cost	Market Value, End of Period
X-Tex..............................	2,000	$15,000	$14,000
Dylan Company...............	500	25,000	32,000

Emory's net income for the year was $124,000, while the accumulated other comprehensive income balance at the beginning of the period was $3,000. The retained earnings had a balance of $521,000 at the beginning of the period. The tax rate on capital gains was 15%. These were the only securities held by Emory during the year, and there were no other comprehensive income items during the year.

Instructions:

(1) Prepare the balance sheet presentation for the temporary investments at the end of the period.

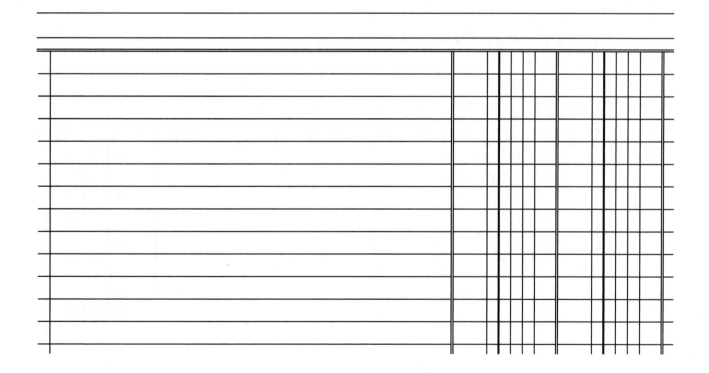

(2) Prepare the balance sheet presentation for retained earnings and accumulated other comprehensive income at the end of the period.

(3) Prepare a statement of comprehensive income for the period.

PROBLEM 12-2

(1) Record the following transactions for Richards Inc.

(a) As a long-term investment, Richards Inc. acquires 40,000 shares of Norris Inc. common stock at a cost of $600,000. Richards Inc. uses the equity method of accounting for this investment because it represents 25% of the voting stock of Norris Inc.

(b) On May 18, a cash dividend of $.75 per share is paid by Norris Inc.

(c) Norris Inc. reports net income of $900,000 for the year.

JOURNAL   PAGE

	DATE	DESCRIPTION	POST. REF.	DEBIT	CREDIT	
1						1
2						2
3						3
4						4
5						5
6						6
7						7
8						8
9						9
10						10
11						11
12						12
13						13
14						14
15						15
16						16
17						17
18						18
19						19
20						20
21						21
22						22
23						23
24						24
25						25
26						26
27						27

(2) Record the following transactions for Smith Inc.

(a) As a long-term investment, Smith Inc. acquires 10,000 shares of Kline Inc. common stock at a cost of $150,000. Smith uses the cost method of accounting for this investment, because it represents 5% of the voting stock of Kline Inc.

(b) On September 3, a cash dividend of $.50 per share is paid by Kline Inc.

(c) Kline Inc. reports a net income of $350,000 for the year.

JOURNAL

PAGE

	DATE	DESCRIPTION	POST. REF.	DEBIT	CREDIT	
1						1
2						2
3						3
4						4
5						5
6						6
7						7
8						8
9						9
10						10
11						11
12						12
13						13
14						14
15						15
16						16
17						17
18						18
19						19
20						20
21						21
22						22
23						23
24						24
25						25
26						26
27						27

PROBLEM 12-3

Summary data for Wess Corp. for the current fiscal year ended March 31 are as follows:

Cost of merchandise sold...	$1,800,000
Restructuring charge...	200,000
Cumulative effect on prior years of changing to a different depreciation method..	80,000
Loss on disposal of a segment of the business	70,000
Income taxes:	
Applicable to a change in depreciation method......................	18,000
Reduction applicable to loss on disposal of segment	20,000
Applicable to ordinary income	176,000
Reduction applicable to loss from earthquake	48,000
Loss from earthquake...	240,000
Operating expenses	100,000
Sales	2,700,000

Instructions: Use the form on the following page to prepare an income statement for Wess Corp., including a section for earnings per share as illustrated in this chapter. There were 50,000 shares of common stock outstanding throughout the year, and the effect of the change in depreciation method was to increase income.

13 Bonds Payable and Investments in Bonds

QUIZ AND TEST HINTS

The following hints may be helpful to you in preparing for a quiz or a test over the material covered in Chapter 13.

1. Study the new terminology introduced in this chapter for possible use in fill-in-the-blank, multiple-choice, or true/false questions. As a review of the key terms, do the Matching exercises included in this Study Guide.

2. It is unlikely that you will see a problem related to the Financing Corporations section of the chapter. Instead, you should focus primarily on being able to prepare the various journal entries illustrated throughout the chapter. The Illustrative Problem is a good study aid for reviewing the various journal entries.

3. If your instructor discussed the computation of present value of bonds payable, you should expect one or more questions on this topic.

4. Be ready to prepare entries for the issuance of bonds at face value, at a discount, and at a premium; for discount and premium amortization; and for bond redemption.

5. Be able to prepare journal entries for bond investments. You will more likely see a question requiring journal entries for the issuance of bonds payable, but occasionally instructors will include short problems on bond investments. You can assess the likelihood of such a problem by the amount of time your instructor spent lecturing on bond investments and whether you were assigned a homework problem on bond investments.

MATCHING

Instructions: Match each of the statements below with its proper term. Some terms may not be used.

A.   annuity
B.   available-for-sale securities
C.   bond
D.   bond fund
E.   bond indenture
F.   carrying amount
G.   contract rate
H.   discount
I.   dividend yield
J.   effective interest rate method

K.   effective rate of interest
L.   future value
M.   held-to-maturity securities
N.   number of times interest charges earned
O.   premium
P.   present value
Q.   present value of an annuity
R.   sinking fund

_____   1.   A form of an interest-bearing note used by corporations to borrow on a long-term basis.

_____   2.   The contract between a corporation issuing bonds and the bond-holders.

_____   3.   The periodic interest to be paid on the bonds that is identified in the bond indenture; expressed as a percentage of the face amount of the bond.

_____   4.   A series of equal cash flows at fixed intervals.

_____   5.   The sum of the present values of a series of equal cash flows to be received at fixed intervals.

_____   6.   The estimated worth today of an amount of cash to be received (or paid) in the future.

_____   7.   The estimated worth in the future of an amount of cash on hand today invested at a fixed rate of interest.

_____   8.   The excess of the face amount of bonds over their issue price.

_____   9.   The excess of the issue price of bonds over their face amount.

_____   10.   A fund in which cash or assets are set aside for the purpose of paying the face amount of the bonds at maturity.

_____   11.   The balance of the bonds payable account (face amount of the bonds) less any unamortized discount or plus any unamortized premium.

_____   12.   Investments in bonds or other debt securities that management intends to hold to their maturity.

_____   13.   A ratio that measures the risk that interest payments to debtholders will continue to be made if earnings decrease.

_____   14.   The market rate of interest at the time bonds are issued.

FILL IN THE BLANK—PART A

Instructions: Answer the following questions or complete the statements by writing the appropriate words or amounts in the answer blanks.

1. A corporation issuing bonds enters into a contract with the bondholders. This contract is known as a(n) _____ _____.

2. A corporation reserves the right to redeem _____ bonds before they mature.

3. Bonds issued on the general credit of the issuing corporation are called _____ _____.

4. The _____ rate determines the periodic interest paid on a bond.

5. When the market rate of interest on bonds is lower than the contract rate, the bonds will sell at a(n) _____.

6. Assuming an interest rate of 10%, $110 to be received a year from today is called the _____ _____ of $100 today.

7. The present value of $1,000 to be paid one year later, using an interest rate of 10% is _____.

8. If the market rate of interest is 11%, the present value of $10,000 to be received in each of the next 2 years is _____ (round to the nearest dollar).

9–10. The two methods for amortizing a bond discount are the _____-_____ method and the _____ _____ _____ method.

11. The amount set aside for the payment of bonds at maturity is called a(n) _____ _____.

12. The balance of the bonds payable account (face amount of the bonds) less any unamortized discount or plus any unamortized premium is called the _____ _____.

13. If the balances of Bonds Payable and Discount on Bonds Payable are $400,000 and $12,000, respectively, the carrying amount of the bonds is _____.

14. If $2,000,000 of bonds are sold at 101½, the amount of cash received is _____.

15. Bonds with a face amount of $100,000 were purchased through a broker at 103 plus accrued interest of $2,000 and brokerage commissions of $650. The amount to be debited to the investment account is _____.

16–17. A corporation purchased bonds at a premium several years ago. When this year ends, the company makes an entry to record the amortization of the premium.

16. The account to be debited is _____ _____.

17. The account to be credited is _____ ____ _____.

18. Jones Company has redeemed bonds at 102. The bonds have a face value of $600,000 and an unamortized premium of $10,000. Jones Company will record a gain (or loss) on redemption of _____ (indicate amount and gain or loss).

19. Smith Company intends to hold 10-year bonds until they mature. This asset is called a(n) _____-____-_____ _____.

20. River Company had interest expenses of $2,500,000 and income before tax of $29,000,000. The number of times interest charges are earned is _____.

FILL IN THE BLANK—PART B

Instructions: Answer the following questions or complete the statements by writing the appropriate words or amounts in the answer blanks.

1. All of Sand Company's bonds mature at the same time. These are known as _____ bonds.

2. Bonds that may be exchanged for other securities are called _____ bonds.

3. When the contract rate of interest on bonds is lower than the market rate of interest, the bonds sell at a(n) _____.

4. The present value of the face amount of a $1,000, 5-year bond, using an interest rate of 7% is _____.

5. Oliver Company issues 10-year, 12% bonds with a face value of $100,000. The present value of the bonds' interest payments using an effective rate of interest of 12% is _____ (round to the nearest dollar).

6. A series of equal cash payments at fixed intervals is called a(n) _____.

7. A firm redeemed bonds at 95. The bonds have a face value of $500,000 and an unamortized discount of $15,000. The firm will record a gain (or loss) on redemption of _____ (indicate amount and gain or loss).

8–11. Under which caption (current assets, investments, fixed assets, current liabilities, long-term liabilities, stockholders' equity) would each of the following appear on the balance sheet?

8. Investment in X Co. Bonds (management intends to hold to maturity in 5 years) would appear in the _____ section of the balance sheet.

9. Premium on Bonds Payable would appear in the _____ _____ section of the balance sheet.

10. Bonds Payable due in ten years would appear in the _____ _____ section of the balance sheet.

11. Bond sinking fund investments would appear in the _____ section of the balance sheet.

12. Bonds with a face value of $75,000 were purchased through a broker at 98 plus accrued interest of $1,000 and brokerage commissions of $350. The amount to be debited to the investment account is _____.

13. If Bonds Payable has a balance of $5,000,000 and Premium on Bonds Payable has a balance of $45,000, the carrying amount of the bonds is _____.

14–16. On April 1, Avery Company issued $4,000,000, 5-year, 12% bonds for $4,280,000 with semiannual interest payable on March 31 and September 30. If the effective rate of interest is 10%, determine the following:

14. The interest paid on September 30 is _____.

15. The amount of premium amortized on September 30, using the straight-line method is _____.

16. The accrued interest payable on December 31 is _____.

17. In No. 14, the total amount of annual interest expense _____ (increases, decreases, or remains the same) over the life of the bonds as the premium on bonds payable is amortized.

18. A ratio that indicates the likelihood a company will be able to continue paying interest to its debtholders if the company's earnings decrease is called the _____ _____ _____ _____ _____ _____.

19. Canary Company had interest expenses of $8,250,000 and income before tax of $60,500,000. The number of times interest charges are earned is _____.

20. The estimated worth today of an amount of cash to be received (or paid) in the future is called the _____ _____.

MULTIPLE CHOICE

Instructions: Circle the best answer for each of the following questions.

1. A bond that gives the bondholder a right to exchange the bond for other securities under certain conditions is called a:

    a. convertible bond

    b. sinking fund bond

    c. term bond

    d. debenture bond

2. What is the present value of $2,000 to be paid in one year if the current interest rate is 6%?

    a. $1,880

    b. $1,887

    c. $2,000

    d. $2,120

3. The entry to record the amortization of a discount on bonds payable is:

    a. debit Bonds Payable; credit Interest Expense

    b. debit Interest Expense; credit Discount on Bonds Payable

    c. debit Discount on Bonds Payable; credit Interest Expense

    d. debit Discount on Bonds Payable; credit Bonds Payable

4. Under the straight-line method of bond discount amortization, as a bond payable approaches maturity, the total yearly amount of interest expense will:

    a. increase

    b. decrease

    c. remain the same

    d. increase or decrease, depending on the size of the original discount

5. On May 1, a $1,000 bond was purchased as a long-term investment at 104, and $8 was paid as the brokerage commission. If the bond bears interest at 6%, which is paid semiannually on January 1 and July 1, what is the total cost to be debited to the investment account?

    a. $1,000

    b. $1,040

    c. $1,048

    d. $1,068

6. What method of amortizing bond discount or premium is required by generally accepted accounting principles?

    a. declining balance method

    b. future value method

    c. principal method

    d. interest method

7. Bonds that do not provide for any interest payments are called:

    a. interest-free bonds

    b. held-to-maturity securities

    c. sinking-fund bonds

    d. zero-coupon bonds

8. The principal of each bond is also called the:

    a. present value

    b. future value

    c. face value

    d. contract value

9. A special fund accumulated over the life of a bond issue and kept separate from other assets in order to provide for payment of bonds at maturity is called a(n):

    a. sinking fund

    b. investment fund

    c. retirement fund

    d. redemption fund

10. Held-to-maturity securities are classified on the balance sheet as:

    a. current assets

    b. investments

    c. long-term liabilities

    d. sinking-fund assets

TRUE/FALSE

Instructions: Indicate whether each of the following statements is true or false by placing a check mark in the appropriate column.

	True	False
1. The interest rate specified on the bond indenture is called the contract rate or effective rate.	____	____
2. If the market rate is lower than the contract rate, the bonds will sell at a discount.	____	____
3. When zero-coupon bonds are issued, the discount is amortized as interest expense over the life of the bonds.	____	____
4. The straight-line method of allocating bond discount provides for a constant amount of interest expense each period.	____	____
5. Bonds that may be exchanged for other securities under certain conditions are called callable bonds.	____	____
6. When cash is transferred to the sinking fund, it is recorded in an account called Sinking Fund Investments.	____	____
7. A corporation's earnings per share can be affected by whether it finances its operations with common stock, preferred stock, or bonds.	____	____
8. If the price paid to redeem bonds is below the bond carrying value, the difference is recorded as a gain.	____	____
9. The balance in a discount on bonds payable account is reported in the balance sheet as a deduction from the related bonds payable.	____	____
10. The present value of a future amount becomes less as the interest rate used to compute the present value increases.	____	____

EXERCISE 13-1

(1) Star Corp. issued $500,000 of 10-year, 12% bonds on June 1 of the current year with interest payable on June 1 and December 1. Journalize the entries to record the following selected transactions for the current year:

June   1.   Issued the bonds for cash at face amount.

Dec.   1.   Paid the interest on the bonds.

JOURNAL   PAGE

	DATE	DESCRIPTION	POST. REF.	DEBIT	CREDIT	
1						1
2						2
3						3
4						4
5						5
6						6
7						7
8						8

(2) On April 1, Turner Inc. issued $1,000,000 of 10-year, 11% bonds, with interest payable semiannually on April 1 and October 1 at an effective interest rate of 12%, receiving cash of $942,645. Journalize the entries to record the following selected transactions for the current year:

Apr.   1.   Sold the bonds.

Oct.   1.   Made first interest payment and amortized discount for six months using the straight-line method.

JOURNAL   PAGE

	DATE	DESCRIPTION	POST. REF.	DEBIT	CREDIT	
1						1
2						2
3						3
4						4
5						5
6						6
7						7
8						8
9						9
10						10
11						11

(3) On March 1, Sullivan Inc. issued $700,000 of 10-year, 11% bonds at an effective interest rate of 10%. Interest is payable semiannually on March 1 and September 1. Journalize the entries to record the following selected transactions for the current year. (Hint: To complete this portion of the exercise, you must compute the present value of the bonds at the issue date.)

Mar. 1. Sold the bonds.

Sept. 1. Made first interest payment and amortized premium for six months using the straight-line method.

JOURNAL

PAGE

	DATE	DESCRIPTION	POST. REF.	DEBIT	CREDIT	
1						1
2						2
3						3
4						4
5						5
6						6
7						7
8						8
9						9
10						10
11						11
12						12

EXERCISE 13-2

Grimes Co. issued $5,000,000 of 10-year bonds at face value on January 1 of the current year.

Instructions:

(1) Assume the bonds are called at 101. Prepare the entry to record the redemption of the bonds.

JOURNAL

PAGE

	DATE	DESCRIPTION	POST. REF.	DEBIT	CREDIT	
1						1
2						2
3						3
4						4
5						5

(2) Assume the bonds are purchased on the open market at 98. Prepare the entry to record the redemption of the bonds.

JOURNAL   PAGE

	DATE	DESCRIPTION	POST. REF.	DEBIT	CREDIT	
1						1
2						2
3						3
4						4
5						5

EXERCISE 13-3

Record the following transactions. (Omit explanations.)

(1) On October 1, 20XA, purchased for cash, as a long-term investment, $400,000 of Elgin Inc. 10% bonds at 99 plus accrued interest of $10,000.

(2) On December 31, 20XA received first semiannual interest.

(3) On December 31, 20XA amortized $120 discount on the bond investment.

(4) On December 1, 20XC, sold the bonds at 102 plus accrued interest of $16,667. The carrying amount of the bonds was $397,040 at the time of sale.

JOURNAL   PAGE

	DATE	DESCRIPTION	POST. REF.	DEBIT	CREDIT	
1						1
2						2
3						3
4						4
5						5
6						6
7						7
8						8
9						9
10						10
11						11
12						12
13						13
14						14
15						15

PROBLEM 13-1

Jackson Inc. issued $2,000,000 of 10-year, 11% bonds with interest payable semiannually.

Instructions:

(1) Compute (a) the cash proceeds and (b) the amount of premium or discount from the sale of the bonds if the effective interest rate is 11%.

(2) Compute (a) the cash proceeds and (b) the amount of premium or discount from the sale of the bonds if the effective interest rate is 12%.

(3) Compute (a) the cash proceeds and (b) the amount of premium or discount from the sale of the bonds if the effective interest rate is 10%.

PROBLEM 13-2

On December 31 of the current fiscal year, Palus Inc. issued $500,000 of 10-year, 11% bonds. The bonds were dated December 31 of the same year. Interest on the bonds is payable on June 30 and December 31 of each year.

Instructions:

Record the following transactions. (Omit explanations and round to the nearest dollar.)

(1) The bonds were sold for $531,161 on December 31 of the current year. The market rate of interest on this date was 10%.

(2) Interest was paid on June 30, and the related amount of bond premium was amortized, based on the straight-line method.

(3) Interest was paid on December 31, and the related amount of bond premium was amortized, based on the straight-line method.

(4) On December 31 (bonds are one year old), one-half of the bonds were redeemed at 103.

JOURNAL

PAGE

	DATE	DESCRIPTION	POST. REF.	DEBIT	CREDIT	
1						1
2						2
3						3
4						4
5						5
6						6
7						7
8						8
9						9
10						10
11						11
12						12
13						13
14						14
15						15
16						16
17						17
18						18
19						19
20						20
21						21
22						22

PROBLEM 13-3

On January 1 of the current fiscal year, Block Co. issued $1,000,000 of 10-year, 10% bonds. The bonds were dated January 1 of the same year. Interest on the bonds is payable on June 30 and December 31 of each year.

Instructions:

Record the following transactions. (Omit explanations and round to the nearest dollar.)

(1) The bonds were sold for $885,295 on January 1 of the current year. The market rate of interest on that date was 12%.

(2) Interest was paid on June 30, and the related amount of bond discount was amortized, based on the straight-line method.

(3) Interest was paid on December 31, and the related amount of bond discount was amortized, based on the straight-line method.

(4) On December 31 (bonds are one year old), one-half of the bonds were redeemed at 98.

JOURNAL

PAGE

	DATE	DESCRIPTION	POST. REF.	DEBIT	CREDIT	
1						1
2						2
3						3
4						4
5						5
6						6
7						7
8						8
9						9
10						10
11						11
12						12
13						13
14						14
15						15
16						16
17						17
18						18
19						19
20						20
21						21

Statement of Cash Flows

QUIZ AND TEST HINTS

The following hints may be helpful to you in preparing for a quiz or a test over the material covered in Chapter 14.

1. Study the new terminology introduced in this chapter for possible use in fill-in-the-blank, multiple-choice, or true/false questions.

2. You should be able to classify different types of cash flows as operating, investing, or financing activities. Test questions on this material often appear in a true/false or multiple-choice format.

3. Instructors may emphasize the indirect method, the direct method, or both methods of preparing the statement of cash flows. Adjust your studying to the method or methods that your instructor emphasized during class lectures and in homework assignments. You should be able to prepare a statement of cash flows using one or both methods. Often, instructors will include a partially completed statement of cash flows on an examination and require students to complete it. The Illustrative Problem is a good study aid for both the indirect and direct methods.

4. The work sheets for preparing the statement of cash flows appear in the Appendix to the chapter. Study the Appendix if your instructor has expressed a preference for use of the work sheet in preparing the statement of cash flows.

5. The statement of cash flows can be prepared by evaluating the changes in the noncash balance sheet accounts. Changes in the noncash current accounts are adjustments to net income in determining cash flows from operating activities under the indirect method. While changes in long-term assets are usually investing activities, changes in long-term liabilities and stockholders' equity paid in capital accounts are usually financing activities. The cash dividends are also financing activities.

MATCHING

Instructions: Match each of the statements below with its proper term. Some terms may not be used.

A. cash conversion cycle
B. cash flows from financing activities
C. cash flows from investing activities
D. cash flows from operating activities

E. direct method
F. free cash flow
G. indirect method
H. statement of cash flows

_____ 1. The section of the statement of cash flows that reports cash flows from transactions affecting the equity and debt of the business.

_____ 2. The section of the statement of cash flows that reports cash flows from transactions affecting investments in noncurrent assets.

_____ 3. A summary of the major cash receipts and cash payments for a period.

_____ 4. The number of days' sales in accounts receivable, plus the number of days' sales in inventory, less the number of days' sales in accounts payable.

_____ 5. A method of reporting the cash flows from operating activities as the difference between the operating cash receipts and the operating cash payments.

_____ 6. The section of the statement of cash flows that reports the cash transactions affecting the determination of net income.

_____ 7. A method of reporting the cash flows from operating activities as the net income from operations adjusted for all deferrals of past cash receipts and payments and all accruals of expected future cash receipts and payments.

_____ 8. The amount of operating cash flow remaining after replacing current productive capacity and maintaining current dividends.

FILL IN THE BLANK—PART A

Instructions: Answer the following questions or complete the statements by writing the appropriate words or amounts in the answer blanks.

1. The financial statement that reports a firm's major cash inflows and outflows for a period is the _____ _____ _____ _____.

2. The two alternative methods of reporting operating activities in the statement of cash flows are the _____ and _____ methods.

3–7. Indicate the section of the statement of cash flows in which each of the following would appear (answer operating activities, investing activities, or financing activities):

3. Depreciation expense on equipment would appear under _____ activities.

4. Sale of long-term investments would appear under _____ activities.

5. Sale of equipment would appear under _____ activities.

6. Issuance of bonds would appear under _____ activities.

7. Sale of patents would appear under _____ activities.

8–10. This year, Young Company issued 500,000 shares of common stock, inventory increased by $20,000, and a new asset was purchased for $1,000,000. For each of these events, indicate whether net cash flows increased or decreased:

8. Common stock issued. Net cash flows _____.

9. Inventory increased. Net cash flows _____.

10. New asset purchased. Net cash flows _____.

11. Cash dividends of $35,000 were declared during the year. Cash dividends payable were $8,000 and $8,750 at the beginning and end of the year, respectively. The amount of cash flows for payment of dividends during the year is _____.

12. The net income from operations was $75,000, and the only revenue or expense item not affecting cash was depreciation expense of $27,000. The amount of net cash flows from operating activities that would appear on the statement of cash flows is _____.

13. A corporation purchased and retired 3,000 shares of its $50 par common stock, originally issued at par, for $65. Cash flows amounted to _____.

14. If a fixed asset having a book value of $54,000 is sold (for cash) at a gain of $6,000, the total amount reported as a cash flow is _____.

15. The $47,000 net income for the year included a loss of $2,500 on the sale of land. Exclusive of the effect of other adjustments, the amount of net cash flows from operating activities is _____.

16. A corporation issued $1,000,000 of bonds payable at 104. Cash flow from this transaction was _____.

17. If 15,000 shares of $20 par common stock were issued at 22, the amount to be reported in the cash flows from financing activities section of the statement of cash flows would be _____.

18. Cash flows resulting from the redemption of debt securities are classified in the statement of cash flows as related to _____ activities.

19. Jones Company had cash flow from operations of $75,000. This year, dividends paid amounted to $6,000, and the company purchased $9,000 in spare parts for machines used on the factory floor. Jones Company's free cash flow is _____.

20. A cash flow term for which an amount should not be reported in the financial statements because it could mislead readers is _____ _____ _____ _____.

FILL IN THE BLANK—PART B

Instructions: Answer the following questions or complete the statements by writing the appropriate words or amounts in the answer blanks.

1. The _____ method of analyzing operating cash flows begins with net income and adjusts it for revenues and expenses that do not involve the receipt or payment of cash.

2. The statement of cash flows groups cash flow activities as financing, investing, or _____.

3. When the _____ method of reporting cash flows is used, a supplemental schedule reconciling net income and net cash flow from operating activities must also be prepared.

4–8. Indicate the section of the statement of cash flows in which each of the following would appear (answer operating activities, investing activities, or financing activities):

4. Retirement of long-term debt would appear under _____ activities.

5. Sale of common stock would appear under _____ activities.

6. Net income would appear under _____ activities.

7. Payment of cash dividends would appear under _____ activities.

8. Purchase of equipment would appear under _____ activities.

9. _____ investing and financing activities that will affect future cash flows are reported in a separate schedule to the statement of cash flows.

10–11. Indicate whether each of the following items would be added to or deducted from net income on the schedule reconciling net income with cash flows from operating activities:

10. Increase in inventories would be _____ _____ net income.

11. Increase in accounts payable would be _____ _____ net income.

12. If a loss of $15,000 is incurred in selling (for cash) store equipment having a book value of $345,000, the total amount reported as a cash flow is _____.

13. A corporation issued $750,000 of 20-year bonds at 99½. Cash flows were _____.

14. A corporation purchased 25,000 shares of its $100 par common stock, originally issued at par, as treasury stock for $125. Cash flows were _____.

15. Cash dividends of $50,000 were declared during the year. Cash dividends payable were $8,500 and $12,500 at the beginning and end of the year, respectively. The amount of cash flows for the payment of dividends during the year is _____.

16. The net loss from operations was $15,000, and the only revenue or expense item not affecting cash was depreciation expense of $35,000. The amount to be reported as net cash flow from operating activities on the statement of cash flows is _____.

17. In preparing a statement of cash flows under the indirect method, it is efficient to analyze the _____ _____ account first.

18. The $55,000 net income for the year included a gain of $4,000 on the sale of equipment. Exclusive of the effect of other adjustments, the amount of net cash flows from operating activities is _____.

19. Cash flow for interest expense is included on the statement of cash flows as an _____ activity.

20. A measure of cash available for corporate purposes, after productive assets are maintained and the business owners are paid dividends, is called _____ _____ _____.

MULTIPLE CHOICE

Instructions: Circle the best answer for each of the following questions.

1. Which of the following is not one of the major sections of the statement of cash flows?

   a. cash flows from financing activities

   b. cash flows from selling activities

   c. cash flows from operating activities

   d. cash flows from investing activities

2. Noncash investing and financing activities which may have a significant effect on future cash flows are reported:

   a. in the statement of cash flows

   b. in a separate schedule to accompany the statement of cash flows

   c. in the retained earnings statement

   d. in a footnote accompanying the balance sheet

3. Under the indirect method, which of the following items must be deducted from reported net income to determine net cash flow from operating activities?

   a. depreciation of fixed assets

   b. decreases in current assets

   c. decreases in current liabilities

   d. loss on sale of equipment

4. During the past year, Lockhart Inc. declared $40,000 in cash dividends. If the beginning and ending balance of the dividends payable account was $12,000 and $10,000, respectively, what amount of cash paid for dividends will appear in the cash flow from financing activities section of the statement of cash flows?

   a. $30,000

   b. $38,000

   c. $40,000

   d. $42,000

5. Under the direct method, which of the following items must be added to operating expenses reported on the income statement to determine cash payments for operating expenses?

   a. increase in accrued expenses

   b. decrease in prepaid expenses

   c. increase in income taxes payable

   d. increase in prepaid expenses

6. An example of a cash flow from a financing activity is:
   a. receipt of cash from sale of land
   b. receipt of cash from collection of accounts receivable
   c. payment of cash for acquisition of treasury stock
   d. payment of cash for new machinery

7. Which of the following items appears first on the statement of cash flows prepared using the direct method?
   a. retained earnings
   b. cash received from customers
   c. net income
   d. depreciation

8. Which of the following would not be considered a noncash investing and financing activity in preparing a statement of cash flows?
   a. withdrawal of cash by the owner of a business
   b. issuance of common stock to retire long-term debt
   c. acquisition of a manufacturing plant by issuing bonds
   d. issuance of common stock in exchange for convertible preferred stock

9. To convert the cost of merchandise sold as reported on the income statement to cash payments for merchandise, the cost of merchandise sold is increased for the:
   a. increase in inventories
   b. increase in accounts payable
   c. decrease in inventories
   d. decrease in accounts receivable

10. Cash payments for income taxes are included on the statement of cash flows as:
    a. financing activities
    b. investing activities
    c. operating activities
    d. nonoperating activities

11. A loss on the sale of land is reflected on the statement of cash flows by:
    a. adding the loss to the book value of the land to determine the cash flow from investing activities.
    b. deducting the loss from net income to determine the cash flow from operating activities.
    c. deducting the loss from the book value of the land to determine the cash flow from investing activities.
    d. both b and c

12. Caldwell Company had cash flows from operating activities of $290,000. Depreciation expense for the year was $25,000. Cash flows for dividends totaled $32,000. Cash flows used for purchasing property, plant, and equipment were $60,000. It is determined that of this amount, $20,000 was used for expansion, while the remainder was used for replacing existing fixed assets. What is the free cash flow?

   a. $193,000

   b. $218,000

   c. $238,000

   d. $250,000

TRUE/FALSE

Instructions: Indicate whether each of the following statements is true or false by placing a check mark in the appropriate column.

	True	False
1. The statement of cash flows is required as part of the basic set of financial statements.	____	____
2. Cash outflows from the payment of cash dividends is a type of financing activity.	____	____
3. Cash receipts from the sale of fixed assets would be classified as a cash flow from investing activities.	____	____
4. Under the direct method, depreciation is the first noncash account balance analyzed.	____	____
5. Under the indirect method, increases in current liabilities are deducted from net income reported on the income statement in determining cash flows from operating activities.	____	____
6. Noncash investing and financing activities that may have a significant effect on future cash flows should be included in a separate schedule to the statement of cash flows.	____	____
7. The correct amount to include in cash flows from financing activities is cash dividends paid, not cash dividends declared.	____	____
8. The analysis of retained earnings provides the starting point for determining cash flows from operating activities under the indirect method only.	____	____
9. The direct method provides a more accurate figure of cash flows from operating activities than does the indirect method.	____	____
10. Under the direct method, the increase in the trade receivables account is deducted from sales to determine the cash received from customers.	____	____

EXERCISE 14-1

Instructions: Listed in the first column below are selected transactions and account balance changes of Mason Inc. for the current year. Indicate by placing a check mark in the appropriate column(s) how each of the items would be reported in the statement of cash flows.

Item	Operating Activities	Investing Activities	Financing Activities	Schedule of Noncash Investing and Financing Activities
1. Decrease in prepaid expenses...........				
2. Retirement of bonds..........................				
3. Proceeds from sale of investments....				
4. Increase in inventories				
5. Issuance of common stock................				
6. Purchase of equipment				
7. Cash dividends paid..........................				
8. Acquisition of building in exchange for bonds				
9. Amortization of patents......................				
10. Amortization of discount on bonds payable..				

Cash Flows From spans Operating, Investing, Financing columns.

EXERCISE 14-2

The net income reported on the income statement of Hunter Inc. for the current year was $150,000. Depreciation recorded on equipment and building amounted to $45,000 for the year. Balances of the current asset and current liability accounts at the beginning and end of the year are as follows:

	End of Year	Beginning of Year
Cash	$ 42,875	$ 36,250
Trade receivables (net)	147,500	137,500
Inventories	109,375	93,750
Prepaid expenses	9,250	11,875
Accounts payable (merchandise creditors)	57,000	40,000
Salaries payable	7,625	10,625

Instructions: Prepare the cash flows from operating activities section of the statement of cash flows using the indirect method.

Exercise 14-3

The income statement of Hunter Inc. for the current year is as follows:

Sales		$530,000
Cost of merchandise sold		130,000
Gross profit		$400,000
Operating expenses:		
Depreciation expense	$ 45,000	
Other operating expenses	160,000	
Total operating expenses		205,000
Income before income tax		$195,000
Income tax		45,000
Net income		$150,000

Instructions: Using the income statement presented above and the account balances provided in Exercise 14-2, prepare the cash flows from operating activities section of the statement of cash flows using the direct method.

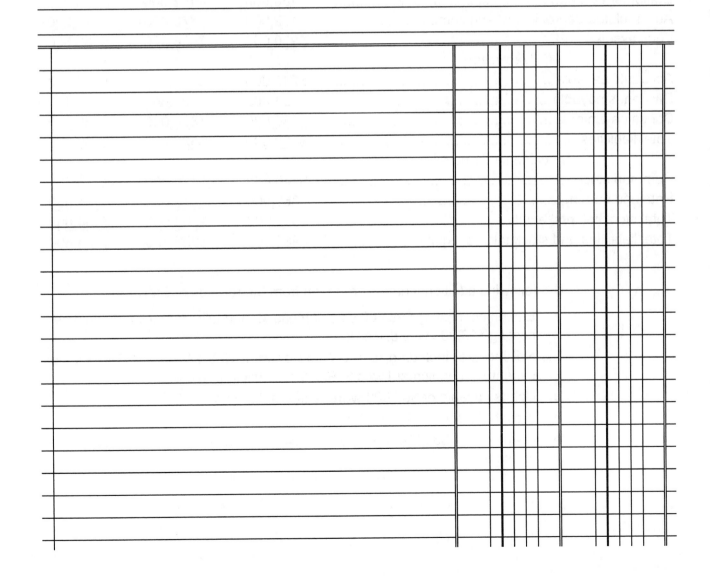

PROBLEM 14-1

The comparative balance sheet of Stellar Inc. at December 31, 2006, appears below.

Stellar Inc.
Comparative Balance Sheet
December 31, 2006 and 2005

	2006	2005	Increase Decrease*
Assets			
Cash	$ 84,000	$ 66,000	$ 18,000
Trade receivables (net)	156,000	144,000	12,000
Inventories	300,000	306,000	6,000*
Prepaid expenses	12,000	14,400	2,400*
Land	80,000	96,000	16,000*
Building	360,000	360,000	0
Accumulated depreciation—building	(120,000)	(91,200)	(28,800)
Equipment	180,000	102,000	78,000
Accumulated depreciation—equipment	(72,000)	(70,800)	(1,200)
Total assets	$980,000	$926,400	$ 53,600
Liabilities			
Accounts payable	$216,000	$208,800	$ 7,200
Dividends payable	24,000	21,600	2,400
Bonds payable	240,000	300,000	60,000*
Total liabilities	$480,000	$530,400	$ 50,400*
Stockholders' Equity			
Common stock	$140,000	$120,000	$ 20,000
Retained earnings	360,000	276,000	84,000
Total stockholders' equity	$500,000	$396,000	$104,000
Total liabilities and stockholders' equity	$980,000	$926,400	$ 53,600

The following additional data were taken from the records of Stellar Inc.:

a. Equipment costing $96,000 was purchased, and fully depreciated equipment costing $18,000 was discarded.

b. Net income, including gain on sale of land, was $114,000. Depreciation expense on equipment was $19,200; on building, $28,800.

c. Bonds payable of $60,000 were retired at face value.

d. A cash dividend of $30,000 was declared.

e. Land costing $36,000 was sold for $54,000, resulting in an $18,000 gain on the sale.

f. Land was acquired by issuing common stock, $20,000.

Instructions: Complete the following statement of cash flows using the indirect method of reporting cash flows from operating activities.

Stellar Inc.
Statement of Cash Flows
For Year Ended December 31, 2006

Cash flows from operating activities:

    Net income, per income statement .... $ _____

    Add: Depreciation .... $ _____

        Decrease in inventories .... _____

        Decrease in prepaid expenses .... _____

        Increase in accounts payable .... _____ _____

         $ _____

    Deduct: Increase in trade receivables .... $ _____

        Gain on sale of land .... _____ _____

    Net cash flow from operating activities .... $ _____

Cash flows from investing activities:

    Cash received from land sold .... $ _____

    Less cash paid for purchase of equipment .... _____

    Net cash flow used for investing activities ..... _____

Cash flows from financing activities:

    Cash used to retire bonds payable .... $ _____

    Cash paid for dividends .... _____

    Net cash flow used for financing activities ..... _____

Increase in cash .... $ _____

Cash, January 1, 2006 .... _____

Cash, December 31, 2006 .... $ _____

Schedule of Noncash Investing and Financing Activities:

Acquisition of land by issuance of common stock .... $ _____

PROBLEM 14-2

The income statement of Stellar Inc. is provided below. Stellar's comparative balance sheet data were provided in Problem 14-1.

Instructions: Complete the statement of cash flows for Stellar Inc. using the direct method of reporting cash flows from operating activities.

Stellar Inc.
Income Statement
For Year Ended December 31, 2006

Sales		$575,000
Cost of merchandise sold		225,000
Gross profit		$350,000
Operating expenses:		
Depreciation expense	$ 48,000	
Other operating expenses	172,000	
Total operating expenses		220,000
Income from operations		$130,000
Other income:		
Gain on sale of land		18,000
Income before income tax		$148,000
Income tax		34,000
Net income		$114,000

Stellar Inc.
Statement of Cash Flows
For Year Ended December 31, 2006

Cash flows from operating activities:

    Cash received from customers .... $ _____

    Deduct: Cash payments for merchandise ...... $ _____

        Cash payments for operating
        expenses .... _____

        Cash payments for income tax .... _____ _____

    Net cash flow from operating activities .... $ _____

Cash flows from investing activities:

    Cash received from land sold .... $ _____

    Less cash paid for purchase of equipment .... _____

    Net cash flow used for investing activities ..... _____

Cash flows from financing activities:

    Cash used to retire bonds payable .... $ _____

    Cash paid for dividends .... _____

    Net cash flow used for financing activities ..... _____

Increase in cash .... $ _____

Cash, January 1, 2006 .... _____

Cash, December 31, 2006 .... $ _____

Schedule of Noncash Investing and Financing Activities:

    Acquisition of land by issuance of common stock .... $ _____

Schedule Reconciling Net Income with Cash Flows from Operating Activities:

    Net income, per income statement .... $ _____

    Add: Depreciation .... $ _____

        Decrease in inventories .... _____

        Decrease in prepaid expenses .... _____

        Increase in accounts payable .... _____ _____

                                           $ _____

    Deduct: Increase in trade receivables .... $ _____

        Gain on sale of land .... _____ _____

    Net cash flow provided by operating activities .... $ _____

Supporting calculations:

15 Financial Statement Analysis

QUIZ AND TEST HINTS

The following hints may be helpful to you in preparing for a quiz or a test over the material covered in Chapter 15.

1. When studying this chapter, you should focus primarily on the various analytical measures described and illustrated. These measures are also summarized in Exhibit 10 on page 629 of the chapter. Pay special attention to each measure's computation, its use, and its classification as either a solvency or profitability measure. A good study aid for the computation of the measures is the Illustrative Problem at the end of the chapter.

2. Instructors will often include exam problems asking you to provide either a horizontal or vertical analysis. Be familiar with both of these.

3. Instructors often use true/false and multiple-choice questions to test this chapter. Such questions may require the computation of ratios or test your understanding of various terms introduced in the chapter.

MATCHING

Instructions: Match each of the statements below with its proper term. Some terms may not be used.

A. accounts receivable turnover
B. asset turnover
C. common-size statement
D. current ratio
E. dividend yield
F. dividends per share
G. earnings per share (EPS) on common stock
H. horizontal analysis
I. inventory turnover
J. leverage
K. Management Discussion and Analysis
L. number of days' sales in inventory
M. number of days' sales in receivables

N. number of times interest charges earned
O. price-earnings (P/E) ratio
P. profitability
Q. quick assets
R. quick ratio
S. rate earned on common stockholders' equity
T. rate earned on stockholders' equity
U. rate earned on total assets
V. ratio of fixed assets to long-term liabilities
W. ratio of liabilities to stockholders' equity
X. solvency
Y. vertical analysis

_____ 1. The percentage of increases and decreases in corresponding items in comparative financial statements.

_____ 2. The sum of cash, receivables, and marketable securities.

_____ 3. The relationship between the volume of sales and inventory, computed by dividing the inventory at the end of the year by the average daily cost of goods sold.

_____ 4. The ability of a firm to pay its debts as they come due.

_____ 5. The relationship between credit sales and accounts receivable, computed by dividing the net accounts receivable at the end of the year by the average daily sales on account.

_____ 6. The relationship between credit sales and accounts receivable, computed by dividing net sales on account by the average net accounts receivable.

_____ 7. The tendency of the rate earned on stockholders' equity to vary from the rate earned on total assets because the amount earned on assets acquired through the use of funds provided by creditors varies from the interest paid to these creditors.

_____ 8. A financial statement in which all items are expressed only in relative terms.

_____ **9.** A measure of profitability computed by dividing net income by total stockholders' equity.

_____ **10.** The ratio of the market price per share of common stock, at a specific date, to the annual earnings per share.

_____ **11.** A measure of the profitability of assets, without regard to the equity of creditors and stockholders in the assets.

_____ **12.** The profitability ratio of net income available to common shareholders to the number of common shares outstanding.

_____ **13.** The number of sales dollars earned for each dollar of total assets, calculated as the ratio of sales to total assets.

_____ **14.** The percentage analysis of component parts in relation to the total of the parts in a single financial statement.

_____ **15.** A measure of profitability computed by dividing net income, reduced by preferred dividend requirements, by common stockholders' equity.

_____ **16.** The ratio of current assets to current liabilities.

_____ **17.** The relationship between the volume of goods sold and inventory, computed by dividing the cost of goods sold by the average inventory.

_____ **18.** The ability of a firm to earn income.

_____ **19.** An annual report disclosure that provides an analysis of the results of operations and financial condition.

FILL IN THE BLANK—PART A

Instructions: Answer the following questions or complete the statements by writing the appropriate words or amounts in the answer blanks.

1. Percentage analysis used to show the relationship of the component parts to the total in a single statement is called _____ _____.

2. _____ _____ focuses primarily on the relationship between operating results as reported in the income statement and resources available to the business as reported in the balance sheet.

3. The use of ratios showing the ability of an enterprise to pay its current liabilities is known as _____ _____ _____.

4. _____ is the ability of a business to meet its financial obligations as they come due.

5. _____-_____ statements are prepared in order to compare percentages of the current period with past periods, to compare individual businesses, or to compare one business with industry percentages published by trade associations or financial information services.

6. The ratio of current assets to current liabilities is called the _____ ratio.

7. The ratio of _____ _____ _____ _____ is a profitability measure that shows how effectively a firm utilizes its assets.

8. The ratio of the sum of cash, receivables, and marketable securities to current liabilities is called the _____ ratio.

9. _____ _____ _____ _____ _____ _____ is the ratio of net income available to common shareholders to the number of common shares outstanding.

10. The excess of the current assets of a business over its current liabilities is called _____ _____.

11. _____ _____ _____ is computed by dividing net sales by the average net accounts receivable.

12. _____ _____ is computed by dividing the cost of goods sold by the average inventory.

13. The ratio of _____ _____ _____ _____ is a solvency measure that indicates the margin of safety for creditors.

14. The number of times _____ _____ _____ _____ is a measure of the risk that dividends to preferred stockholders may not be paid.

15. If significant amounts of nonoperating income and expense are reported on the income statement, it may be desirable to compute the ratio of _____ _____ _____ to total assets as a profitability measure.

16. The rate earned on _____ _____ focuses only on the rate of profits earned on the amount invested by common stockholders.

17. Earnings per share and _____ per share on common stock are commonly used by investors in assessing alternative stock investments.

18. All publicly held corporations are required to have a(n) _____ _____ of their financial statements.

19. The ratio of _____ _____ _____ _____-_____ _____ is a solvency measure that indicates the margin of safety of the noteholders or bondholders.

20. In a vertical analysis of the income statement, each item is stated as a percent of _____ _____.

FILL IN THE BLANK—PART B

Instructions: Answer the following questions or complete the statements by writing the appropriate words or amounts in the answer blanks.

1. The percentage analysis of increases and decreases in corresponding items in comparative financial statements is called _____ _____.

2. The _____ _____ is a profitability measure that shows the rate of return to common stockholders in terms of cash dividend distributions.

3. The _____ _____ report describes the results of an independent examination of the financial statements.

4. The _____ _____ _____ _____ _____ _____ is computed by dividing the net accounts receivable at the end of the year by the average daily net sales.

5. The _____ _____ _____ _____ _____ _____ is computed by dividing the inventory at the end of the year by the average daily cost of goods sold.

6. The number of times _____ _____ _____ is a measure of the risk that interest payments will not be made if earnings decrease.

7. The _____ _____ _____ _____ _____ measures the profitability of total assets, without considering how the assets are financed.

8. The _____ _____ _____ _____ _____ is computed by dividing net income by average total stockholders' equity.

9. The difference between the rate earned by a business on the equity of its stockholders and the rate earned on total assets is called _____.

10. The _____-_____ ratio is computed by dividing the market price per share of common stock at a specific date by the annual earnings per share.

11. The _____ _____ _____ _____ section of a corporate annual report includes management's analysis of the results of operations, financial condition, and significant risks.

12. _____ _____ are cash and other current assets that can be quickly converted to cash.

13. In a(n) _____-_____ statement, all items are expressed as percentages.

14. _____ _____ focuses on the ability of a business to pay or otherwise satisfy its current and noncurrent liabilities.

15. The current ratio is sometimes called the working capital ratio or the _____ ratio.

16. Two measures that are useful for evaluating the management of inventory are the inventory turnover and the _____ _____ _____ _____ _____ _____.

17. A profitability measure often quoted in the financial press and normally reported in the income statement in corporate annual reports is _____ _____ _____.

18. All items in _____-_____ statements are expressed only in relative terms.

19. Quick assets normally include cash, marketable securities, and _____.

20. Beginning in 2004, the Sarbanes-Oxley Act will require independent auditors to attest to management's assessment of _____ _____.

MULTIPLE CHOICE

Instructions: Circle the best answer for each of the following questions.

1. Statements in which all items are expressed only in relative terms (percentages of a common base) are:

   a. relative statements

   b. horizontal statements

   c. vertical statements

   d. common-size statements

2. Which one of the following measures is a solvency measure?

   a. rate earned on total assets

   b. price-earnings ratio

   c. accounts receivable turnover

   d. ratio of net sales to assets

3. Based on the following data for the current year, what is the inventory turnover?

Net sales	$6,500,000
Cost of goods sold	$4,000,000
Inventory, beginning of year	$250,000
Inventory, end of year	$345,000
Accounts receivable, beginning of year	$175,000
Accounts receivable, end of year	$297,000

   a. 26.7

   b. 16

   c. 13.4

   d. 11.6

4. Based on the following data for the current year, what is the accounts receivable turnover?

Net sales	$6,500,000
Cost of goods sold	$4,000,000
Inventory, beginning of year	$250,000
Inventory, end of year	$345,000
Accounts receivable, beginning of year	$175,000
Accounts receivable, end of year	$297,000

   a. 37.1

   b. 27.5

   c. 21.8

   d. 17

5. Which of the following sections of corporate annual reports normally includes a statement concerning future prospects and risks?

   a. independent auditor's report

   b. footnotes to the financial statements

   c. management's internal control assertion

   d. management discussion and analysis

6. A measure used in evaluating the efficiency in collecting receivables is:

   a. working capital ratio

   b. quick ratio

   c. receivables/inventory ratio

   d. number of days' sales in receivables

7. Based on the following data for the current year, compute the number of times interest charges are earned.

Income before income tax.........	$510,000
Interest expense.......................	$30,000
Total assets.............................	$4,080,000

   a. 8

   b. 17

   c. 18

   d. 136

8. Based on the following data for the current year, what is the quick ratio?

Cash...	$27,000
Marketable securities................	$23,000
Receivables..............................	$90,000
Inventory	$105,000
Current liabilities.......................	$70,000

   a. 2.0

   b. 3.5

   c. 0.7

   d. 1.5

9. In vertical analysis of the balance sheet, each asset item is stated as a percent of total:

   a. current assets

   b. assets

   c. current liabilities

   d. liabilities

10. Based on the following data for the current year, what is the earnings per share on common stock?

Net income..	$460,000
Preferred dividends..................................	$50,000
Interest expense	$24,000
Shares of common stock outstanding	50,000

    a. $9.20

    b. $8.68

    c. $8.20

    d. $7.72

11. Companies with high P/E ratios are usually associated with:

    a. a high-dividend yield

    b. high-profit growth

    c. low long-term debt to total assets

    d. strong current position

12. Based on the following data, what is the rate earned on total assets?

Net income..	$240,000
Preferred dividends..................................	$60,000
Interest expense	$120,000
Interest income	$40,000
Average total assets	$1,000,000

    a. 18%

    b. 28%

    c. 30%

    d. 36%

TRUE/FALSE

Instructions: Indicate whether each of the following statements is true or false by placing a check mark in the appropriate column.

		True	**False**
1.	In horizontal analysis of the income statement, each item is stated as a percentage of total sales...............................	____	____
2.	Solvency is the ability of a business to meet its financial obligations as they come due.	____	____
3.	The ratio of net sales to assets provides a solvency measure that shows the margin of safety of the debt-holders.	____	____
4.	The quick ratio or acid-test ratio is the ratio of the sum of cash, receivables, and marketable securities to current liabilities...	____	____
5.	Net sales divided by the year-end net accounts receivable gives the accounts receivable turnover...............................	____	____
6.	Net income minus the amount required for preferred dividends divided by the average common stockholders' equity gives the rate earned on common stockholders' equity...	____	____
7.	The rate earned on total assets is calculated by subtracting interest expense from net income and dividing this sum by the average total assets.	____	____
8.	The tendency on the rate earned on stockholders' equity to vary disproportionately from the rate earned on total assets is referred to as financial leverage.	____	____
9.	A profitability measure that shows the rate of return to common stockholders in terms of cash dividends is known as the dividend yield on common stock.	____	____
10.	The excess of the current assets of an enterprise over its current liabilities and stockholders' equity is called working capital..	____	____

EXERCISE 15-1

Instructions: Using the condensed income statement information presented below, perform a vertical analysis for Delta Corp. for the years ending December 31, 2007 and 2006, stating each item as a percent of revenues.

	2007	Percent	2006	Percent
Revenues	$450,000		$389,000	
Costs and expenses:				
Cost of sales	$200,000		$176,000	
Selling and administrative expenses	100,000		73,000	
Total costs and expenses	$300,000		$249,000	
Earnings before income taxes	$150,000		$140,000	
Income taxes	34,500		32,200	
Net earnings	$115,500		$107,800	

EXERCISE 15-2

Instructions: Using the condensed balance sheet data presented below, perform a horizontal analysis for Carson Inc. on December 31, 2007. Indicate the amount and percent increase (decrease) in the columns provided.

			Increase (Decrease)	
	2007	2006	Amount	Percent
Current assets	$250,000	$219,500		
Fixed assets	435,000	401,600		
Intangible assets	43,700	46,000		
Current liabilities	88,000	80,000		
Long-term liabilities	225,000	250,000		
Common stock	214,000	167,600		
Retained earnings	200,000	170,000		

PROBLEM 15-1

Instructions: Using the information below and on the following page, perform a horizontal analysis for Nordic Inc. by filling in the Amount and Percent columns that are provided. (Round all percents to one decimal place.)

Nordic Inc.
Comparative Income Statement
For the Years Ended December 31, 2007 and 2006

	2007	2006	Increase (Decrease) Amount	Percent
Sales	$690,500	$585,000		
Sales returns and allowances	25,500	23,000		
Net sales	$665,000	$562,000		
Cost of goods sold	420,000	330,000		
Gross profit	$245,000	$232,000		
Selling expenses	$ 43,000	$ 47,700		
Administrative expenses	31,000	31,000		
Total operating expenses	$ 74,000	$ 78,700		
Operating income	$171,000	$153,300		
Other income	13,000	16,400		
	$184,000	$169,700		
Other expense	58,000	53,500		
Income before income taxes	$126,000	$116,200		
Income taxes	34,000	32,400		
Net income	$ 92,000	$ 83,800		

Nordic Inc.
Comparative Balance Sheet
December 31, 2007 and 2006

Assets	2007	2006	Increase (Decrease) Amount	Percent
Cash	$ 76,000	$ 69,000		
Marketable securities	98,900	130,000		
Accounts receivable (net)	199,000	195,000		
Inventory	450,000	375,000		
Prepaid expenses	28,000	26,300		
Long-term investments	35,000	35,000		
Fixed assets (net)	871,000	835,000		
Intangible assets	18,000	22,800		
Total assets	$1,775,900	$1,688,100		
Liabilities				
Current liabilities	$ 129,000	$ 107,000		
Long-term liabilities	420,000	440,000		
Total liabilities	$ 549,000	$ 547,000		
Stockholders' Equity				
Preferred 3% stock, $100 par	$ 102,000	$ 93,000		
Common stock, $50 par	549,900	530,100		
Retained earnings	575,000	518,000		
Total stockholders' equity	$1,226,900	$1,141,100		
Total liabilities and stockholders' equity ...	$1,775,900	$1,688,100		

PROBLEM 15-2

Instructions: Using the information below and on the following page, perform a vertical analysis for Voyageur Inc. by filling in the Percent columns on the statements provided. (Round all percents to one decimal place.)

Voyageur Inc.
Comparative Balance Sheet
December 31, 2006 and 2005

	2006		2005	
Assets	Amount	Percent	Amount	Percent
Cash	$ 500,000		$ 425,000	
Marketable securities	200,000		185,000	
Accounts receivable (net)	680,000		575,000	
Inventory	860,000		740,000	
Prepaid expenses	104,000		95,000	
Long-term investments	450,000		410,000	
Fixed assets	6,556,000		5,420,000	
Total assets	$9,350,000	100%	$7,850,000	100%
Liabilities				
Current liabilities	$1,090,000		$1,050,000	
Long-term liabilities	2,150,000		2,050,000	
Total liabilities	$3,240,000		$3,100,000	
Stockholders' Equity				
Preferred 5% stock, $100 par	$ 350,000		$ 350,000	
Common stock, $10 par	2,550,000		2,550,000	
Retained earnings	3,210,000		1,850,000	
Total stockholders' equity	$6,110,000		$4,750,000	
Total liabilities and stockholders' equity ..	$9,350,000	100%	$7,850,000	100%

Voyageur Inc.
Income Statement
For the Year Ended December 31, 2006

	Amount	Percent
Sales	$12,800,000	
Sales returns and allowances	300,000	
Net sales	$12,500,000	100%
Cost of goods sold	7,550,000	
Gross profit	$ 4,950,000	
Selling expenses	$ 1,550,000	
Administrative expenses	825,000	
Total operating expenses	$ 2,375,000	
Operating income	$ 2,575,000	
Other income	125,000	
	$ 2,700,000	
Other expense (interest)	150,000	
Income before income taxes	$ 2,550,000	
Income taxes	937,000	
Net income	$ 1,613,000	

PROBLEM 15-3

Voyageur Inc. declared $250,000 of common stock dividends during 2006. The price of Voyageur's common stock on December 31, 2006 is $29.75.

Instructions: Using the data for Voyageur Inc. from Problem 15-2, determine the following amounts and ratios for 2006. (Round all ratios to one decimal point.)

		Calculation	Final Result
a.	Working capital		
b.	Current ratio		
c.	Quick ratio		
d.	Accounts receivable turnover		
e.	Number of days' sales in receivables		
f.	Inventory turnover		
g.	Number of days' sales in inventory		
h.	Ratio of fixed assets to long-term liabilities		
i.	Ratio of liabilities to stockholders' equity		

	Calculation	Final Result
j. Number of times interest charges earned		
k. Number of times preferred dividends earned		
l. Ratio of net sales to assets		
m. Rate earned on total assets		
n. Rate earned on stockholders' equity		
o. Rate earned on common stockholders' equity		
p. Earnings per share on common stock		
q. Price-earnings ratio		
r. Dividends per share of common stock		
s. Dividend yield		

CHAPTER 1

MATCHING

1. H	**8.** Y	**14.** T	**20.** X	**26.** C	**32.** QQ
2. BB	**9.** SS	**15.** Z	**21.** HH	**27.** S	**33.** CC
3. DD	**10.** J	**16.** U	**22.** E	**28.** OO	**34.** A
4. KK	**11.** AA	**17.** I	**23.** L	**29.** W	**35.** M
5. II	**12.** D	**18.** RR	**24.** B	**30.** NN	**36.** Q
6. N	**13.** R	**19.** F	**25.** JJ	**31.** G	**37.** MM
7. K					

FILL IN THE BLANK—PART A

1. business
2. corporation
3. business stakeholder
4. accounting
5. ethics
6. managerial
7. unit of measure
8. assets
9. owner's equity
10. accounting equation
11. $70,000
12. account payable
13. $130,000
14. $80,000
15. revenue
16. $15,000 net income
17. retained earnings statement
18. $38,000 net income
19. account
20. $94,000 increase

FILL IN THE BLANK—PART B

1. manufacturing
2. merchandising
3. proprietorship
4. managers
5. financial
6. Financial Accounting Standards Board (FASB)
7. business entity
8. liabilities
9. business transaction
10. prepaid expenses
11. account receivable
12. $80,000
13. $65,500
14. expenses
15. income statement
16. ($5,000) net loss
17. balance sheet
18. $13,500 increase
19. statement of cash flows
20. $29,000 net income

MULTIPLE CHOICE

1. a. Incorrect. General accounting is not a category of employment by accountants.
   b. Incorrect. Accountants and their staffs who provide services on a fee basis are said to be employed in public accounting.
   c. Incorrect. Independent accounting is not a category of employment by accountants.
   d. **Correct.** Accountants employed by a particular business firm or not-for-profit organization, perhaps as chief accountant, controller, or financial vice-president, are said to be engaged in private accounting.

2. a. Incorrect. Service businesses provide services rather than products to customers.
   b. **Correct.** Manufacturing businesses change basic inputs into products that are sold to individual customers.
   c. Incorrect. Merchandising businesses do not make the products, but instead they purchase them from other businesses and sell them to customers.
   d. Incorrect. A proprietorship is a form of business organization rather than a type of business.

3. a. Incorrect. The cost concept is the basis for entering the exchange price, or cost, into the accounting records.
   b. Incorrect. The objectivity concept requires that the accounting records and reports be based upon objective evidence.
   c. Incorrect. The business entity concept limits the economic data in the accounting system to data related directly to the activities of the business or entity.
   d. **Correct.** The unit of measure concept requires that economic data be recorded in dollars.

4. a. Incorrect. The business entity concept limits the economic data in the accounting system to data related directly to the activities of the business or entity.
   b. **Correct.** The cost concept is the basis for recording the amounts, or cost, into the accounting records.
   c. Incorrect. The matching principle emphasizes matching the expenses with the revenue generated during a period by those expenses.
   d. Incorrect. Proprietorship is not a principle, but instead it is a form of business organization.

5. a. Incorrect.
   b. Incorrect.
   c. Incorrect.
   d. **Correct.** The accounting equation (Assets = Liabilities + Owner's Equity) may also be expressed as Assets – Liabilities = Owner's Equity.

6. a. Incorrect.
   b. Incorrect.
   c. Incorrect.
   d. **Correct.** If total liabilities increased by $20,000 during a period of time and owner's equity increased by $5,000 during the same period, total assets must increase by $25,000. That is, if the right side of the accounting equation increases by $25,000 (Liabilities + Owner's Equity), the left side of the equation must also increase by the same amount, $25,000.

7. a. Incorrect.
   b. Incorrect.
   c. **Correct.** The payment of a credit of $6,000 decreases the asset, Cash, and decreases the liability, Accounts Payable.
   d. Incorrect.

8. a. Incorrect.
   b. Incorrect.
   c. Incorrect.
   d. **Correct.** The amount of net income for the year is $40,000. It is computed as ending owner's equity $135,000 ($355,000 – $220,000) less beginning owner's equity $100,000 ($290,000 – $190,000), which equals the change in owner's equity, $35,000. The change in owner's equity of $35,000, plus dividends of $30,000, less the additional issuance of capital stock of $25,000, equals the net income for the year, $40,000.

9. a. **Correct.** The amount of net income of $11,000 is determined by subtracting expenses, $59,000, from the revenues, $70,000. The dividends of $25,000 do not affect the determination of net income.
   b. Incorrect.
   c. Incorrect.
   d. Incorrect.

10. a. **Correct.** The statement of cash flows does not contain a section for cash flows from marketing activities.
   b. Incorrect. The statement of cash flows contains a section for investing activities.
   c. Incorrect. The statement of cash flows contains a section for financing activities.
   d. Incorrect. The statement of cash flows contains a section for cash flows from operating activities.

TRUE/FALSE

1. T

2. F Accountants and their staffs who provide services on a fee basis are said to be employed in public accounting, not private accounting.

3. F Managerial accounting uses both financial accounting and estimated data to aid management in running day-to-day operations.

4. F The concept that expenses incurred in generating revenue should be matched against the revenue in determining net income or net loss is the matching concept, not the cost concept.

5. F The operating activities section, not the financing activities section, of the statement of cash flows includes cash transactions that enter into the determination of net income.

6. F The debts of a business are called its accounts payable, not accounts receivable.

7. F A partnership is owned by two or more individuals.

8. T

9. F A summary of the changes in the earnings retained in the business that have occurred during a specific period of time, such as a month or a year, is called the retained earnings statement, not the statement of cash flows.

10. F A claim against a customer for sales made on credit is an account receivable, not an account payable.

EXERCISE 1-1

	A	L	OE			A	L	OE
1.	+	0	+	**6.**	+,–	0	0
2.	+	+	0	**7.**	+,–	0	0
3.	+	0	+	**8.**	–	–	0
4.	+	0	+	**9.**	–	–	0
5.	–	0	–	**10.**	–	0	–

PROBLEM 1-1

	Assets				=	Liabilities	+	Owner's Equity		
	Cash	+	Supplies	+	Land =	Accounts Payable	+	Capital Stock	+	Retained Earnings	
(1)	+$40,000							+$40,000			I
(2)			+$2,000			+$2,000				
Bal.	$40,000		$2,000			$2,000		$40,000		
(3)	–14,000				+$14,000					
Bal.	$26,000		$2,000		$14,000	$2,000		$40,000		
(4)	– 1,800					–1,800				
Bal.	$24,200		$2,000		$14,000	$ 200		$40,000		
(5)	+ 5,000									+$5,000	R
Bal.	$29,200		$2,000		$14,000	$ 200		$40,000		$5,000
(6)						+ 900				– 900	E
Bal.	$29,200		$2,000		$14,000	$1,100		$40,000		$4,100
(7)	+10,000							+10,000			I
Bal.	$39,200		$2,000		$14,000	$1,100		$50,000		$4,100
(8)	– 2,800									–2,800	E
Bal.	$36,400		$2,000		$14,000	$1,100		$50,000		$1,300
(9)	– 200									– 200	D
Bal.	$36,200		$2,000		$14,000	$1,100		$50,000		$1,100
(10)			– 600							– 600	E
Bal.	$36,200		$1,400		$14,000	$1,100		$50,000		$ 500

PROBLEM 1-2

(1)

Tom's Painting Service Inc.
Income Statement
For Year Ended December 31, 20--

Sales..		$27,450
Operating expenses:		
Supplies expense	$5,450	
Advertising expense	4,825	
Truck rental expense	1,525	
Utilities expense..	700	
Misc. expense...	1,400	13,900
Net income		$13,550

(2)

Tom's Painting Service Inc.
Retained Earnings Statement
For Year Ended December 31, 20--

Income for the year	$13,550
Less dividends...	(1,000)
Retained earnings, Dec. 31, 20--	$12,550

(3)

Tom's Painting Service Inc.
Balance Sheet
December 31, 20--

Assets		Liabilities		
Cash	$10,050	Accounts payable......................		$ 4,450
Accounts receivable	8,950	Stockholders' Equity		
Supplies.....................................	4,000	Capital stock	$ 6,000	
		Retained earnings....................	12,550	18,550
		Total liabilities and		
Total assets	$23,000	stockholders' equity..............		$23,000

CHAPTER 2

MATCHING

1. A	**6.** R	**10.** F	**14.** M	**18.** S	**22.** P
2. N	**7.** T	**11.** E	**15.** L	**19.** Y	**23.** W
3. D	**8.** I	**12.** C	**16.** H	**20.** Z	**24.** U
4. B	**9.** V	**13.** K	**17.** G	**21.** X	**25.** J
5. O					

FILL IN THE BLANK—PART A

1. account	**6.** debit	**11.** credit	**16.** double-entry
2. chart of accounts	**7.** credit	**12.** debit	accounting
3. revenue	**8.** debit	**13.** credit	**17.** posting
4. T account	**9.** credit	**14.** journal	**18.** two-column journal
5. debits	**10.** liability	**15.** journalizing	**19.** materiality
			20. transposition

FILL IN THE BLANK—PART B

1. ledger	6. credits	11. debit	16. asset
2. assets	7. balance	12. debit	17. debit
3. liabilities	8. journalizing	13. credit	18. credit
4. owner's equity	9. dividends	14. horizontal	19. trial balance
5. expenses	10. unearned revenue	15. liability	20. slide

MULTIPLE CHOICE

1. a. Incorrect.
   b. **Correct.** The receipt of cash from customers in payment of their accounts would be recorded by a debit to Cash and a credit to Accounts Receivable.
   c. Incorrect.
   d. Incorrect.

2. a. Incorrect. The third step in recording a transaction in a two-column journal is to list the account to be credited.
   b. Incorrect. The fourth step in recording a transaction in a two-column journal is to list the amount to be credited.
   c. Incorrect. The second step in recording a transaction in a two-column journal is to list the amount to be debited.
   d. **Correct.** The first step in recording a transaction in a two-column journal is to list the account to be debited.

3. a. Incorrect. Cash is debited when the owner invests cash.
   b. **Correct.** The dividends account of a corporation is debited when cash is paid to stockholders from earnings retained in the business.
   c. Incorrect. Accounts Payable is debited when a liability is paid.
   d. Incorrect. An expense account is debited when an expense is paid.

4. a. Incorrect.
   b. Incorrect.
   c. **Correct.** The equality of debits and credits in the ledger should be verified at the end of each accounting period by preparing a trial balance.
   d. Incorrect.

5. a. **Correct.** Incorrectly computing an account balance will cause an inequality in the trial balance totals.
   b. Incorrect. A failure to record a transaction will not cause an inequality in the trial balance totals.
   c. Incorrect. Recording the same transaction more than once will not cause an inequality in the trial balance totals.
   d. Incorrect. Posting a transaction to the wrong account will not cause an inequality in the trial balance totals.

6. a. Incorrect.
   b. **Correct.** Since cash is an asset, credits to Cash result in a decrease in assets.
   c. Incorrect.
   d. Incorrect.

7. a. Incorrect.
   b. **Correct.** Under the rules of double-entry accounting, debits to expense accounts signify a decrease in owner's equity.
   c. Incorrect.
   d. Incorrect.

8. a. Incorrect.
   b. Incorrect.
   c. Incorrect.
   d. **Correct.**   Under the rules of double-entry accounting, when rent is prepaid for several months in advance, the debit is to Prepaid Rent, an asset account.

9. a. Incorrect.
   b. Incorrect.
   c. **Correct.**   Under the rules of double-entry accounting, when an asset is purchased on account, the credit is to Accounts Payable, a liability account.
   d. Incorrect.

10. a. Incorrect.
    b. **Correct.**   Under the rules of double-entry accounting, when a payment is made to a supplier for goods previously purchased on account, the debit is to Accounts Payable, a liability account.
    c. Incorrect.
    d. Incorrect.

TRUE/FALSE

1. F   Amounts entered on the left side of an account, regardless of the account title, are called debits or charges to the account, not credits.
2. T
3. T
4. F   Accounts receivable are reported as assets, not liabilities, on the balance sheet.
5. T
6. F   Every business transaction affects a minimum of two accounts, not one account.
7. F   The process of recording a transaction in a journal is called journalizing, not posting.
8. F   The group of accounts for a business entity is called its ledger, not a journal.
9. T
10. F   A recording error caused by the erroneous rearrangement of digits, such as writing $627 as $672, is called a transposition, not a slide.

EXERCISE 2-1

Transaction	Account Debited Type	Effect	Account Credited Type	Effect
(1)	asset	+	owner's equity (capital stock)	+
(2)	asset	+	liability	+
(3)	asset	+	liability	+
(4)	asset	+	revenue	+
(5)	liability	–	asset	–
(6)	expense	+	liability	+
(7)	asset	+	asset	–
(8)	owner's equity (dividends)	+	asset	–

PROBLEM 2-1

(1)

Date		Account	Ref.	Debit	Credit
June	1	Cash..	11	5,000	
		Equipment......................................	18	14,500	
		Vehicles	19	21,000	
		Capital Stock	31		40,500
	16	Equipment......................................	18	5,500	
		Accounts Payable.....................	21		5,500
	28	Supplies	12	500	
		Accounts Payable.....................	21		500
	30	Accounts Payable	21	2,100	
		Cash	11		2,100

(2)

ACCOUNT   *Cash*   ACCOUNT NO.   *11*

| | | POST. | | | BALANCE | |
DATE	ITEM	REF.	DEBIT	CREDIT	DEBIT	CREDIT
20--						
June 1		1	5,000		5,000	
30		1		2,100	2,900	

ACCOUNT   *Supplies*   ACCOUNT NO.   *12*

DATE	ITEM	REF.	DEBIT	CREDIT	DEBIT	CREDIT
20--						
June 28		1	500		500	

ACCOUNT   *Equipment*   ACCOUNT NO.   *18*

DATE	ITEM	REF.	DEBIT	CREDIT	DEBIT	CREDIT
20--						
June 1		1	14,500		14,500	
16		1	5,500		20,000	

ACCOUNT   *Vehicles*   ACCOUNT NO.   *19*

DATE	ITEM	REF.	DEBIT	CREDIT	DEBIT	CREDIT
20--						
June 1		1	21,000		21,000	

ACCOUNT   *Accounts Payable*   ACCOUNT NO.   *21*

DATE	ITEM	REF.	DEBIT	CREDIT	DEBIT	CREDIT
20--						
June 16		1		5,500		5,500
28		1		500		6,000
30		1	2,100			3,900

ACCOUNT   *Capital Stock*   ACCOUNT NO.   *31*

DATE	ITEM	REF.	DEBIT	CREDIT	DEBIT	CREDIT
20--						
June 1		1		40,500		40,500

(3)

Star Service Corporation
Trial Balance
June 30, 20--

	Debit	Credit
Cash	2,900	
Supplies..	500	
Equipment	20,000	
Vehicles..	21,000	
Accounts Payable...		3,900
Capital Stock		40,500
	44,400	44,400

PROBLEM 2-2

(1)

Cash			
(a)	20,000	(b)	2,500
(d)	19,600	(c)	1,000
		(e)	1,100
		(g)	2,600
		(h)	5,000
		(i)	800
		(k)	240
		(l)	1,700
		(m)	2,000
		(n)	5,000
		(o)	500

Office Equipment			
(a)	13,200		

Auto			
(g)	13,000		

Accounts Payable			
(k)	240	(f)	200
(m)	2,000	(g)	10,400
		(j)	240

Rent Expense		
(b)	2,500	

Salary Expense		
(e)	1,100	

Telephone Expense		
(j)	240	

Auto Repairs & Maintenance Expense		
(i)	800	

Office Supplies		
(c)	1,000	
(f)	200	

Capital Stock		
	(a)	33,200

Janitor Expense		
(o)	500	

Prepaid Insurance		
(l)	1,700	

Dividends		
(h)	5,000	

Legal Fees		
	(d)	19,600

Library		
(n)	5,000	

(2)

Turner Law Services, P.C.
Trial Balance
January 31, 20--

Cash	17,160	
Office Supplies	1,200	
Prepaid Insurance	1,700	
Library	5,000	
Office Equipment	13,200	
Auto	13,000	
Accounts Payable		8,600
Capital Stock		33,200
Dividends	5,000	
Legal Fees		19,600
Rent Expense	2,500	
Salary Expense	1,100	
Telephone Expense	240	
Auto Repairs & Maintenance Expense	800	
Janitor Expense	500	
	61,400	61,400

PROBLEM 2-3

(a)	Prepaid Insurance	1,000	
	Prepaid Rent..		1,000
	To correct erroneous debit to prepaid rent.		
(b)	Accounts Receivable..	200	
	Accounts Payable		200
	To correct erroneous credit to accounts receivable.		
(c)	Dividends	3,000	
	Cash		3,000
	To correct erroneous entry debiting cash and crediting dividends.		

CHAPTER 3

MATCHING

1.	A	**5.**	T	**8.**	M	**11.**	D	**14.**	P	**17.** F
2.	J	**6.**	H	**9.**	N	**12.**	R	**15.**	E	**18.** X
3.	B	**7.**	G	**10.**	C	**13.**	O	**16.**	I	**19.** L
4.	W									

FILL IN THE BLANK—PART A

1. accounting period
2. cash
3. revenue recognition
4. adjusting
5. deferred expenses
6. accrued expenses
7. advertising expense
8. accumulated depreciation—equipment
9. unearned fees
10. taxes payable
11. overstated
12. understated
13. understated
14. $10,700
15. $800
16. fixed assets
17. depreciation
18. book value
19. $88,700
20. adjusted

FILL IN THE BLANK—PART B

1. accrual
2. matching
3. adjusting
4. deferred revenues
5. accrued revenues
6. depreciation
7. accumulated depreciation
8. understated
9. overstated
10. interest expense
11. prepaid rent
12. depreciation expense
13. fees earned
14. vertical
15. balance sheet
16. expense
17. overstated
18. overstated
19. $1,950
20. $800

MULTIPLE CHOICE

1. a. Incorrect.
   b. **Correct.** Entries required at the end of an accounting period to bring the accounts up to date and to assure the proper matching of revenues and expenses are called adjusting entries.
   c. Incorrect.
   d. Incorrect. Correcting entries correct errors in the accounting records. Entries required at the end of an accounting period to bring the accounts up to date and to assure the proper matching of revenues and expenses are called adjusting entries.

2. a. **Correct.** The amount of accrued but unpaid expenses at the end of the fiscal period is both an expense and a liability.
   b. Incorrect. The amount of accrued but unpaid expenses at the end of the fiscal period is both an expense and a liability, not an asset.
   c. Incorrect. The amount of accrued but unpaid expenses at the end of the fiscal period is both an expense and a liability, not a deferral.
   d. Incorrect. The amount of accrued but unpaid expenses at the end of the fiscal period is both an expense and a liability, not a revenue.

3. a. Incorrect.
   b. Incorrect.
   c. **Correct.** If the effect of the debit portion of an adjusting entry is to increase the balance of an expense account, the effect of the credit portion of the entry is a decrease in the balance of an asset account.
   d. Incorrect.

4. a. Incorrect.
   b. Incorrect.
   c. Incorrect.
   d. **Correct.** If the effect of the credit portion of an adjusting entry is to increase the balance of a liability account, the effect of the debit portion of the entry is an increase in the balance of an expense account.

5. a. Incorrect.
   b. **Correct.** The balance in the prepaid rent account before adjustment at the end of the year is $12,000, which represents three months' rent paid on December 1. The adjusting entry required on December 31 debits Rent Expense, $4,000, and credits Prepaid Rent, $4,000.
   c. Incorrect.
   d. Incorrect.

6. a. **Correct.** At the end of the preceding fiscal year, the usual adjusting entry for accrued salaries owed to employees was omitted. The error was not corrected, and the accrued salaries were included in the first salary payment in the current fiscal year. As a result, Salary Expense was overstated and net income was understated for the current year.
   b. Incorrect. Salaries Payable is understated at the end of the preceding fiscal year, not the current year.
   c. Incorrect. Salary Expense was overstated and net income was understated for the current fiscal year, not the preceding year.
   d. Incorrect. Salary Expense and Salaries Payable were understated, rather than overstated, for the preceding year.

7. a. Incorrect.
   b. Incorrect.
   c. **Correct.** The decrease in usefulness of fixed assets as time passes is called depreciation.
   d. Incorrect.

8. a. **Correct.** The difference between the fixed asset account and the related accumulated depreciation account is called the book value of the asset.
   b. Incorrect.
   c. Incorrect.
   d. Incorrect.

9. a. Incorrect. Expenses will be understated, not overstated.
   b. Incorrect. Net income will be overstated, not understated.
   c. Incorrect. Assets will be overstated, not understated.
   d. **Correct.** If a $250 adjustment for depreciation is not recorded, retained earnings will be overstated.

10. a. **Correct.** The corrected net income is computed as $50,000 less the adjusting entry for supplies expense of $500 and accrued salaries of $1,300.
   b. Incorrect.
   c. Incorrect.
   d. Incorrect.

TRUE/FALSE

1. T

2. F   When the reduction in prepaid expenses is not properly recorded, the asset accounts will be overstated and the expense accounts will be understated.

3. T

4. F If the adjusting entry to record accrued wages at the end of the year is omitted, net income and retained earnings will be overstated, but total assets will not be affected. Instead, liabilities will be understated.

5. T

6. T

7. T

8. F Expenses that have not been paid or revenues that have not been received are accruals, not deferrals.

9. T

10. F The amount of accrued revenue is recorded by debiting an asset account, not a liability account. The credit is to a revenue account.

EXERCISE 3-1

(1)

Cash		Prepaid Insurance		Insurance Expense	
	May 1 5,400	May 1 5,400	Dec. 31 1,200	Dec. 31 1,200	

(2) Unexpired insurance $4,200

(3) Insurance expense $1,200

EXERCISE 3-2

(1)

Cash		Salary Expense		Salaries Payable	
	Oct. 7 250	Oct. 7 250			Oct. 31 50
	14 250	14 250			
	21 250	21 250			
	28 250	28 250			
		31 50			

(2) Salary expense $1,050

(3) Salaries payable $50

EXERCISE 3-3

Unearned Rent		Rent Revenue	
Dec. 31 500	Dec. 1 6,000		Dec. 31 500

Dec. 31	Unearned Rent	500	
	Rent Revenue		500

EXERCISE 3-4

Interest Receivable		Interest Revenue	
Dec. 31 320			Dec. 31 320

Dec. 31	Interest Receivable	320	
	Interest Revenue		320

PROBLEM 3-1

(1) **(a)** Salaries Expense.......................................   2,000
        Salaries Payable   2,000

    (b) Rent Expense   726
        Prepaid Rent   726

    (c) Supplies Expense....................................   1,750
        Supplies   1,750

    (d) Depreciation Expense   400
        Accumulated Depreciation.................   400

    (e) Accounts Receivable..............................   2,100
        Service Fees.....................................   2,100

(2)

Bob's Service Inc.
Adjusted Trial Balance
July 31, 20--

Cash	9,218	
Accounts Receivable..	9,377	
Supplies..	1,000	
Prepaid Rent	7,986	
Tools & Equipment..	21,829	
Accumulated Depreciation		1,935
Accounts Payable...		7,117
Salaries Payable		2,000
Capital Stock		10,000
Retained Earnings		27,417
Dividends..	3,234	
Service Fees		30,799
Salary Expense	17,929	
Rent Expense..	726	
Supplies Expense...	1,750	
Depreciation Expense	400	
Miscellaneous Expense..	5,819	
	79,268	79,268

CHAPTER 4

MATCHING

1. T	**4.** F	**7.** O	**10.** A	**13.** G	**15.** P
2. E	**5.** J	**8.** H	**11.** R	**14.** D	**16.** S
3. L	**6.** I	**9.** K	**12.** U		

FILL IN THE BLANK—PART A

1. work sheet
2. note receivable
3. current liabilities
4. balance sheet
5. balance sheet
6. net income
7. net loss
8. income summary
9. retained earnings
10. income summary
11. retained earnings
12. post-closing
13. natural business year
14. accounting cycle
15. working capital

FILL IN THE BLANK—PART B

1. current assets
2. property, plant, and equipment
3. long-term liabilities
4. income statement
5. income statement
6. net loss
7. net income
8. closing entries
9. income summary
10. retained earnings
11. income summary
12. retained earnings
13. fiscal year
14. solvency
15. current

MULTIPLE CHOICE

1. a. Incorrect. Notes receivable are written claims against customers not creditors.
   b. Incorrect. Notes receivable are written claims against customers not owner's equity.
   c. ***Correct.*** Notes receivable are written claims against customers.
   d. Incorrect. Notes payable, not notes receivable, are written claims against assets.

2. a. Incorrect. A work sheet is completed by extending the adjusted trial balance amounts to the Income Statement and Balance Sheet columns as well as totaling the Adjustment columns and extending the work sheet adjustments to the Adjusted Trial Balance columns.
   b. Incorrect. A work sheet is completed by totaling the Adjustment columns as well as extending the adjusted trial balance amounts to the Income Statement and Balance Sheet columns and extending the work sheet adjustments to the Adjusted Trial Balance columns.
   c. Incorrect. A work sheet is completed by extending the work sheet adjustments to the Adjusted Trial Balance columns as well as totaling the Adjustment columns and extending the adjusted trial balance amounts to the Income Statement and Balance Sheet columns.
   d. ***Correct.*** A work sheet is completed by extending the adjusted trial balance amounts to the income Statement and Balance Sheet columns, totaling the Adjustment columns, and extending the work sheet adjustments to the Adjusted Trial Balance columns.

3. a. ***Correct.*** If the Income Statement Credit column is greater than the Income Statement Debit column, a net income exists.
   b. Incorrect. If the Income Statement Credit column is greater than the Income Statement Debit column, a net income exists, not a net loss.
   c. Incorrect.
   d. Incorrect.

4. a. Incorrect. After all of the account balances have been extended to the Balance Sheet columns of the work sheet, the totals of the Debit and Credit columns are $377,750 and $387,750, respectively. The amount of net loss for the period is $10,000—the difference between the Balance Sheet Debit and Credit columns. Because the Balance Sheet Credit column is larger than the Debit column, a net loss has been incurred, rather than a net income.
   b. ***Correct.*** After all of the account balances have been extended to the Balance Sheet columns of the work sheet, the totals of the Debit and Credit columns are $377,750 and $387,750, respectively. The amount of net loss for the period is $10,000—the difference between the Debit and Credit columns. Because the Balance Sheet Credit column is larger than the Debit column, a net loss has been incurred.
   c. Incorrect. The net income or net loss is computed as the difference between the Balance Sheet Debit and Credit columns, not the total of the Debit column.
   d. Incorrect. The net income or net loss is computed as the difference between the Balance Sheet Debit and Credit column, not the total of the Credit column.

5. a. ***Correct.*** After all of the account balances have been extended to the Income Statement columns of the work sheet, the totals of the Debit and Credit columns are $62,300 and $67,600, respectively. The amount of the net income for the period is $5,300—the difference between the Debit and Credit columns. Because the Income Statement Credit column is larger than the Debit column, a net income has been incurred.
   b. Incorrect. After all of the account balances have been extended to the Income Statement columns of the work sheet, the totals of the Debit and Credit columns are $62,300 and $67,600, respectively. The amount of the net income for the period is $5,300—the difference between the Debit and Credit columns. Because the Income Statement Credit column is larger than the Debit column, a net income has been incurred, rather than a net loss.
   c. Incorrect. The net income or net loss is computed as the difference between the Income Statement Debit and Credit columns, not the total of the Debit column.
   d. Incorrect. The net income or net loss is computed as the difference between the Income Statement Debit and Credit columns, not the total of the Credit column.

6. a. Incorrect. Dividends should be closed to Retained Earnings at the end of the fiscal year, not to Income Summary.
   b. Incorrect. Accumulated Depreciation—Equipment is not closed at the end of the fiscal year.
   c. **Correct.** Sales should be closed to Income Summary at the end of the fiscal year.
   d. Incorrect. Accounts Payable is not closed at the end of the fiscal year.

7. a. Incorrect. Salaries Expense is closed at the end of the fiscal year to Income Summary.
   b. Incorrect. Sales is closed at the end of the fiscal year to Income Summary.
   c. **Correct.** Dividends should be closed to Retained Earnings at the end of the fiscal year.
   d. Incorrect. Accounts Receivable is not closed at the end of the fiscal year.

8. a. Incorrect. Salaries Expense is closed to Income Summary at the end of the period and does not appear in the post-closing trial balance.
   b. Incorrect. Dividends is closed to Retained Earnings at the end of the period and does not appear in the post-closing trial balance.
   c. Incorrect. Sales is closed to Income Summary at the end of the period and does not appear in the post-closing trial balance.
   d. **Correct.** Capital Stock is not closed at the end of the period and does appear in the post-closing trial balance.

9. a. Incorrect. The maximum length of an accounting period is normally greater than 6 months.
   b. **Correct.** The maximum length of an accounting period is normally 1 year.
   c. Incorrect. The maximum length of an accounting period is normally less than 2 years.
   d. Incorrect. The maximum length of an accounting period is normally less than 3 years.

10. a. Incorrect.
   b. Incorrect.
   c. **Correct.** The complete sequence of accounting procedures for a fiscal period is frequently called the accounting cycle.
   d. Incorrect.

TRUE/FALSE

1. F   The balance of Accumulated Depreciation—Equipment is extended to the Balance Sheet columns of the work sheet, not the Income Statement columns.
2. F   The difference between the Debit and Credit columns of the Income Statement section of the work sheet is the same as the difference between the Debit and Credit columns of the Balance Sheet section. This difference is the net income or net loss for the period.
3. T
4. T
5. F   The balances of the accounts reported in the balance sheet are carried from year to year and are called real or permanent accounts, not temporary accounts.
6. T
7. F   If the Income Statement Debit column is greater than the Income Statement Credit column, the difference is a net loss, not a net income.
8. F   A type of working paper frequently used by accountants prior to the preparation of financial statements is called a work sheet, not a post-closing trial balance. The post-closing trial balance is prepared after the closing entries have been recorded to verify the equality of the debit and credit balances.
9. T
10. T

EXERCISE 4-1

Aug.	31	Salary Expense	1,500	
		Salaries Payable		1,500
	31	Rent Expense	560	
		Prepaid Rent		560
	31	Supplies Expense	700	
		Supplies		700
	31	Depreciation Expense	1,000	
		Accumulated Depreciation		1,000
	31	Accounts Receivable	3,200	
		Repair Fees		3,200

EXERCISE 4-2

(1) 20--

Mar.	31	Service Fees	50	19,225	
		Income Summary	45		19,225
	31	Income Summary	45	13,980	
		Salary Expense	58		8,550
		Supplies Expense	67		5,430

(2)

ACCOUNT *Income Summary* — ACCOUNT NO. 45

DATE	ITEM	POST. REF.	DEBIT	CREDIT	BALANCE DEBIT	BALANCE CREDIT
20--						
Mar. 31		7		19,225		19,225
31		7	13,980			5,245

ACCOUNT *Service Fees* — ACCOUNT NO. 50

DATE	ITEM	POST. REF.	DEBIT	CREDIT	BALANCE DEBIT	BALANCE CREDIT
20--						
Mar. 15		5		4,850		4,850
31		6		14,375		19,225
31		7	19,225			–0–

ACCOUNT *Salary Expense* — ACCOUNT NO. 58

DATE	ITEM	POST. REF.	DEBIT	CREDIT	BALANCE DEBIT	BALANCE CREDIT
20--						
Mar. 31		5	8,550		8,550	
31		7		8,550	–0–	

ACCOUNT *Supplies Expense* — ACCOUNT NO. 67

DATE	ITEM	POST. REF.	DEBIT	CREDIT	BALANCE DEBIT	BALANCE CREDIT
20--						
Mar. 15		5	2,430		2,430	
25		6	1,720		4,150	
31		6	1,280		5,430	
31		7		5,430	–0–	

PROBLEM 4-1

(1)

Castle Shop Inc.
Work Sheet
For Year Ended April 30, 20--

Account Title	Trial Balance Dr.	Trial Balance Cr.	Adjustments Dr.	Adjustments Cr.	Adjusted Trial Balance Dr.	Adjusted Trial Balance Cr.	Income Statement Dr.	Income Statement Cr.	Balance Sheet Dr.	Balance Sheet Cr.
Cash	10,056				10,056				10,056	
Accts. Rec.	7,938		(e) 3,000		10,938				10,938	
Supplies	3,000			(a) 1,200	1,800				1,800	
Prepaid Rent	9,504			(b) 792	8,712				8,712	
Tools & Equipment	23,814				23,814				23,814	
Acc. Depreciation		1,674		(c) 1,000		2,674				2,674
Accounts Payable		7,764				7,764				7,764
Unearned Fees		2,000	(f) 500			1,500				1,500
Capital Stock		10,000				10,000				10,000
Retained Earnings		28,818				28,818				28,818
Dividends	3,528				3,528				3,528	
Service Fees		31,308		(e) 3,000		34,808		34,808		
				(f) 500						
Wages Expense	17,376		(d) 2,000		19,376		19,376			
Misc. Expense	6,348				6,348		6,348			
	81,564	81,564								
Wages Payable				(d) 2,000		2,000				2,000
Rent Expense			(b) 792		792		792			
Supplies Expense			(a) 1,200		1,200		1,200			
Depr. Expense			(c) 1,000		1,000		1,000			
			8,492	8,492	87,564	87,564	28,716	34,808	58,848	52,756
Net Income							6,092			6,092
							34,808	34,808	58,848	58,848

(2)

Castle Shop Inc.
Income Statement
For Year Ended April 30, 20--

Service fees..		$34,808
Operating expenses:		
Wages expenses	$19,376	
Supplies expense	1,200	
Depreciation expense...	1,000	
Rent expense...	792	
Misc. expenses	6,348	
Total operating expenses		28,716
Net income		$ 6,092

Castle Shop Inc.
Retained Earnings Statement
For Year Ended April 30, 20--

Retained earnings, May 1, 20--..		$28,818
Income for the year	$6,092	
Less dividends for the year	3,528	
Increase in retained earnings..		2,564
Retained earnings, April 30, 20--		$31,382

Castle Shop Inc.
Balance Sheet
April 30, 20--

Assets			Liabilities		
Current assets:			Current liabilities:		
Cash...	$10,056		Accounts payable	$7,764	
Accounts receivable.................	10,938		Wages payable.............	2,000	
Supplies	1,800		Unearned fees.............	1,500	
Prepaid rent..............................	8,712		Total liabilities.................		$11,264
Total current assets..............		$31,506	**Stockholders' Equity**		
Property, plant, and equipment:			Capital stock...................	$10,000	
Tools & equipment	$23,814		Retained earnings...........	31,382	41,382
Less accumulated depreciation	2,674	21,140	Total liabilities and		
Total assets		$52,646	stockholders' equity.....		$52,646

PROBLEM 4-2

(1)

20--		Adjusting Entries		
Apr.	30	Supplies Expense...	1,200	
		Supplies..		1,200
	30	Rent Expense	792	
		Prepaid Rent		792
	30	Depreciation Expense...................................	1,000	
		Accumulated Depreciation		1,000
	30	Wages Expense..	2,000	
		Wages Payable		2,000
	30	Accounts Receivable	3,000	
		Service Fees		3,000
	30	Unearned Fees...	500	
		Service Fees		500

(2) 20--   Closing Entries
 Apr. 30   Service Fees...   34,808
                Income Summary   34,808

      30   Income Summary...   28,716
                Wages Expense   19,376
                Miscellaneous Expense   6,348
                Supplies Expense....................................   1,200
                Depreciation Expense............................   1,000
                Rent Expense..   792

      30   Income Summary...   6,092
                Retained Earnings.................................   6,092

      30   Retained Earnings   3,528
                Dividends..   3,528

CHAPTER 5

MATCHING

1. D	**6.** CC	**11.** V	**16.** E	**21.** AA	**26.** Q
2. J	**7.** T	**12.** W	**17.** DD	**22.** B	**27.** BB
3. O	**8.** S	**13.** F	**18.** H	**23.** K	**28.** L
4. C	**9.** U	**14.** Y	**19.** G	**24.** N	**29.** A
5. I	**10.** M	**15.** Z	**20.** P	**25.** R	**30.** X

FILL IN THE BLANK—PART A

1. cost of merchandise sold
2. merchandise inventory
3. control
4. general
5. periodic
6. merchandise available for sale
7. purchases return or allowance
8. sales discounts
9. credit
10. FOB shipping point
11. $50
12. $60
13. $700
14. multiple-step
15. administrative
16. loss from operations
17. other
18. inventory shrinkage
19. $240,000
20. report

FILL IN THE BLANK—PART B

1. gross profit
2. subsidiary
3. perpetual
4. physical inventory
5. purchases discounts
6. debit
7. sales return or allowance
8. trade discounts
9. FOB destination
10. $160
11. $15,100
12. $33
13. $9,900
14. $6,600
15. selling
16. income from operations
17. other income
18. single-step
19. $215,000
20. account

MULTIPLE CHOICE

1. a. Incorrect. Cost of merchandise sold is not included in the stockholders' equity section of the balance sheet.
   b. Incorrect. Cost of merchandise sold is not included in the other income section of the income statement.
   c. **Correct.** The basic differences between the financial statements of a merchandising business and a service business include reporting cost of merchandise sold on the income statement and the balance sheet as a current asset.
   d. Incorrect. Cost of merchandise sold is not included in the owner's equity statement.

2. a. Incorrect. The sales discount should be deducted in determining the amount the seller will received.
   b. *Correct.*   The seller will receive $58.80, computed as $60 less the sales discount of $1.20 ($60 × 2%).
   c. Incorrect.
   d. Incorrect. $1.20 is the amount of the sales discount, not the amount received by the seller.

3. a. Incorrect. A debit memorandum is issued by the buyer, not the seller.
   b. *Correct.*   A credit memorandum is issued by the seller when a customer is allowed a reduction from the original price for defective goods.
   c. Incorrect.
   d. Incorrect.

4. a. *Correct.*   When the seller prepays the transportation costs and the terms of sale are FOB shipping point, the seller records the payment of the transportation costs by debiting Accounts Receivable. This is because transportation costs are the responsibility of the buyer when the terms are FOB shipping point.
   b. Incorrect.
   c. Incorrect.
   d. Incorrect.

5. a. Incorrect.
   b. Incorrect.
   c. *Correct.*   If the seller collects sales tax at the time of sale, the seller credits the tax to Sales Tax Payable.
   d. Incorrect.

6. a. Incorrect. Accounts Receivable normally appears in the chart of accounts of both a merchandising and a service business.
   b. Incorrect. Advertising Expense normally appears in the chart of accounts of both a merchandising and a service business.
   c. *Correct.*   Sales Returns and Allowances appears in the chart of accounts for a merchandising business but not for a service business.
   d. Incorrect. Accumulated Depreciation normally appears in the chart of accounts of both a merchandising and a service business.

7. a. *Correct.*   The excess of net revenue from sales over the cost of merchandise sold is gross profit.
   b. Incorrect. Operating profit, sometimes called income from operations, is gross profit less selling and administrative expenses.
   c. Incorrect.
   d. Incorrect.

8. a. Incorrect. Income from operations is computed by subtracting from gross profit both selling and administrative expenses.
   b. Incorrect. Income from operations is computed by subtracting from gross profit both selling and administrative (general) expenses.
   c. Incorrect. Income from operations is computed by subtracting from gross profit both selling and administrative expenses.
   d. *Correct.*   Income from operations is computed by subtracting operating expenses from gross profit. Operating expenses include both selling and administrative expenses.

9. a. Incorrect.
   b. Incorrect.
   c. Incorrect.
   d. *Correct.*   After all adjusting entries are posted, the balances of all asset, liability, revenue, and expense accounts correspond exactly to the amounts in the financial statements.

10. a. Incorrect. Sales appears as revenue from operations.
   b. **Correct.** In a multiple-step income statement of a merchandising business, interest revenue would appear as "other income."
   c. Incorrect. Sales discounts are deducted from sales in reporting revenue from sales.
   d. Incorrect. Sales returns and allowances are deducted from sales in reporting revenue from sales.

TRUE/FALSE

1. T

2. F   In a perpetual inventory system, purchases of merchandise are recorded in the merchandise inventory account, not the purchases account.

3. T

4. F   A discount offered the purchaser of goods as a means of encouraging payment before the end of the credit period is known as a purchases discount, not a bank discount.

5. T

6. F   If the seller is to absorb the cost of delivering the goods, the terms are stated FOB (free on board) destination, not FOB shipping point.

7. F   The liability for the sales tax is incurred at the time the seller sells the merchandise, not when the seller receives payment from the buyer.

8. T

9. T

10. F   The work sheet procedures for a merchandising business are similar to, not significantly different from, those of a service business.

11. F   The physical inventory taken at the end of the period is normally smaller, not larger, than the amount of the balance of the merchandise inventory account.

12. F   Any merchandise inventory shrinkage is normally debited to the cost of merchandise sold account, not the merchandise inventory account.

13. F   Expenses incurred directly and entirely in connection with the sale of merchandise are called selling expenses, not administrative expenses.

14. F   Revenue from sources such as income from interest, rent, dividends, and gains resulting from the sale of fixed assets is classified as "other income," not income from operations.

15. T

16. T

17. T

18. F   The traditional balance sheet arrangement of assets on the left-hand side with the liabilities and owner's equity on the right-hand side is called the account form, not the report form.

19. F   After the adjusting and closing entries have been recorded and posted, the general ledger accounts that appear on the balance sheet *do* have balances. The general ledger accounts that appear in the income statement *do not* have balances. In addition, the owner's drawing account *does not* have a balance.

20. T

EXERCISE 5-1

Sales			$875,000
Cost of merchandise sold:			
Merchandise inventory, July 1, 2005.........................		$130,000	
Purchases..	$600,000		
Less: Purchases returns and allowances................... $45,000			
Purchases discounts.. 10,000	55,000		
Net purchases	$545,000		
Add transportation in	7,500		
Cost of merchandise purchased		552,500	
Merchandise available for sale..................................		$682,500	
Less merchandise inventory, June 30, 2006..............		125,000	
Cost of merchandise sold...			557,500
Gross profit..			$317,500

EXERCISE 5-2

(1)	Merchandise Inventory..	5,000	
	Accounts Payable		5,000
(2)	Accounts Payable..	5,000	
	Cash..		4,900
	Merchandise Inventory		100
(3)	Merchandise Inventory..	3,580	
	Accounts Payable		3,580
(4)	Accounts Payable..	900	
	Merchandise Inventory		900
(5)	Accounts Payable..	2,680	
	Cash..		2,680

EXERCISE 5-3

(1)	Accounts Receivable...	3,150	
	Sales		3,150
	Cost of Merchandise Sold	2,000	
	Merchandise Inventory		2,000
(2)	Cash	2,850	
	Sales		2,850
	Cost of Merchandise Sold	1,380	
	Merchandise Inventory		1,380
(3)	Cash	3,050	
	Credit Card Expense	100	
	Accounts Receivable		3,150

(4) Accounts Receivable.. 4,500
                Sales.. 4,500

        Accounts Receivable.. 150
                Cash.. 150

        Cost of Merchandise Sold....................................... 3,100
                Merchandise Inventory 3,100

(5) Sales Returns and Allowances 400
                Accounts Receivable 400

        Merchandise Inventory... 275
                Cost of Merchandise Sold................................ 275

(6) Cash 4,168
        Sales Discounts... 82
                Accounts Receivable 4,250

EXERCISE 5-4

20--
Jan. 3   Merchandise Inventory 25,000
                Accounts Payable 25,000

      5   Accounts Payable..................................... 5,000
                Merchandise Inventory............................. 5,000

      12 Accounts Receivable.................................. 50,000
                Sales 50,000

      12 Cost of Merchandise Sold 35,000
                Merchandise Inventory............................. 35,000

      13 Accounts Payable..................................... 20,000
                Cash... 19,600
                Merchandise Inventory............................ 400

      15 Sales Returns and Allowances...................... 8,000
                Accounts Receivable 8,000

      15 Merchandise Inventory 5,600
                Cost of Merchandise Sold...................... 5,600

      22 Cash 41,580
          Sales Discounts.. 420
                Accounts Receivable 42,000

PROBLEM 5-1

20--

Sept.	3	Merchandise Inventory	8,500	
		Accounts Payable		8,500
	4	Office Supplies	800	
		Cash		800
	6	Accounts Receivable	4,000	
		Sales		4,000
	6	Cost of Merchandise Sold	3,000	
		Merchandise Inventory		3,000
	7	Accounts Payable	2,000	
		Merchandise Inventory		2,000
	10	Merchandise Inventory	5,000	
		Cash		5,000
	12	Accounts Receivable	5,500	
		Sales		5,500
	12	Cost of Merchandise Sold	3,200	
		Merchandise Inventory		3,200
	13	Accounts Payable	6,500	
		Cash		6,435
		Merchandise Inventory		65
	16	Cash	3,920	
		Sales Discounts	80	
		Accounts Receivable		4,000
	20	Cash	5,200	
		Credit Card Expense	300	
		Accounts Receivable		5,500
	24	Accounts Receivable	3,000	
		Sales		3,000
	24	Cost of Merchandise Sold	1,750	
		Merchandise Inventory		1,750
	26	Cash	2,200	
		Sales		2,200
	26	Cost of Merchandise Sold	1,400	
		Merchandise Inventory		1,400
	30	Sales Returns and Allowances	1,000	
		Accounts Receivable		1,000
	30	Merchandise Inventory	600	
		Cost of Merchandise Sold		600

PROBLEM 5-2

(a)

Miller Inc.
Income Statement
For Year Ended March 31, 20--

Revenue from sales:			
Sales		$1,016,700	
Less: Sales returns and allowances		13,010	
Net sales			$1,003,690
Cost of merchandise sold			681,060
Gross profit			$ 322,630
Operating expenses:			
Selling expenses:			
Sales salaries expense	$78,250		
Delivery expense	42,100		
Advertising expense	13,090		
Depr. expense—delivery equip.	9,050		
Misc. selling expense	13,950		
Total selling expenses		$ 156,440	
Administrative expenses:			
Office salaries expense	$55,800		
Insurance expense	16,000		
Office supplies expense	9,100		
Misc. administrative expenses	6,870		
Total administrative expenses		87,770	
Total operating expenses			244,210
Income from operations			$ 78,420
Other income:			
Interest revenue			1,020
Net income			$ 79,440

(b)

Miller Inc.
Income Statement
For Year Ended March 31, 20--

Revenues:		
Net sales		$1,003,690
Interest revenue		1,020
Total revenues		$1,004,710
Expenses:		
Cost of merchandise sold	$681,060	
Selling expenses	156,440	
Administrative expenses	87,770	
Total expenses		925,270
Net income		$ 79,440

(c)

Cost of Merchandise Sold	4,200	
Merchandise Inventory		4,200

PROBLEM 5-3

Miller Inc.
Retained Earnings Statement
For Year Ended March 31, 20--

Retained earnings, April 1, 20--		$143,650
Net income for year..	$79,440	
Less dividends	30,000	
Increase in retained earnings..		49,440
Retained earnings, March 31, 20--		$193,090

PROBLEM 5-4

Miller Inc.
Balance Sheet
March 31, 20--

Assets

Current assets:		
Cash	$ 49,620	
Accounts receivable	107,780	
Merchandise inventory	115,800	
Office supplies	1,250	
Prepaid insurance..	8,740	
Total current assets...		$283,190
Property, plant, and equipment:		
Delivery equipment...	$ 60,150	
Less accumulated depreciation..	22,950	
Total property, plant, and equipment		37,200
Total assets...		$320,390

Liabilities

Current liabilities:		
Accounts payable	$ 75,300	
Salaries payable	2,000	
Total current liabilities..		$ 77,300

Stockholders' Equity

Capital stock...	$ 50,000	
Retained earnings..	193,090	243,090
Total liabilities and stockholders' equity................................		$320,390

CHAPTER 6

MATCHING

1. D	3. N	5. M	7. E	9. J	11. K
2. O	4. H	6. B	8. G	10. A	12. I

FILL IN THE BLANK—PART A

1. accounting
2. cash
3. voucher
4. due
5. electronics fund transfer (EFT)
6. bank reconciliation
7. deducted from
8. deducted from
9. depositor's records
10. cash equivalents

FILL IN THE BLANK—PART B

1. internal controls
2. elements
3. employee fraud

4. Other income
5. voucher
6. petty cash

7. added to
8. added to

9. deducted from
10. doomsday

MULTIPLE CHOICE

1. a. Incorrect. Installation is not a phase of installing or changing an accounting system.
   b. Incorrect. Verification is not a phase of installing or changing an accounting system.
   c. Incorrect. Management is not a phase of installing or changing an accounting system.
   d. **Correct.** The job of installing or changing an accounting system is made up of three phases: (1) analysis, (2) design, and (3) implementation.

2. a. Incorrect. Risk assessment is an element of the internal control framework.
   b. Incorrect. Control environment is an element of the internal control framework.
   c. **Correct.** Management is not an element of the internal control framework.
   d. Incorrect. Monitoring is an element of the internal control framework.

3. a. Incorrect. Rotating duties among employees is a control procedure.
   b. Incorrect. Separating responsibilities for custody of assets and accounting for assets is a control procedure.
   c. **Correct.** Management's operating style is not a control procedure.
   d. Incorrect. Proofs and security measures is a control procedure.

4. a. Incorrect. Internal control policies and procedures do not necessarily provide reasonable assurance that all liabilities will be paid.
   b. Incorrect. Internal control policies and procedures do not necessarily provide reasonable assurance that a net income will be earned.
   c. Incorrect. Internal control policies and procedures do not necessarily provide reasonable assurance that they are being effectively applied.
   d. **Correct.** Internal control policies and procedures provide reasonable assurance that business information is accurate.

5. a. Incorrect. Since the treasurer is responsible for the custody of cash, the remittance advices should not be sent to the treasurer.
   b. Incorrect. Since the cashier's department handles cash, the remittance advices should not be sent to the cashier's department.
   c. **Correct.** For good internal control over cash receipts, remittance advices should be separated from cash received by mail and sent directly to the accounting department.
   d. Incorrect. Voucher clerks do not use remittance advices in carrying out their responsibilities.

6. a. Incorrect. Vouchers are not prepared by the treasurer.
   b. Incorrect. Vouchers are not paid immediately after they are prepared; they are filed and paid by the due date.
   c. Incorrect. The account distribution is normally shown on the back of the voucher, not on its face.
   d. **Correct.** An important characteristic of the voucher system is the requirement that a voucher be prepared for each major expenditure.

7. a. Incorrect. The drawer is the one who signs the check, ordering payment by the bank.
   b. **Correct.** The bank on which a check is drawn is known as the drawee.
   c. Incorrect. The payee is the party to whom payment is to be made.
   d. Incorrect. The creditor is the party to whom payment is owed.

8. a. **Correct.** In a bank reconciliation, deposits not recorded by the bank are added to the balance according to the bank statement.
   b. Incorrect.
   c. Incorrect.
   d. Incorrect.

9. a. Incorrect.
   b. **Correct.** The amount of the outstanding checks is included on the bank reconciliation as a deduction from the balance per bank statement.
   c. Incorrect.
   d. Incorrect.

10. a. Incorrect.
   b. **Correct.** The entry required in the depositor's accounts for receipts from cash sales of $7,500, recorded incorrectly as $5,700, is a debit to Cash and a credit to Sales for $1,800.
   c. Incorrect.
   d. Incorrect.

11. a. Incorrect.
   b. **Correct.** The entry required in the depositor's accounts for a credit memorandum for a short-term, non-interest-bearing note collected by the bank is a debit to Cash and a credit to Notes Receivable.
   c. Incorrect.
   d. Incorrect.

12. a. Incorrect.
   b. Incorrect.
   c. Incorrect.
   d. **Correct.** No entry is required in the depositor's accounts to record outstanding checks.

13. a. Incorrect. Journal entries based on the bank reconciliation are also required on the depositor's books for deductions from the balance according to the depositor's records.
   b. Incorrect. Journal entries based on the bank reconciliation are also required on the depositor's books for additions to the balance according to the depositor's records.
   c. **Correct.** Journal entries based on the bank reconciliation are required on the depositor's books for both additions to the balance according to the depositor's records and deductions from the balance according to the depositor's records.
   d. Incorrect. Journal entries based on the bank reconciliation are not required on the depositor's books for additions to and deductions from the balance according to the bank's records.

14. a. Incorrect.
   b. **Correct.** In a bank reconciliation, a note receivable collected by the bank is added to the balance according to the depositor's records.
   c. Incorrect.
   d. Incorrect.

15. a. **Correct.** The entry to record the replenishment of the petty cash fund includes a debit to various expense and asset accounts and a credit to Cash.
   b. Incorrect.
   c. Incorrect.
   d. Incorrect.

TRUE/FALSE

1. F   Systems analysis, not design, determines information needs, the sources of such information, and the deficiencies in procedures and data processing methods presently used.

2. T

3. T

4. F   Checks issued that have not been paid by the bank are deducted, not added, to the balance according to the bank statement.

5. T

6. T

7. F A debit balance in the cash short and over account at the end of the fiscal period represents miscellaneous administrative expense, not income.

8. T

9. F When a petty cash fund is replenished, the accounts debited are determined by summarizing the petty cash receipts. Petty Cash is only debited when the fund is initially established or increased.

10. T

EXERCISE 6-1

(2)	Cash	1,920	
	Notes Receivable		1,800
	Interest Revenue		120
(3)	Miscellaneous Administrative Expense	28	
	Cash		28
(6)	Accounts Payable—Charlie's Optical Supply	100	
	Cash		100

EXERCISE 6-2

(1)	Petty Cash	400.00	
	Cash		400.00
(2)	Office Supplies	80.25	
	Miscellaneous Selling Expense	115.33	
	Miscellaneous Administrative Expense	78.05	
	Cash Short and Over		1.97
	Cash		271.66

PROBLEM 6-1

(1)

Dumont Co.
Bank Reconciliation
September 30, 20--

Balance according to bank statement		$ 8,510
Add deposit not recorded		1,900
		$10,410
Deduct outstanding checks:		
No. 255	$325	
No. 280	100	
No. 295	700	1,125
Adjusted balance		$ 9,285
Balance according to depositor's records		$ 7,540
Add: Error in recording Check No. 289	$270	
Error in a deposit	720	
Note and interest collected by bank	780	1,770
		$ 9,310
Deduct bank service charge		25
Adjusted balance		$ 9,285

(2) Sept. 30	Cash	1,745	
	Miscellaneous Administrative Expense	25	
	Accounts Payable		270
	Accounts Receivable		720
	Notes Receivable		700
	Interest Revenue		80

CHAPTER 7

MATCHING

1. L	**3.** I	**5.** D	**7.** C	**9.** G	**11.** B
2. A	**4.** M	**6.** F	**8.** H	**10.** J	**12.** K

FILL IN THE BLANK—PART A

1. receivables
2. note receivable
3. allowance
4. aging of receivables
5. $7,150
6. $32,500
7. $309,000
8. October 10
9. dishonored
10. accounts receivable turnover

FILL IN THE BLANK—PART B

1. account
2. uncollectible accounts
3. direct write-off
4. $310,000
5. $10,400
6. maturity value
7. $153,750
8. December 16
9. number of days' sales in receivables
10. promissory

MULTIPLE CHOICE

1. a. ***Correct.*** When the allowance method is used in accounting for uncollectible accounts, any uncollectible account is written off against the allowance account. The entry is a debit to the allowance account and a credit to the accounts receivable account.
   b. Incorrect.
   c. Incorrect.
   d. Incorrect. When the direct write-off method is used in accounting for uncollectible accounts, any uncollectible account is written off against the uncollectible accounts expense account.

2. a. Incorrect. When the allowance method is used in accounting for uncollectible accounts, any uncollectible account is written off against the allowance account.
   b. Incorrect.
   c. Incorrect.
   d. ***Correct.*** When the direct write-off method is used in accounting for uncollectible accounts, any uncollectible account is written off against the uncollectible accounts expense account. The entry is a debit to the uncollectible accounts expense account and a credit to the accounts receivable account.

3. a. Incorrect.
   b. Incorrect.
   c. Incorrect.
   d. ***Correct.*** The allowance for doubtful accounts is a contra asset account, normally with a credit balance.

4. a. Incorrect.
   b. ***Correct.*** If the allowance account has a credit balance of $170 at the end of the year before adjustments and if the estimate of uncollectible accounts based on aging the receivables is $3,010, the amount of the adjusting entry for uncollectible accounts is $2,840 ($3,010 − $170).
   c. Incorrect.
   d. Incorrect.

5. a. Incorrect.
   b. Incorrect.
   c. **Correct.** If the allowance account has a debit balance of $250 at the end of the year before adjustments and if the estimate of uncollectible accounts based on sales for the period is $2,200, the amount of the adjusting entry for uncollectible accounts is $2,200. The balance of the allowance account does not affect the amount of the adjusting entry when the estimate is based upon sales.
   d. Incorrect.

6. a. Incorrect.
   b. **Correct.** After the accounts are adjusted and closed at the end of the fiscal year, Accounts Receivable has a balance of $430,000 and Allowance for Doubtful Accounts has a balance of $25,000. The expected realizable value of the accounts receivable is $405,000 ($430,000 – $25,000).
   c. Incorrect.
   d. Incorrect.

7. a. Incorrect. The payee is the one to whose order the note is payable.
   b. Incorrect.
   c. **Correct.** On a promissory note, the one making the promise to pay is called the maker.
   d. Incorrect.

8. a. Incorrect.
   b. Incorrect.
   c. Incorrect.
   d. **Correct.** The amount that is due on a note at the maturity or due date is called the maturity value.

9. a. Incorrect.
   b. **Correct.** The due date of a 90-day note dated July 1 is September 29, determined as follows: 30 days in July; 31 days in August; and 29 days in September.
   c. Incorrect.
   d. Incorrect.

10. a. Incorrect.
   b. Incorrect.
   c. **Correct.** The maturity value of a 60-day, 12% note for $15,000, dated May 1, is $15,300 computed as follows: [$15,000 + ($15,000 × 60/360 × 12%)].
   d. Incorrect.

TRUE/FALSE

1. T
2. T
3. F The direct write-off method of accounting for uncollectible receivables provides for uncollectible accounts in the year when the account is determined to be worthless (uncollectible), not in the year of sale.
4. T
5. T
6. F Notes do not include all money claims against people, organizations, or other debtors. An account receivable is another example of a money claim against people, organizations, or other debtors.
7. T
8. T
9. F When a note is received from a customer on account, it is recorded by debiting Notes Receivable and crediting Accounts Receivable, not Sales.
10. T

EXERCISE 7-1

(1)	Mar. 31	Allowance for Doubtful Accounts............................	3,150	
		Accounts Receivable—Jane Eades		3,150
(2)	May 8	Accounts Receivable—Jane Eades.....................	3,150	
		Allowance for Doubtful Accounts		3,150
	8	Cash..	3,150	
		Accounts Receivable—Jane Eades		3,150

EXERCISE 7-2

(1)	Aug. 31	Uncollectible Accounts Expense	550	
		Accounts Receivable—Don Shore		550
(2)	Oct. 8	Accounts Receivable—Don Shore	550	
		Uncollectible Accounts Expense....................		550
	8	Cash..	550	
		Accounts Receivable—Don Shore		550

EXERCISE 7-3

1. $80	**3.** $60	**5.** $75	**7.** $210
2. $35	**4.** $60	**6.** $270	

EXERCISE 7-4

Walton Company
Balance Sheet
December 31, 20--

Assets

Current assets:		
Cash		$ 37,500
Notes receivable..		20,000
Accounts receivable	$35,000	
Less allowance for doubtful accounts	1,200	33,800
Interest receivable		9,900
Total current assets		$101,200

PROBLEM 7-1

(1)	Uncollectible Accounts Expense...............................	24,000	
	Allowance for Doubtful Accounts.........................		24,000
(2)	Uncollectible Accounts Expense...............................	5,955	
	Allowance for Doubtful Accounts.........................		5,955
(3)	Allowance for Doubtful Accounts	3,500	
	Accounts Receivable—Bentley Co.		3,500
(4)	Accounts Receivable—Apple Co.	1,235	
	Allowance for Doubtful Accounts.........................		1,235
	Cash	1,235	
	Accounts Receivable—Apple Co.		1,235

PROBLEM 7-2

(1)   Notes Receivable 8,000.00

          Accounts Receivable—Dave Davidson 8,000.00

(2)   Accounts Receivable—Dave Davidson.....................   8,160.00*

          Interest Revenue 160.00

          Notes Receivable...   8,000.00

(3)   Cash 8,184.93

          Interest Revenue 24.93**

          Accounts Receivable—Dave Davidson 8,160.00

(4)   Notes Receivable 3,000.00

          Accounts Receivable—Sue Smith 3,000.00

(5)   Accounts Receivable—Sue Smith...........................   3,075.00

          Interest Revenue 75.00

          Notes Receivable...   3,000.00

        * $8,000 × 60/360 × 12% = $160; $8,000 + $160 = $8,160

  ** $8,160 × 10/360 × 11% = $24.93

CHAPTER 8

MATCHING

1.	I	**3.**	E	**5.**	F	**7.**	J	**9.**	D
2.	B	**4.**	A	**6.**	G	**8.**	C	**10.**	H

FILL IN THE BLANK—PART A

1. physical inventory
2. understated
3. understated
4. last-in, first-out (lifo)
5. $1,270
6. lifo
7. lower-of-cost-or-market (LCM)
8. $15,000
9. gross profit
10. inventory turnover

FILL IN THE BLANK—PART B

1. overstated
2. understated
3. first-in, first-out (fifo)
4. average cost
5. $1,388
6. net realizable value
7. $45
8. retail inventory
9. $120,000
10. number of days' sales in inventory

MULTIPLE CHOICE

1. a. Incorrect. If merchandise inventory at the end of the period is understated, gross profit will be understated, not overstated.
   b. Incorrect. If merchandise inventory at the end of the period is understated, owner's equity will be understated, not overstated.
   c. ***Correct.*** If merchandise inventory at the end of the period is understated, net income will be understated because cost of merchandise sold will be overstated.
   d. Incorrect. If merchandise inventory at the end of the period is understated, cost of merchandise sold will be overstated, not understated.

2. a. **Correct.** If merchandise inventory at the end of period 1 is overstated and at the end of period 2 is correct, gross profit in period 2 will be understated because cost of merchandise sold will be overstated in period 2.
   b. Incorrect. If merchandise inventory at the end of period 1 is overstated and at the end of period 2 is correct, assets at the end of period 2 will be correct, not overstated.
   c. Incorrect. If merchandise inventory at the end of period 1 is overstated and at the end of period 2 is correct, owner's equity at the end of period 2 will be correct, not understated.
   d. Incorrect. If merchandise inventory at the end of period 1 is overstated and at the end of period 2 is correct, cost of merchandise sold in period 2 will be overstated, not understated.

3. a. **Correct.** The total cost of the 15 units on hand at the end of the period, as determined under a perpetual inventory system and the lifo costing method, is $80 [(5 units × $6) + (10 units × $5)].
   b. Incorrect.
   c. Incorrect.
   d. Incorrect.

4. a. Incorrect.
   b. Incorrect.
   c. Incorrect.
   d. **Correct.** The total cost of the 15 units on hand at the end of the period, as determined under a perpetual inventory system and the fifo costing method, is $120 (15 units × $8).

5. a. **Correct.** The total cost of the 15 units on hand at the end of the period, as determined under a periodic inventory system and the lifo costing method, is $80 [(5 units × $6) + (10 units × $5)].
   b. Incorrect.
   c. Incorrect.
   d. Incorrect.

6. a. Incorrect.
   b. Incorrect.
   c. Incorrect.
   d. **Correct.** The total cost of the 15 units on hand at the end of the period, as determined under a periodic inventory system and the fifo costing method, is $120 (15 units × $8).

7. a. Incorrect.
   b. Incorrect.
   c. **Correct.** The total cost of the 15 units on hand at the end of the period, as determined under a periodic inventory system and the average costing method, is $99 (15 units × $6.60).
   d. Incorrect.

8. a. Incorrect. During a period of rising prices, the fifo inventory costing method will result in the highest amount of net income.
   b. **Correct.** During a period of rising prices, the lifo inventory costing method will result in the lowest amount of net income.
   c. Incorrect. During a period of rising prices, the average inventory costing method will result in an amount of net income that is higher than lifo and lower than fifo.
   d. Incorrect. The perpetual inventory system is not an inventory costing method.

9. a. Incorrect. The lower of cost or market method is permitted under both the periodic and the perpetual inventory systems.
   b. Incorrect.
   c. Incorrect.
   d. **Correct.** If the replacement price of an item of inventory is lower than its cost, the use of the lower of cost or market method reduces gross profit for the period in which the decline occurred.

10. a. Incorrect.
 b. Incorrect.
 c. **_Correct._** When lifo is strictly applied to a perpetual inventory system, the unit cost prices assigned to the ending inventory will not necessarily be those associated with the earliest unit costs of the period if at any time during a period the number of units of a commodity sold exceeds the number previously purchased during the same period.
 d. Incorrect.

TRUE/FALSE

1. F If merchandise inventory at the end of the period is understated, gross profit will be understated, not overstated. This is because cost of merchandise sold will be overstated.

2. F The two principal systems of inventory accounting are periodic and perpetual. Physical is not an inventory system.

3. T

4. F If merchandise inventory at the end of the period is overstated, owner's equity at the end of the period will be overstated, not understated. This is because cost of merchandise sold will be understated.

5. F During a period of rising prices, the inventory costing method that will result in the highest amount of net income is fifo, not lifo. This is because fifo will assign the highest costs to inventory, and thus, cost of merchandise sold will be lower than lifo.

6. T

7. T

8. F As used in the phrase "lower of cost or market," _market_ is the cost to replace the merchandise on the inventory date, not the selling price.

9. F When the retail inventory method is used, inventory at retail is converted to cost by multiplying the inventory at retail by the ratio of cost to selling (retail) price for the merchandise available for sale. The denominator is the selling (retail) price for the merchandise available for sale, not the replacement cost of the merchandise available for sale.

10. T

EXERCISE 8-1

Sales
(1) Correct
(2) N/A

Cost of Merchandise Sold
(1) Overstated
(2) $5,000

Gross Profit
(1) Understated
(2) $5,000

Net Income
(1) Understated
(2) $5,000

Merchandise Inventory (October 31, 2006)
(1) Understated
(2) $5,000

Current Assets
(1) Understated
(2) $5,000

Total Assets
(1) Understated
(2) $5,000

Liabilities
(1) Correct
(2) N/A

Owner's Equity
(1) Understated
(2) $5,000

EXERCISE 8-2

	Cost	Total Lower of Cost or Market
Commodity A	$3,750	$3,600
Commodity B	2,760	2,760
Commodity C	1,450	1,200
Commodity D	1,440	1,290
Total	$9,400	$8,850

PROBLEM 8-1

(1)

Date Purchased	Units	Price	Total Cost
November 1	12	$58	$696
Total	12		$696

(2)

Date Purchased	Units	Price	Total Cost
January 10	2	$48	$ 96
February 15	5	54	270
November 1	5	58	290
Total	12		$656

(3)

Date Purchased	Units	Price	Total Cost
November 1	12	$58	$696
Total	12		$696

(4)

Date Purchased	Units	Price	Total Cost
January 10	10	$48	$480
February 15	2	54	108
Total	12		$588

(5) Average unit cost: $\dfrac{\$11,485}{210} = \$54.69$

12 units in inventory @ $54.69 = $656.28

PROBLEM 8-2

	(1) Fifo	(2) Lifo	(3) Average Cost
Sales	$2,240,000	$2,240,000	$2,240,000
Purchases	$1,783,900	$1,783,900	$1,783,900
Less ending inventory	145,600	100,000	118,920
Cost of merchandise sold	$1,638,300	$1,683,900	$1,664,980
Gross profit.............................	$ 601,700	$ 556,100	$ 575,020

Computation of Ending Inventory

Fifo:

Date Purchased	Units	Price	Total Cost
November 1	100	$69	$ 6,900
December 1	1,900	73	138,700
Total	2,000		$145,600

Lifo:

	Date Purchased	Units	Price	Total Cost
Lifo:	January 1	2,000	50	$100,000

Average Cost: $\dfrac{\$1,783,900}{30,000} = \$59.46$

$59.46 × 2,000 = $118,920

PROBLEM 8-3

	Cost	Retail
(1) Merchandise inventory, August 1...	$118,500	$170,000
Purchases in August (net)...	299,125	472,500
Merchandise available for sale..	$417,625	$642,500

Ratio of cost to retail

$$\frac{\$417,625}{\$642,500} = 65\%$$

	Cost	Retail
Sales in August (net)..		479,000
Merchandise inventory, August 31, at retail...........................		$163,500
Merchandise inventory, August 31, at estimated cost ($163,500 × 65%)		$106,275

	Cost	Retail
(2) Merchandise inventory, August 1...		$118,500
Purchases in August (net)...		299,125
Merchandise available for sale..		$417,625
Sales in August (net)..	$479,000	
Less estimated gross profit ($479,000 × 30%)	143,700	
Estimated cost of merchandise sold		335,300
Estimated merchandise inventory, August 31..........................		$ 82,325

CHAPTER 9

MATCHING

1. K	**5.** W	**9.** E	**13.** F	**17.** B	**20.** G
2. J	**6.** H	**10.** S	**14.** N	**18.** L	**21.** V
3. R	**7.** C	**11.** U	**15.** I	**19.** O	**22.** P
4. T	**8.** A	**12.** D	**16.** M		

FILL IN THE BLANK—PART A

1. fixed
2. land
3. machine
4. residual
5. units-of-production
6. book
7. 25%
8. $11,250
9. $25,000
10. $12,600
11. capital
12. revenue expenditures
13. trade-in allowance
14. $65,000
15. capital
16. depletion
17. amortization
18. patents
19. Patents
20. trademark

FILL IN THE BLANK—PART B

1. land
2. depreciation
3. straight-line
4. declining-balance
5. 20%
6. $14,000
7. $32,000
8. $16,800
9. accelerated
10. revenue
11. capital expenditures
12. boot
13. $70,000
14. operating
15. intangible
16. goodwill
17. copyright
18. Accumulated Depletion
19. current operating expenses
20. fixed assets to long-term liabilities

MULTIPLE CHOICE

1. a. Incorrect.
   b. Incorrect.
   c. **Correct.** If unwanted buildings are located on land acquired for a plant site, the cost of their removal, less any salvage recovered, should be charged to the land account.
   d. Incorrect.

2. a. ***Correct.*** The depreciation method used most often in the financial statements is the straight-line method.
   b. Incorrect. The declining-balance method is the third most used method for financial statements.
   c. Incorrect. The units-of-production method is the second most used method for financial statements.
   d. Incorrect. The MACRS method is used to compute depreciation for tax purposes.

3. a. ***Correct.*** The depreciation method that would provide the highest reported net income in the early years of an asset's life would be the straight-line method.
   b. Incorrect. The declining-balance depreciation method is an accelerated depreciation method that provides more depreciation in the early years of an asset's life.
   c. Incorrect. The 150% straight-line depreciation method is an accelerated depreciation method that provides more depreciation in the early years of an asset's life.
   d. Incorrect. Accelerated depreciation methods provide more depreciation in the early years of an asset's life.

4. a. Incorrect.
   b. Incorrect.
   c. Incorrect.
   d. ***Correct.*** Using the declining-balance method (at twice the straight-line rate), the amount of depreciation for the first year of use of the equipment is $6,000 ($15,000 × 40%).

5. a. Incorrect.
   b. ***Correct.*** The depreciation expense on the equipment in Year 3 using the straight-line method would be $5,900, computed as follows: depreciation in Years 1 and 2 is $3,600 per year [($20,000 – $2,000) / 5 years]; book value at the end of Year 2 is $12,800 ($20,000 – $3,600 – $3,600); remaining depreciation is computed as $5,900 [($12,800 – $1,000) / 2 years].
   c. Incorrect.
   d. Incorrect.

6. a. Incorrect.
   b. ***Correct.*** The cost of rebuilding the drill press is a replacement component and should be capitalized.
   c. Incorrect.
   d. Incorrect.

7. a. Incorrect. $15,600 is the list price of the new equipment. It must be reduced by the unrecognized gain on the old equipment to determine the cost of the new equipment.
   b. Incorrect. $15,300 is the accumulated depreciation of the old equipment plus the cash (boot) given of $9,000. It is not the cost of the new equipment.
   c. ***Correct.*** The new equipment should be recorded at $13,700 determined as follows: book value of old equipment is $4,700 ($11,000 – $6,300); trade-in value allowed on the old equipment is $6,600 ($15,600 – $9,000); gain on trade-in of the old equipment of $1,900 ($6,600 – $4,700) is not recognized and instead reduces the cost of the new equipment; thus, the cost of the new equipment is $13,700 ($15,600 – $1,900). Alternatively, the cost of the new equipment is the cash (boot) given, $9,000, plus the book value of the old equipment, $4,700.
   d. Incorrect. $9,000 is the cash (boot) given. It must be added to the book value of the old equipment to determine the cost of the new equipment.

8. a. Incorrect.
   b. ***Correct.*** The new equipment should be recorded at $15,600, the price of the new equipment. A loss of $600 would also be recorded on the trade-in of the old equipment computed as follows: book value of the old equipment is $4,700 ($11,000 – $6,300); trade-in value allowed on the old equipment is $4,100 ($15,600 – $11,500); loss on trade-in of the old equipment is $600 ($4,700 – $4,100).
   c. Incorrect.
   d. Incorrect.

9. a. Incorrect.
   b. Incorrect.
   c. Incorrect. The lessee is the party to whom the rights to use the asset are granted by the lessor.
   d. *Correct.* The lessor legally owns the asset.

10. a. *Correct.*   Mineral ore deposits are natural resources with tangible characteristics.
    b. Incorrect. Patents do not have tangible characteristics and are intangible assets.
    c. Incorrect. Copyright do not have tangible characteristics and are intangible assets.
    d. Incorrect. Goodwill do not have tangible characteristics and are intangible assets.

TRUE/FALSE

1. T
2. T
3. F   In using the declining-balance method, the asset should not be depreciated below the asset's residual value, not below the net book value.
4. T
5. T
6. T
7. F   A lease that transfers ownership of the leased asset to the lessee at the end of the lease term should be classified as a capital lease, not an operating lease.
8. F   Long-lived assets that are without physical characteristics but useful in the operations of a business are classified as intangible assets, not fixed assets.
9. T
10. F   Intangible assets are usually reported on the balance sheet in a separate section immediately following fixed assets, not in the current asset section.

EXERCISE 9-1

(a)	Straight-line method	Depreciation
	Year 1	$50,000
	Year 2	$50,000

(b)	Declining-balance method	Depreciation
	Year 1	$105,000
	Year 2	$78,750

EXERCISE 9-2

Dec. 31	Depreciation Expense—Equipment	20,800	
	Accumulated Depreciation—Equipment		20,800

EXERCISE 9-3

Mar. 8	Accumulated Depreciation—Fixtures	2,500	
	Cash	2,000	
	Fixtures		4,000
	Gain on Disposal of Assets		500

EXERCISE 9-4

Dec. 31	Depletion Expense	240,000	
	Accumulated Depletion—Mineral Rights		240,000

EXERCISE 9-5

Dec. 31	Amortization Expense—Patents		20,000	
	Patents			20,000

PROBLEM 9-1

	Depreciation Expense		
Year	Straight-Line	Declining-Balance	Units-of-Production
20xA	$18,750	$40,000	$17,000
20xB	18,750	20,000	20,000
20xC	18,750	10,000	30,000
20xD	18,750	5,000	8,000
Total	$75,000	$75,000	$75,000

PROBLEM 9-2

(1)	Dec. 31	Depreciation Expense—Automobile	5,000	
		Accumulated Depreciation—Automobile		5,000
	Dec. 31	Depreciation Expense—Automobile	5,000	
		Accumulated Depreciation—Automobile		5,000
(2)	Dec. 31	Depreciation Expense—Automobile	10,000	
		Accumulated Depreciation—Automobile		10,000
	Dec. 31	Depreciation Expense—Automobile	2,500	
		Accumulated Depreciation—Automobile		2,500
(3)	Dec. 31	Depreciation Expense—Automobile	7,000	
		Accumulated Depreciation—Automobile		7,000
	Dec. 31	Depreciation Expense—Automobile	5,600	
		Accumulated Depreciation—Automobile		5,600

PROBLEM 9-3

(a)	Apr. 30	Accumulated Depreciation—Truck	12,000	
		Truck	20,200	
		Truck		15,000
		Cash		17,200
(b)	Apr. 30	Accumulated Depreciation—Truck	12,000	
		Truck	20,700	
		Loss on Disposal of Fixed Assets	2,000	
		Truck		15,000
		Cash		19,700

CHAPTER 10

MATCHING

1. E	**4.** I	**7.** G	**10.** L	**13.** N
2. K	**5.** M	**8.** D	**11.** J	**14.** C
3. A	**6.** B	**9.** H	**12.** F	

FILL IN THE BLANK—PART A

1. $30,900
2. $84,600
3. gross
4. net pay
5. Federal Insurance Contributions Act (FICA)
6. employee's earnings record
7. paid
8. defined benefit
9. postretirement
10. quick

FILL IN THE BLANK—PART B

1. $77,250
2. $232,000
3. discount
4. discount
5. net
6. payroll register
7. Medicare Tax
8. payroll
9. fringe
10. defined contribution

MULTIPLE CHOICE

1. a. Incorrect.
   b. **Correct.** The interest charged by the bank, at the rate of 12%, on a 90-day, non-interest-bearing note payable for $75,000 is $2,250 ($75,000 × 12% × 90/360).
   c. Incorrect.
   d. Incorrect.

2. a. **Correct.** The cost of a product warranty should be included as an expense in the period of the sale of the product.
   b. Incorrect.
   c. Incorrect.
   d. Incorrect.

3. a. Incorrect. $440 is the employee's gross pay.
   b. Incorrect. $374 doesn't deduct the FICA or Medicare withholdings.
   c. **Correct.** The employee's net pay for the week is $341, computed as follows: gross pay is $440 [($8 × 40 hours) + ($12 × 10 hours)]; thus, net pay is [$440 − ($440 × 6%) − ($440 × 1.5%) − ($440 × 15%)].
   d. Incorrect.

4. a. Incorrect. The gross pay is the earnings before any deductions.
   b. Incorrect. The gross pay is the earnings before any deductions such as federal income tax withholding.
   c. Incorrect. The gross pay is the earnings before any deductions.
   d. **Correct.** The gross pay for the employee is $855, computed as [($18 × 40 hours) + ($27 × 5 hours)].

5. a. Incorrect.
   b. Incorrect.
   c. **Correct.** The employer's total FICA tax (social security and Medicare) for this payroll period is $120, computed as [($200 × 6%) + ($1,000 × 6%) + ($1,000 × 1.5%) + ($1,000 × 1.5%)].
   d. Incorrect. The FICA tax is limited to $200 on the first employee ($80,000 − $79,800) rather than the full $1,000.

6. a. Incorrect.
   b. Incorrect.
   c. Incorrect.
   d. **Correct.** Payroll taxes levied against employees become liabilities at the time the liability for the employee's wages is paid.

7. a. Incorrect. Vacations are a fringe benefit.
   b. Incorrect. Employee pension plans are a fringe benefit.
   c. Incorrect. Health insurance is a fringe benefit.
   d. **Correct.** FICA benefits are not considered a fringe benefit.

8. a. ***Correct.*** For proper matching of revenues and expenses, the estimated cost of fringe benefits must be recognized as an expense of the period the employee earns the benefit.
   b. Incorrect.
   c. Incorrect.
   d. Incorrect.

9. a. Incorrect. Number of hours worked is a variable input in a payroll system.
   b. Incorrect. Vacation credits is a variable input in a payroll system.
   c. ***Correct.*** Number of income tax withholding allowances is a constant in a payroll system, not a variable input.
   d. Incorrect. Number of days sick leave with pay is a variable input in a payroll system.

10. a. Incorrect. A payroll register is an aid in internal control, but it does not aid in indicating employee attendance.
    b. Incorrect. An employee earnings record is an aid in internal control, but it does not aid in indicating employee attendance.
    c. ***Correct.*** "In and Out" cards are an aid in internal control over payrolls that indicates employee attendance.
    d. Incorrect. Payroll checks are an aid in internal control, but they do not aid in indicating employee attendance.

TRUE/FALSE

1. T
2. F Both employers and employees are required to contribute to the Federal Insurance Contributions Act program.
3. F Not all states require that unemployment compensation taxes be withheld from employees' pay.
4. F Employers are subject to federal and state payroll taxes based on the amount paid to their employees, not the amount earned by their employees.
5. F The amounts withheld from employees' earnings do not have an effect on the firm's debits to the salary or wage expense accounts.
6. T
7. F The recording procedures when special payroll checks are used are the same as when the checks are drawn on the regular bank account.
8. T
9. T
10. F In order for revenues and expenses to be matched properly, a liability to cover the cost of a product warranty should be recorded in the period when the product is sold, not repaired.
11. T
12. T
13. F The net periodic pension cost of a defined benefit plan is debited to Pension Expense, the amount funded is credited to Cash, and any unfunded amount is credited to Unfunded Pension Liability, not Revenue.
14. T
15. F The rate used by a bank in discounting a note is called the discount rate, not the prime rate.

EXERCISE 10-1

(1) $770   (3) $45
(2) $60   (4) $727.50

EXERCISE 10-2

(1)	Dec. 31	Vacation Pay Expense......................................	3,225	
		Vacation Pay Payable		3,225

(2)	Dec. 31	Product Warranty Expense...............................	4,500	
		Product Warranty Payable		4,500

(3)	Dec. 31	Pension Expense...	40,000	
		Cash..		27,500
		Unfunded Accrued Pension Cost...................		12,500

PROBLEM 10-1

(1)	Dec. 7	Sales Salaries Expense.....................................	34,000	
		Office Salaries Expense	16,000	
		Social Security Tax Payable		3,000
		Medicare Tax Payable		750
		Employees Income Tax Payable....................		7,500
		Union Dues Payable		900
		United Way Payable..		450
		Salaries Payable		37,400

(2)	Dec. 7	Salaries Payable...	37,400	
		Cash..		37,400

(3)	Dec. 7	Payroll Taxes Expense	6,850	
		Social Security Tax Payable		3,000
		Medicare Tax Payable		750
		State Unemployment Tax Payable...................		2,700
		Federal Unemployment Tax Payable..............		400

(4)	Dec. 7	Payroll Taxes Expense	3,150	
		Social Security Tax Payable		2,400
		Medicare Tax Payable		750

PROBLEM 10-2

		Employer's Taxes				
Employee	Annual Earnings	Social Security Tax	Medicare Tax	State Unemploy- ment	Federal Unemploy- ment	Total
Avery	$ 12,000	$ 720	$ 180	$ 378	$ 56	$ 1,334
Johnson	5,000	300	75	270	40	685
Jones	59,000	3,540	885	378	56	4,859
Smith	73,000	4,380	1,095	378	56	5,909
Wilson	141,000	4,800	2,115	378	56	7,349
Total	$290,000	$13,740	$4,350	$1,782	$264	$20,136

PROBLEM 10-3

(1)	Accounts Payable—Mayday Co.............................	2,000	
	Notes Payable—Mayday Co.............................		2,000

(2)	Notes Payable—Mayday Co.	2,000	
	Interest Expense	60	
	Cash...		2,060

(3)	Cash	8,000	
	Notes Payable		8,000
(4)	Notes Payable	8,000	
	Interest Expense	220	
	Cash...		8,220
(5)	Cash	5,910	
	Interest Expense	90	
	Notes Payable		6,000
(6)	Notes Payable	6,000	
	Cash...		6,000

CHAPTER 11

MATCHING

1. M	**4.** K	**7.** F	**10.** D	**13.** A	**16.** H
2. P	**5.** B	**8.** C	**11.** Q	**14.** N	**17.** L
3. G	**6.** I	**9.** J	**12.** O	**15.** E	

FILL IN THE BLANK—PART A

1. stock
2. public
3. limited
4. $995,000
5. outstanding
6. common
7. nonparticipating
8. $100,000
9. premium
10. $160,000
11. treasury
12. none
13. dividend
14. $32,500
15. retained earnings

FILL IN THE BLANK—PART B

1. stockholders
2. article of incorporation
3. organizational expenses
4. stated
5. preferred
6. cumulative
7. $140,000
8. discount
9. $32,500 decrease
10. $895,000
11. stock split
12. $36
13. stock dividend
14. par
15. dividend yield

MULTIPLE CHOICE

1. a. Incorrect. Ownership represented by shares of stock is a characteristic of the corporate form of organization.
   b. Incorrect. Separate legal existence is a characteristic of the corporate form of organization.
   c. **Correct.** Unlimited liability of stockholders is not a characteristic of the corporate form of organization. Rather, stockholders of a corporation have limited liability that limits the liability to the amount invested.
   d. Incorrect. Earnings subject to the federal income tax is a characteristic of the corporate form of organization.

2. a. Incorrect. The stated value is the amount the board of directors assigns to no-par stock.
   b. Incorrect. The premium is the amount by which the issue price of a stock exceeds its par.
   c. Incorrect. The discount is the amount by which the par value of a stock exceeds its issue price.
   d. **Correct.** The amount printed on a stock certificate is known as par value.

3. a. Incorrect.
   b. Incorrect.
   c. **Correct.** The amount of preferred dividends that must be declared in the current year before a dividend can be declared on common stock is $150,000, computed as $120,000 dividends in arrears [(5,000 shares × $6) × 4 years] plus the current year dividend of $30,000 (5,000 shares × $6).
   d. Incorrect.

4. a. Incorrect.
  b. **Correct.** When a corporation purchases its own stock, Treasury Stock is debited for the cost of the stock.
  c. Incorrect.
  d. Incorrect.

5. a. Incorrect. Retained Earnings is credited for the income of a period, not for the excess of proceeds from selling treasury stock over its cost.
  b. Incorrect. Premium on Capital Stock is credited for the issuance of new stock at a price exceeding the par or stated value of the stock.
  c. Incorrect. A corporation cannot have gains and losses from trading its stock.
  d. **Correct.** The excess of the proceeds from selling treasury stock over its cost should be credited to Paid-In Capital from Sale of Treasury Stock.

6. a. Incorrect. The claims of preferred stockholders are satisfied after the claims of creditors upon liquidation of a corporation.
  b. Incorrect. The claims of preferred stockholders are satisfied after the claims of creditors upon liquidation of a corporation.
  c. Incorrect. The claims of common stockholders are satisfied last upon liquidation of a corporation
  d. **Correct.** The claims of the creditors must first be satisfied upon liquidation of a corporation.

7. a. **Correct.** The amount transferred from the retained earnings account to paid-in capital accounts as a result of the stock dividend is $36,000, computed as [(12,000 shares × 5%) × $60].
  b. Incorrect.
  c. Incorrect. The amount transferred from the retained earnings account to paid-in capital accounts as a result of the stock dividend is based upon the market price of the stock, not the par value.
  d. Incorrect.

8. a. Incorrect. 5,000 is the number of shares reacquired.
  b. **Correct.** The number of shares outstanding is 55,000 shares, determined as the 60,000 shares issued minus the 5,000 shares reacquired.
  c. Incorrect. 60,000 is the number of shares issued.
  d. Incorrect. 100,000 is the number of shares authorized.

9. a. Incorrect. Donated Capital is credited for the fair value of assets donated to a corporation as an incentive to locate or remain in a community.
  b. Incorrect. Retained Earnings is credited for the income of the period.
  c. Incorrect. Treasury Stock is credited when reacquired shares are sold.
  d. **Correct.** The entry to record the issuance of common stock at a price above par would include a credit to Paid-In Capital in Excess of Par—Common Stock.

10. a. Incorrect. The total stockholders' equity will decrease, not increase.
  b. Incorrect. The total stockholders' equity will decrease, not increase.
  c. Incorrect. The decrease is based upon the cost of the reacquired stock, not its par value.
  d. **Correct.** The effect on total stockholders' equity of purchasing 10,000 shares of its own $20 par common stock for $35 per share is a decrease of $350,000 (10,000 shares × $35).

TRUE/FALSE

1. T

2. T

3. F The two main sources of stockholders' equity are paid-in capital and retained earnings, not long-term debt.

4. F The preferred stockholders have a greater chance of receiving regular dividends than do common stockholders, not vice versa.

5. T

6. T

7. F Preferred stock for which dividend rights are limited to a certain amount is said to be nonparticipating, not noncumulative.

8. T

9. F Sales of treasury stock result in a net increase, not decrease, in paid-in capital.

10. F Expenditures incurred in organizing a corporation, such as legal fees, taxes, fees paid to the state, and promotional costs, are charged to an expense account entitled Organization Expenses, not Goodwill.

11. F A commonly used method for accounting for the purchase and resale of treasury stock is the cost method, not the derivative method.

12. F A major objective of a stock split is to reduce the market price per share of the stock. A stock split does not affect the amount of total stockholders' equity.

13. T

14. F A liability for a dividend is normally recorded in the accounting records on the date of declaration, not the date of record.

15. T

EXERCISE 11-1

| (1) | Cash | 700,000 | |
| | Common Stock | | 700,000 |

| (2) | Cash | 500,000 | |
| | Common Stock | | 500,000 |

(3)	Cash	1,200,000	
	Common Stock		1,000,000
	Paid-In Capital in Excess of Par—Common Stock		200,000

(4)	Equipment	145,000	
	Common Stock		100,000
	Paid-In Capital in Excess of Par—Common Stock		45,000

(5)	Cash	300,000	
	Preferred Stock		250,000
	Paid-In Capital in Excess of Par—Preferred Stock		50,000

EXERCISE 11-2

| (1) | Oct. 1 | Treasury Stock | 150,000 | |
| | | Cash | | 150,000 |

(2)	Oct. 31	Cash	65,600	
		Treasury Stock		60,000
		Paid-In Capital from Sale of Treasury Stock		5,600

(3)	Nov. 20	Cash	7,000	
		Paid-In Capital from Sale of Treasury Stock	500	
		Treasury Stock		7,500

EXERCISE 11-3

(1) Feb. 20   Cash Dividends..   60,000
                        Cash Dividends Payable   60,000

(2) Mar. 22   Cash Dividends Payable...   60,000
                        Cash   60,000

(3) Dec. 15   Stock Dividends   200,000
                        Stock Dividends Distributable   160,000
                        Paid-In Capital in Excess of Par—Common Stock ...   40,000

(4) Jan. 14   Stock Dividends Distributable......................................   160,000
                        Common Stock..   160,000

(5) Feb. 20   None

PROBLEM 11-1

(1)

Year	Total Dividends	Preferred Dividends		Common Dividends	
		Total	Per Share	Total	Per Share
1	$ 7,000	$7,000	$7	–0–	–0–
2	9,000	9,000	9	–0–	–0–
3	28,000	8,000	8	$20,000	$ 5
4	48,000	8,000	8	40,000	10

(2)

Year	Total Dividends	Preferred Dividends		Common Dividends	
		Total	Per Share	Total	Per Share
1	$ 7,000	$7,000	$7	–0–	–0–
2	9,000	8,000	8	$ 1,000	$ .25
3	28,000	8,000	8	20,000	5.00
4	48,000	8,000	8	40,000	10.00

PROBLEM 11-2

	(1)	(2)	(3)
	Column A	**Column B**	**Column C**
	Before Any Dividend	After Cash Dividend	After Stock Dividend
a. Total number of shares outstanding..........	100,000	100,000	105,000
b. Total par value of shares outstanding.......	$2,500,000	$2,500,000	$2,625,000
c. Total additional paid-in capital..................	$1,500,000	$1,500,000	$1,525,000
d. Total retained earnings............................	$6,440,000	$6,290,000	$6,290,000
e. Total stockholders' equity........................	$10,440,000	$10,290,000	$10,440,000
f. Amount required to pay a $1.50 per share cash dividend next year	$150,000	$150,000	$157,500

	(1)	(2)	(3)
	Column A	**Column B**	**Column C**
	Before Any Dividend	After Cash Dividend	After Stock Dividend
g. Percentage of total stock owned by Rafael	1%	1%	1%
h. Total number of shares owned by Rafael .	1,000	1,000	1,050
i. Total par value of Rafael's shares.............	$25,000	$25,000	$26,250
j. Total equity of Rafael's shares..................	$104,400	$102,900	$104,400

PROBLEM 11-3

Paid-in capital:
Preferred $10 stock, $100 par (10,000 shares authorized; 7,500 issued)	$ 750,000	
Excess over par...	375,000	$1,125,000
Common stock, $25 par (150,000 shares authorized; 100,000 issued)	$2,500,000	
Excess over par...	500,000	3,000,000
From sale of treasury stock		4,000
Total paid-in capital		$4,129,000
Retained earnings..		1,000,000
Total		$5,129,000
Deduct treasury common stock (1,000 shares at cost)		50,000
Total stockholders' equity..		$5,079,000

CHAPTER 12

MATCHING

1. U	**6.** A	**10.** X	**14.** L	**18.** E	**22.** O
2. V	**7.** S	**11.** B	**15.** K	**19.** P	**23.** D
3. F	**8.** C	**12.** W	**16.** H	**20.** T	**24.** N
4. J	**9.** I	**13.** Y	**17.** M	**21.** R	**25.** Q
5. G					

FILL IN THE BLANK—PART A

1. taxable
2. $150,000
3. restructuring charges
4. discontinued
5. extraordinary items
6. loss from discontinued operations
7. earnings per share (EPS)
8. preferred dividends
9. comprehensive
10. trading
11. temporary investments
12. equity
13. consolidation
14. subsidiary
15. minority interest

FILL IN THE BLANK—PART B

1. temporary
2. $25,000
3. fixed asset impairment
4. extraordinary item
5. stockholders' equity
6. equity
7. available-for-sale
8. unrealized
9. cost
10. merger
11. investments
12. parent
13. accumulated other comprehensive income
14. consolidated
15. price-earnings

MULTIPLE CHOICE

1. a. *Correct.* The amount of income tax deferred to future years is $40,000 [($300,000 – $200,000) × 40%].
   b. Incorrect.
   c. Incorrect.
   d. Incorrect.

2. a. Incorrect. A method of recognizing revenue when the sale is made is used for financial statements, and a method of recognizing revenue at the time the cash is collected is used for tax reporting *does* result in a temporary difference.
   b. Incorrect. Warranty expense is recognized in the year of sale for financial statements and when paid for tax reporting *does* result in a temporary difference.
   c. Incorrect. An accelerated depreciation method is used for tax reporting, and the straight-line method is used for financial statements *does* result in a temporary difference.
   d. *Correct.* Interest income on municipal bonds is recognized for financial statements and not for tax reporting *does not* result in a temporary difference.

3. a. Incorrect. A correction of an error in the prior year's financial statements is a prior-period adjustment and would be reported in the statement of retained earnings.
   b. Incorrect. A gain resulting from the sale of fixed assets is not an extraordinary item, but it is reported as other income on the income statement.
   c. Incorrect. A loss on sale of temporary investments is not an extraordinary item, but it is reported as other income or loss on the income statement.
   d. *Correct.* A loss on condemnation of land is an extraordinary item on the income statement.

4. a. Incorrect. Earnings per share is not required to be presented on the face of the income statement for extraordinary items.
   b. Incorrect. Earnings per share is not required to be presented on the face of the income statement for discontinued operations.
   c. *Correct.* Earnings per share is required to be presented on the face of the income statement for income from continuing operations and net income.
   d. Incorrect.

5. a. Incorrect.
   b. *Correct.* All changes in stockholders' equity during a period except those resulting from investments by stockholders and dividends is the definition of comprehensive income.
   c. Incorrect.
   d. Incorrect.

6. a. Incorrect. Under the equity method, the receipt of cash dividends on a long-term investment in common stock is accounted for as a debit to Cash and a credit to the investment account, not Dividend Revenue.
   b. Incorrect.
   c. *Correct.* Under the cost method, the receipt of cash dividends on a long-term investment in common stock is accounted for as a debit to Cash and a credit to Dividend Revenue.
   d. Incorrect.

7. a. *Correct.* Under the equity method, the receipt of cash dividends on a long-term investment in common stock is accounted for as a debit to Cash and a credit to Investment in Spacek Inc.
   b. Incorrect.
   c. Incorrect. Under the cost method, the receipt of cash dividends on a long-term investment in common stock is accounted for as a debit to Cash and a credit to Dividend Revenue, not a credit to Investment in Spacek Inc.
   d. Incorrect.

8. a. Incorrect.
   b. **Correct.** The amount of net increase in the Investment in Subsidiary account for the year is $112,500, determined as [($200,000 × 75%) – ($50,000 × 75%)].
   c. Incorrect.
   d. Incorrect.

9. a. **Correct.** The amount of loss on the sale is $1,000, determined as [($96,000 / 800 shares) – $115] × 200 shares sold.
   b. Incorrect. A loss, not gain, was incurred on the sale.
   c. Incorrect.
   d. Incorrect.

10. a. Incorrect.
    b. Incorrect.
    c. **Correct.** The balance of the account Investment in Subsidiary would appear in the investments section of the parent company's balance sheet.
    d. Incorrect.

11. a. Incorrect.
    b. **Correct.** The beginning balance of $12,000 would be reduced by the $5,000 loss, to $7,000.
    c. Incorrect.
    d. Incorrect. The accumulated other comprehensive amount wasn't a deficit of $12,000 at the beginning of the period.

TRUE/FALSE

1. F Income that is exempt from federal taxes, such as interest income on municipal bonds, is not an example of a temporary tax difference since it will not reverse or turn around in later years. Instead, such differences are sometimes called permanent differences.

2. F Only extraordinary items, discontinued items, and cumulative effects of changes in accounting principle have separate earnings per share disclosures.

3. T

4. T

5. T

6. F Over the life of a business, temporary differences do not reduce the total amount of tax paid. Rather, temporary differences only affect when the taxes are paid.

7. T

8. F The accumulated other comprehensive income should be disclosed in the stockholders' equity section of the balance sheet.

9. F Under the cost method of accounting for investments in stocks, the investor records its share of cash dividends as an increase in Dividend Revenue, not a decrease in the investment account. The cash account is also increased for the dividends received.

10. T

11. T

12. F When two or more corporations transfer their assets and liabilities to a corporation that has been created for the purpose of the takeover, the combination is called a consolidation, not a merger. A merger is when one corporation acquires all the assets and liabilities of another corporation, which is then dissolved.

13. T

14. T

15. T

EXERCISE 12-1

(1)	Income Tax Expense	220,000	
	Income Tax Payable		128,000
	Deferred Income Tax Payable		92,000

(2)	Income Tax Expense	200,000	
	Deferred Income Tax Payable	40,000	
	Income Tax Payable		240,000

EXERCISE 12-2

(1)	Income Tax Expense	62,500	
	Cash		62,500

(2)	Income Tax Expense	30,000	
	Income Tax Payable		30,000

PROBLEM 12-1

(1)

Emory Corporation
Balance Sheet (selected items)
December 31, 20--

Current Assets

Temporary investments in marketable securities as cost	$40,000	
Add: Unrealized gain net of applicable income tax of $900	5,100	$45,100

(2)

Emory Corporation
Balance Sheet (selected items)
December 31, 20--

Stockholders' Equity

Retained earnings	$645,000
Accumulated other comprehensive income	8,100

(3)

Emory Corporation
Statement of Comprehensive Income

Net income	$124,000
Other comprehensive income:	
Unrealized gain on temporary investments in marketable securities net of applicable income tax of $1,200	4,800
Comprehensive income	$128,800

PROBLEM 12-2

(1)	(a)	Investment in Norris Inc. Stock	600,000	
		Cash		600,000

	(b)	Cash (40,000 × $.75)	30,000	
		Investment in Norris Inc. Stock		30,000

	(c)	Investment in Norris Inc. Stock ($900,000 × 25%)	225,000	
		Income of Norris Inc.		225,000

(2) (a) Investment in Kline Inc... 150,000

        Cash   150,000

(b) Cash 5,000

        Dividend Revenue   5,000

(c) None

PROBLEM 12-3

Wess Corp.
Income Statement
For Year Ended March 31, 20--

Sales	$2,700,000
Cost of merchandise sold	1,800,000
Gross profit	$ 900,000
Operating expenses	100,000
Restructuring charge	200,000
Income from continuing operations before income tax	$ 600,000
Income tax	176,000
Income from continuing operations	$ 424,000
Loss on discontinued operations, net of applicable income tax of $20,000	(50,000)
Income before extraordinary item and cumulative effect of a change in accounting principle	$ 374,000
Extraordinary item:	
Loss from earthquake, net of applicable income tax of $48,000	(192,000)
Cumulative effect on prior years of changing to a different depreciation method, net of applicable income tax of $18,000	62,000
Net income	$ 244,000
Earnings per common share:	
Income from continuing operations	$ 8.48
Loss on discontinued operations	(1.00)
Income before extraordinary item and cumulative effect of a change in accounting principle	$ 7.48
Extraordinary item	(3.84)
Cumulative effect on prior years of changing to a different depreciation method	1.24
Net income	$ 4.88

CHAPTER 13

MATCHING

1. C		**4.** A		**7.** L		**10.** R		**13.** N	
2. E		**5.** Q		**8.** H		**11.** F		**14.** K	
3. G		**6.** P		**9.** O		**12.** M			

FILL IN THE BLANK—PART A

1. bond indenture (or trust indenture)
2. callable
3. debenture bonds
4. contract (or coupon)
5. premium
6. future value
7. $909.09 ($1,000 × 0.90909)
8. $17,125 ($10,000 × 1.71252)
9. straight-line
10. effective interest rate
11. sinking fund
12. carrying amount
13. $388,000 ($400,000 – $12,000)
14. $2,030,000
15. $103,650 [($100,000 × 1.03) + $650]
16. Interest Revenue
17. Investment in Bonds
18. $2,000 (loss)
19. held-to-maturity security
20. 12.6 [(29,000,000 + 2,500,000) / 2,500,000]

FILL IN THE BLANK—PART B

1. term
2. convertible
3. discount
4. $712.99 ($1,000 × .71299)
5. $67,803 ($12,000 × 5.65022)
6. annuity
7. $10,000 (gain)
8. Investments
9. Long-term liabilities
10. Long-term liabilities
11. Investments
12. $73,850 [($75,000 × .98) + $350]
13. $5,045,000
14. $240,000 ($4,000,000 × .12 × 6/12)
15. $28,000 ($280,000 / 10 periods)
16. $120,000 ($4,000,000 × .12 × 3/12)
17. remains the same
18. number of times interest charges earned
19. 8.33 [(60,500,000 + 8,250,000) / 8,250,000]
20. present value

MULTIPLE CHOICE

1. a. **Correct.** A bond that gives the bondholder a right to exchange the bond for other securities under certain conditions is called a convertible bond.
   b. Incorrect. A bond sinking fund is a special fund in which amounts are set aside for the payment of a bond issue at its maturity date.
   c. Incorrect. Term bonds refer to bonds of an issue that all mature at the same time.
   d. Incorrect. Bonds issued on the basis of the general credit of the corporation are called debenture bonds.

2. a. Incorrect.
   b. **Correct.** The present value of $2,000 to be paid in one year at a current interest rate of 6% is $1,887 ($2,000 / 1.06).
   c. Incorrect. The present value must be less than the amount to be received at the end of one year.
   d. Incorrect. The present value must be less than the amount to be received at the end of one year.

3. a. Incorrect.
   b. **Correct.** The entry to record the amortization of a discount on bonds payable is a debit to Interest Expense and a credit to Discount on Bonds Payable.
   c. Incorrect.
   d. Incorrect.

4. a. Incorrect.
   b. Incorrect.
   c. **Correct.** Under the straight-line method of bond discount amortization, as a bond payable approaches maturity, the total yearly amount of interest expense will remain the same.
   d. Incorrect.

5. a. Incorrect. The cost of the bond is more than its face value, since it was purchased at a premium.
   b. Incorrect. The cost of the bond also includes the brokerage commission.
   c. **Correct.** The total cost to be debited to the investment account is $1,048 [($1,000 × 1.04) + $8].
   d. Incorrect.

6. a. Incorrect.
   b. Incorrect.
   c. Incorrect.
   d. ***Correct.*** The interest method of amortizing bond discount or premium is required by generally accepted accounting principles.

7. a. Incorrect.
   b. Incorrect. Investments in bonds or other debt securities that management intends to hold to their maturity are called held-to-maturity securities.
   c. Incorrect. Sinking-bond funds are special funds in which amounts are set aside for the payment of bond issues at their maturity dates.
   d. ***Correct.*** Bonds that do not provide for any interest payments are called zero-coupon bonds.

8. a. Incorrect. The present value is the value today of an amount to be received at a future date.
   b. Incorrect. The estimated worth in the future of an amount of cash on hand today invested at a fixed rate of interest is the future value.
   c. ***Correct.*** The principal of each bond is also called the face value.
   d. Incorrect.

9. a. ***Correct.*** A special fund accumulated over the life of a bond issue and kept separate from other assets in order to provide for payment of bonds at maturity is called a sinking fund.
   b. Incorrect.
   c. Incorrect.
   d. Incorrect.

10. a. Incorrect.
    b. ***Correct.*** Held-to-maturity securities are classified on the balance sheet as investments.
    c. Incorrect.
    d. Incorrect.

TRUE/FALSE

1. F The interest rate specified on the bond indenture is called the contract rate. It is not called the effective rate, which is sometimes called the market rate.

2. F If the market rate is lower than the contract rate, the bonds will sell at a premium, not a discount.

3. T

4. T

5. F Bonds that may be exchanged for other securities under certain conditions are called convertible bonds, not callable bonds. Callable bonds are bonds that a corporation reserves the right to redeem before their maturity.

6. F When cash is transferred to the sinking fund, it is recorded in an account called Sinking Fund Cash, not Sinking Fund Investments. When investments are purchased with the sinking fund cash, the investments are recorded in Sinking Fund Investments.

7. T

8. T

9. T

10. T

EXERCISE 13-1

(1)	June	1	Cash..	500,000	
			Bonds Payable		500,000
	Dec.	1	Interest Expense..	30,000	
			Cash		30,000

(2) Apr. 1 Cash... 942,645

Discount on Bonds Payable............................... 57,355

Bonds Payable 1,000,000

Oct. 1 Interest Expense.. 57,868

Discount on Bonds Payable ($57,355 / 20) 2,868

Cash 55,000

(3) Mar. 1 Cash... 743,625*

Premium on Bonds Payable................................ 43,625

Bonds Payable 700,000

*$700,000 × .3769 (present value of $1 for 20 periods at 5%)   263,830

$38,500 × 12.4622 (present value of an annuity of $1 for 20 periods at 5%)   479,795

Total present value of bonds   743,625

Sept. 1 Interest Expense.. 36,319

Premium on Bonds Payable ($43,625 / 20)..................... 2,181

Cash 38,500

EXERCISE 13-2

(1) Bonds Payable 5,000,000

Loss on Redemption of Bonds Payable.............................. 50,000

Cash... 5,050,000

(2) Bonds Payable 5,000,000

Cash... 4,900,000

Gain on Redemption of Bonds Payable 100,000

EXERCISE 13-3

(1) Oct. 1 Investment in Elgin Inc. Bonds ($400,000 × .99)............. 396,000

Interest Revenue 10,000

Cash 406,000

(2) Dec. 31 Cash... 20,000

Interest Revenue... 20,000

(3) Dec. 31 Investment in Elgin Inc. Bonds 120

Interest Revenue... 120

(4) Dec. 1 Cash... 424,667

Investment in Elgin Inc. Bonds............................. 397,040

Interest Revenue... 16,667

Gain on Sale of Investments 10,960

PROBLEM 13-1

(1) **(a)** Present value of $1 at compound interest of 5½% in 20

semiannual periods .... .3427

Face amount of bonds.. × $2,000,000 $ 685,400

Present value of annuity of $1 for 20 periods at 5½%..................... 11.9504

Semiannual interest payments .... × $ 110,000   1,314,544

Proceeds of bonds (present value)... $1,999,944

Note: The difference of $56 between the face value of the bonds and the present value is due to rounding.

(b) There is no premium or discount on the bond issuance.

(2) (a)

Present value of $1 at compound interest of 6% in 20 semiannual periods	.3118	
Face amount of bonds	× $2,000,000	$ 623,600
Present value of annuity of $1 for 20 periods at 6%	11.4699	
Semiannual interest payments	× $ 110,000	1,261,689
Proceeds of bonds (present value)		$1,885,289

(b) The discount is $114,711 on the bond issuance.

(3) (a)

Present value of $1 at compound interest of 5% in 20 semiannual periods	.3769	
Face amount of bonds	× $2,000,000	$ 753,800
Present value of annuity of $1 for 20 periods at 5%	12.4622	
Semiannual interest payments	× $ 110,000	1,370,842
Proceeds of bonds (present value)		$2,124,642

(b) The premium is $124,642 on the bond issuance.

PROBLEM 13-2

(1) Dec. 31

Cash...	531,161	
Bonds Payable		500,000
Premium on Bonds Payable		31,161

(2) June 30

Interest Expense ($27,500 – $1,558)	25,942	
Premium on Bonds Payable ($31,161 / 20)	1,558	
Cash		27,500

(3) Dec. 31

Interest Expense ($27,500 – $1,558)	25,942	
Premium on Bonds Payable ($31,161 / 20)	1,558	
Cash		27,500

(4) Dec. 31

Bonds Payable..	250,000	
Premium on Bonds Payable [($31,161 – $1,558 – $1,558) / 2]	14,023	
Gain on Redemption of Bonds		6,523
Cash		257,500

PROBLEM 13-3

(1) Jan. 1

Cash...	885,295	
Discount on Bonds Payable...	114,705	
Bonds Payable		1,000,000

(2) June 30

Interest Expense ($50,000 + $5,735)	55,735	
Discount on Bonds Payable ($114,705 / 20)		5,735
Cash		50,000

(3) Dec. 31

Interest Expense ($50,000 + $5,735)	55,735	
Discount on Bonds Payable ($114,705 / 20)		5,735
Cash		50,000

(4) Dec. 31

Bonds Payable..	500,000	
Loss on Redemption of Bonds..	41,618	
Discount on Bonds Payable [($114,705 – $5,735 – $5,735) / 2]...		51,618
Cash		490,000

CHAPTER 14

MATCHING

1. B
2. C
3. H
4. A
5. E
6. D
7. G
8. F

FILL IN THE BLANK—PART A

1. statement of cash flows
2. direct; indirect
3. operating
4. investing
5. investing
6. financing
7. investing
8. increased
9. decreased
10. decreased
11. $34,250
12. $102,000
13. $195,000
14. $60,000
15. $49,500
16. $1,040,000
17. $330,000
18. financing
19. $60,000
20. cash flow per share

FILL IN THE BLANK—PART B

1. indirect
2. operating
3. direct
4. financing
5. financing
6. operating
7. financing
8. investing
9. noncash
10. deducted from
11. added to
12. $330,000
13. $746,250
14. $3,125,000
15. $46,000
16. $20,000
17. retained earnings
18. $51,000
19. operating
20. free cash flow

MULTIPLE CHOICE

1. a. Incorrect. The cash flows from financing activities is a major section of the statement of cash flows.
   b. **Correct.** The cash flows from selling activities is not a major section of the statement of cash flows.
   c. incorrect. The cash flows from operating activities is a major section of the statement of cash flows.
   d. Incorrect. The cash flows from investing activities is a major section of the statement of cash flows.

2. a. Incorrect. Noncash investing and financing activities are not reported within the statement of cash flows because cash is not affected by these transactions.
   b. **Correct.** Although noncash investing and financing activities do not affect cash, these transactions are disclosed in a separate schedule that accompanies the statement of cash flows. This helps users interpret major investing and financing transactions that involve stock swaps, asset swaps, and other noncash events.
   c. Incorrect. Noncash investing and financing activities are not reported within the statement of retained earnings because this statement shows the events that influence retained earnings, such as net income and dividends.
   d. Incorrect. Noncash investing and financing activities are not reported in the footnotes to the balance sheet.

3. a. Incorrect. Depreciation is added to net income in deriving cash flows from operating activities under the indirect method.
   b. Incorrect. Decreases in current assets are added to net income in deriving cash flows from operating activities under the indirect method.
   c. **Correct.** Decreases in current liabilities are subtracted from net income in deriving cash flows from operating activities under the indirect method. This is because expenses have been accrued but not paid. Thus, the expenses overstate the amount of cash that has been spent on operating activities.
   d. Incorrect. A loss on sale of equipment is added to net income in deriving cash flows from operating activities under the indirect method.

4. a. Incorrect.
   b. Incorrect.
   c. Incorrect.
   d. **Correct.** The cash paid for dividends is $40,000 declared plus the difference between the beginning and ending dividend payable ($12,000 – $10,000), or $40,000 + $12,000 – $10,000.

5. a. Incorrect. The increase in accrued expenses is deducted from operating expenses under the direct method.

   b. Incorrect. The decrease in prepaid expenses is deducted from operating expenses under the direct method.

   c. Incorrect. The increase in income taxes payable is deducted from operating expenses under the direct method.

   d. **Correct.** The increase in prepaid expenses is added to operating expenses under the direct method. The increase in a prepaid expense causes cash to be paid before the expense is recorded; hence, the increase must be added to the expense to reflect the cash outflow.

6. a. Incorrect. The receipt of cash from the sale of land is a cash flow from an investing activity.

   b. Incorrect. The receipt of cash from the collection of accounts receivable is a cash flow from operating activities.

   c. **Correct.** The payment of cash for the acquisition of treasury stock is a cash flow from a financing activity.

   d. Incorrect. The payment of cash for new machinery is a cash flow from an investing activity.

7. a. Incorrect. The retained earnings does not appear on the statement of cash flows.

   b. **Correct.** Cash received from customers is the first line when preparing the statement of cash flows under the direct method.

   c. Incorrect. The net income appears first when preparing the statement of cash flows under the indirect method.

   d. Incorrect. Depreciation is added to net income in the statement of cash flows under the indirect method, but it does not even appear under the direct method.

8. a. **Correct.** The withdrawal of cash by the owner of a business is a financing activity, similar to a dividend.

   b. Incorrect. The issuance of common stock to retire long-term debt is a transaction that exchanges long-term debt for capital stock, so it is a noncash investing and financing activity.

   c. Incorrect. The acquisition of a manufacturing plant by issuing bonds exchanges a fixed asset for long-term debt, so it is a noncash investing and financing activity.

   d. Incorrect. The issuance of common stock in exchange for convertible preferred stock exchanges two types of capital stock, so it is a noncash investing and financing activity.

9. a. **Correct.** The increase in inventories uses more cash than is shown by the cost of goods sold; thus, the increase in inventories must be added to cost of goods sold to reflect the payment of cash for merchandise.

   b. Incorrect. The increase in accounts payable uses less cash than is shown by the cost of goods sold; thus, the increase in accounts payable must be deducted from cost of goods sold to reflect the payment of cash for merchandise.

   c. Incorrect. The decrease in inventories uses less cash than is shown by the cost of goods sold; thus, the decrease in inventories must be deducted from cost of goods sold to reflect the payment of cash for merchandise.

   d. Incorrect. The decrease in accounts receivable does not impact the cash paid for merchandise, but it impacts the cash received from customers.

10. a. Incorrect.

   b. Incorrect.

   c. **Correct.** The cash paid for income taxes is part of the cash flow from operating activities under the direct method.

   d. Incorrect.

11. a. Incorrect. The loss should not be added to the book value of the land.

   b. Incorrect. The loss should not be deducted from net income on the statement of cash flows.

   c. **Correct.** The loss should be deducted from the book value of the land in determining the cash flow from investing activities.

   d. Incorrect. The loss should not be deducted from net income on the statement of cash flows.

12. a. Incorrect.
   b. *Correct.* $290,000 – $32,000 – $40,000. The free cash flows are the cash flows available after paying dividends and replacing productive capacity. The depreciation expense would not be used in the calculation, since it is known that $40,000 was required to maintain productive capacity.
   c. Incorrect.
   d. Incorrect.

TRUE/FALSE

1. T
2. T
3. T
4. F Only cash receipts and payments from operations are evaluated under the direct method; thus, depreciation is not analyzed under the direct method.
5. F Increases in current liabilities are added to net income under the indirect method because expense accruals exceed cash payments when current liabilities increase.
6. T
7. T
8. T
9. F Both the direct and indirect methods report the same cash flows from operating activities; thus, neither method is more accurate than the other.
10. T

EXERCISE 14-1

Item	Cash Flows From			Schedule of Noncash Investing and Financing Activities
	Operating Activities	Investing Activities	Financing Activities	
1. Decrease in prepaid expenses	✔			
2. Retirement of bonds...............................			✔	
3. Proceeds from sale of investments...........		✔		
4. Increase in inventories	✔			
5. Issuance of common stock			✔	
6. Purchase of equipment.............................		✔		
7. Cash dividends paid.................................			✔	
8. Acquisition of building in exchange for bonds				✔
9. Amortization of patents	✔			
10. Amortization of discount on bonds payable..	✔			

EXERCISE 14-2

Cash flows from operating activities:

Net income, per income statement		$150,000
Add: Depreciation	$45,000	
Decrease in prepaid expenses	2,625	
Increase in accounts payable	17,000	64,625
		$214,625
Deduct: Increase in trade receivables	$10,000	
Increase in inventories	15,625	
Decrease in salaries payable	3,000	28,625
Net cash flow from operating activities		$186,000

EXERCISE 14-3

Cash flows from operating activities:

Cash received from customers		$520,000
Deduct: Cash payments for merchandise	$128,625	
Cash payments for operating expenses	160,375	
Cash payments for income tax	45,000	334,000
Net cash flow from operating activities		$186,000

Supporting calculations:

Sales (reported on income statement)	$530,000
Less increase in trade receivables	(10,000)
Cash received from customers	$520,000
Cost of merchandise sold	$130,000
Plus increase in inventories	15,625
Less increase in accounts payable	(17,000)
Cash payments for merchandise	$128,625
Operating expenses (other than depreciation)	$160,000
Less decrease in prepaid expenses	(2,625)
Plus decrease in salaries payable	3,000
Cash payments for operating expenses	$160,375

PROBLEM 14-1

Stellar Inc.
Statement of Cash Flows
For Year Ended December 31, 2006

Cash flows from operating activities:			
Net income, per income statement..		$114,000	
Add: Depreciation..	$48,000		
Decrease in inventories	6,000		
Decrease in prepaid expenses	2,400		
Increase in accounts payable	7,200	63,600	
		$177,600	
Deduct: Increase in trade receivables.....................................	$12,000		
Gain on sale of land...	18,000	30,000	
Net cash flow from operating activities......................................			$147,600
Cash flows from investing activities:			
Cash received from land sold...		$ 54,000	
Less cash paid for purchase of equipment		96,000	
Net cash flow used for investing activities..................................			(42,000)
Cash flows from financing activities:			
Cash used to retire bonds payable..		$ 60,000	
Cash paid for dividends...		27,600*	
Net cash flow used for financing activities................................			(87,600)
Increase in cash...			$ 18,000
Cash, January 1, 2006..			66,000
Cash, December 31, 2006...			$ 84,000

*30,000 + 21,600 – 24,000

Schedule of Noncash Investing and Financing Activities:

Acquisition of land by issuance of common stock..	$ 20,000

PROBLEM 14-2

Stellar Inc.
Statement of Cash Flows
For Year Ended December 31, 2006

Cash flows from operating activities:			
Cash received from customers...		$563,000	
Deduct: Cash payments for merchandise	$211,800		
Cash payments for operating expenses	169,600		
Cash payments for income tax	34,000	415,400	
Net cash flow from operating activities....................................			$147,600
Cash flows from investing activities:			
Cash received from land sold...		$ 54,000	
Less cash paid for purchase of equipment		96,000	
Net cash flow used for investing activities..............................			(42,000)
Cash flows from financing activities:			
Cash used to retire bonds payable..		$ 60,000	
Cash paid for dividends..		27,600*	
Net cash flow used for financing activities			(87,600)
Increase in cash..			$ 18,000
Cash, January 1, 2006...			66,000
Cash, December 31, 2006...			$ 84,000

*30,000 + 21,600 – 24,000

Schedule of Noncash Investing and Financing Activities:

Acquisition of land by issuance of common stock...		$ 20,000

Schedule Reconciling Net Income with Cash Flows from Operating Activities:

Net income, per income statement..		$114,000
Add: Depreciation	$48,000	
Decrease in inventories	6,000	
Decrease in prepaid expenses	2,400	
Increase in accounts payable	7,200	63,600
		$177,600
Deduct: Increase in trade receivables...	$12,000	
Gain on sale of land..	18,000	30,000
Net cash flow provided by operating activities		$147,600

Supporting calculations:

Sales (reported on income statement)...	$575,000
Less increase in trade receivables	(12,000)
Cash received	$563,000
Cost of merchandise sold	$225,000
Less decrease in inventories	(6,000)
Less increase in accounts payable..	(7,200)
Cash payments for merchandise	$211,800
Operating expenses (other than depreciation)	$172,000
Less decrease in prepaid expenses	(2,400)
Cash payments for operating expenses	$169,600

CHAPTER 15

MATCHING

1. H	**5.** M	**8.** C	**11.** U	**14.** Y	**17.** I
2. Q	**6.** A	**9.** T	**12.** G	**15.** S	**18.** P
3. L	**7.** J	**10.** O	**13.** B	**16.** D	**19.** K
4. X					

FILL IN THE BLANK—PART A

1. vertical analysis
2. profitability analysis
3. current position analysis
4. solvency
5. common-size
6. current
7. net sales to assets
8. quick
9. earnings per share on common stock
10. working capital
11. accounts receivable turnover
12. inventory turnover
13. liabilities to stockholders' equity
14. preferred dividends are earned
15. income from operations
16. stockholders' equity
17. dividends
18. independent audit
19. fixed assets to long-term liabilities
20. net sales

FILL IN THE BLANK—PART B

1. horizontal analysis
2. dividend yield
3. independent auditors'
4. number of days' sales in receivables
5. number of days' sales in inventory
6. interest charges earned
7. rate earned on total assets
8. rate earned on stockholders' equity
9. leverage
10. price-earnings
11. management discussion and analysis (MDA)
12. quick assets
13. common-size
14. solvency analysis
15. bankers'
16. number of days' sales in inventory
17. earnings per share (on common stock)
18. common-size
19. receivables
20. internal control

MULTIPLE CHOICE

1. a. Incorrect.
    b. Incorrect. Horizontal statements are one type of statement that uses both relative comparisons and dollar amounts.
    c. Incorrect. Vertical statements are one type of statement that uses both relative comparisons and dollar amounts.
    d. *Correct.* In common-size statements, all items are expressed in percentages.

2. a. Incorrect. The rate of return on total assets is a profitability ratio.
    b. Incorrect. The price-earnings ratio is a profitability ratio.
    c. *Correct.* The accounts receivable turnover is a measure of solvency (short-term).
    d. Incorrect. The ratio of net sales to assets is a profitability ratio.

3. a. Incorrect.
    b. Incorrect.
    c. *Correct.* $4,000,000 / [$250,000 + $345,000) / 2]
    d. Incorrect.

4. a. Incorrect.
    b. *Correct.* $6,500,000 / [($175,000 + $297,000) / 2]
    c. Incorrect.
    d. Incorrect.

5. a. Incorrect. The independent auditor's report attests to the fairness of financial statements.
   b. Incorrect. The footnotes provide additional descriptive details of the financial statements, but rarely include forward-looking statements by management.
   c. Incorrect. This is a new management assertion required by the Sarbanes-Oxley Act on the effectiveness of internal controls, but it does not include forward-looking statements about prospects and risks.
   d. **Correct.** The management discussion and analysis provides an in-depth discussion of prior results and statements regarding future prospects and business risks.

6. a. Incorrect. The working capital ratio provides a measure of the short-term, debt-paying ability.
   b. Incorrect. The quick ratio provides a measure of the short-term, debt-paying ability.
   c. Incorrect. The receivables to inventory ratio is not an interpretable financial ratio.
   d. **Correct.** The number of days' sales in receivables is a measure of the efficiency in collecting receivables.

7. a. Incorrect.
   b. Incorrect.
   c. **Correct.** ($510,000 + $30,000) / $30,000
   d. Incorrect.

8. a. **Correct.** ($27,000 + $23,000 + $90,000) / $70,000
   b. Incorrect.
   c. Incorrect.
   d. Incorrect.

9. a. Incorrect.
   b. **Correct.** In a vertical analysis balance sheet, items are expressed as a percentage of total assets.
   c. Incorrect.
   d. Incorrect.

10. a. Incorrect.
    b. Incorrect.
    c. **Correct.** ($460,000 – $50,000) / 50,000 shares
    d. Incorrect.

11. a. Incorrect. A high dividend yield is usually associated with low P/E companies, since most of the shareholder return is in the form of predictable dividends, rather than share appreciation.
    b. **Correct.** High P/E firms are usually associated with high growth companies.
    c. Incorrect. Debt position is not usually associated with the P/E ratio.
    d. Incorrect. Current position is not usually associated with the P/E ratio.

12. a. Incorrect.
    b. Incorrect.
    c. Incorrect.
    d. **Correct.** ($240,000 + $120,000) / $1,000,000

TRUE/FALSE

1. F   This statement is true for a vertical analysis, not a horizontal analysis.
2. T
3. F   The net sales to assets ratio is a profitability ratio that shows how effectively and efficiently assets are used to generate sales.
4. T
5. F   The receivable turnover is determined by dividing the net sales by the average accounts receivable outstanding during the period.
6. T
7. F   The rate earned on total assets is determined by adding interest expense to net income, then dividing this sum by average total assets during the period.
8. T
9. T
10. F   Working capital is the excess of current assets over current liabilities.

EXERCISE 15-1

	2007	Percent	2006	Percent
Revenues	$450,000	100%	$389,000	100%
Costs and expenses:				
Cost of sales	$200,000	44%	$176,000	45%
Selling and administrative expenses	100,000	23%	73,000	19%
Total costs and expenses	$300,000	67%	$249,000	64%
Earnings before income taxes	$150,000	33%	$140,000	36%
Income taxes	34,500	8%	32,200	8%
Net earnings	$115,500	25%	$107,800	28%

EXERCISE 15-2

			Increase (Decrease)	
	2007	2006	Amount	Percent
Current assets	$250,000	$219,500	$ 30,500	14%
Fixed assets	435,000	401,600	33,400	8%
Intangible assets	43,700	46,000	(2,300)	−5%
Current liabilities	88,000	80,000	8,000	10%
Long-term liabilities	225,000	250,000	(25,000)	−10%
Common stock	214,000	167,600	46,400	28%
Retained earnings	200,000	170,000	30,000	18%

PROBLEM 15-1

Nordic Inc.
Comparative Income Statement
For the Years Ended December 31, 2007 and 2006

	2007	2006	Increase (Decrease) Amount	Percent
Sales	$690,500	$585,000	$105,500	18.0%
Sales returns and allowances	25,500	23,000	2,500	10.9%
Net sales	$665,000	$562,000	$103,000	18.3%
Cost of goods sold	420,000	330,000	90,000	27.3%
Gross profit	$245,000	$232,000	$ 13,000	5.6%
Selling expenses	$ 43,000	$ 47,700	$ (4,700)	−9.9%
Administrative expenses	31,000	31,000	0	0.0%
Total operating expenses	$ 74,000	$ 78,700	$ (4,700)	−6.0%
Operating income	$171,000	$153,300	$ 17,700	11.5%
Other income	13,000	16,400	(3,400)	−20.7%
	$184,000	$169,700	$ 14,300	8.4%
Other expense	58,000	53,500	4,500	8.4%
Income before income taxes	$126,000	$116,200	$ 9,800	8.4%
Income taxes	34,000	32,400	1,600	4.9%
Net income	$ 92,000	$ 83,800	$ 8,200	9.8%

Nordic Inc.
Comparative Balance Sheet
December 31, 2007 and 2006

Assets	2007	2006	Increase (Decrease) Amount	Percent
Cash	$ 76,000	$ 69,000	$ 7,000	10.1%
Marketable securities	98,900	130,000	(31,100)	−23.9%
Accounts receivable (net)	199,000	195,000	4,000	2.1%
Inventory	450,000	375,000	75,000	20.0%
Prepaid expenses	28,000	26,300	1,700	6.5%
Long-term investments	35,000	35,000	0	0.0%
Fixed assets (net)	871,000	835,000	36,000	4.3%
Intangible assets	18,000	22,800	(4,800)	−21.1%
Total assets	$1,775,900	$1,688,100	$ 87,800	5.2%
Liabilities				
Current liabilities	$ 129,000	$ 107,000	$ 22,000	20.6%
Long-term liabilities	420,000	440,000	(20,000)	−4.5%
Total liabilities	$ 549,000	$ 547,000	$ 2,000	0.4%
Stockholders' Equity				
Preferred 3% stock, $100 par	$ 102,000	$ 93,000	$ 9,000	9.7%
Common stock, $50 par	549,900	530,100	19,800	3.7%
Retained earnings	575,000	518,000	57,000	11.0%
Total stockholders' equity	$1,226,900	$1,141,100	$ 85,800	7.5%
Total liabilities and stockholders' equity	$1,775,900	$1,688,100	$ 87,800	5.2%

PROBLEM 15-2

Voyageur Inc.
Comparative Balance Sheet
December 31, 2006 and 2005

	2006		2005	
Assets	Amount	Percent	Amount	Percent
Cash...	$ 500,000	5.3%	$ 425,000	5.4%
Marketable securities	200,000	2.1%	185,000	2.4%
Accounts receivable (net)	680,000	7.3%	575,000	7.3%
Inventory	860,000	9.2%	740,000	9.4%
Prepaid expenses	104,000	1.1%	95,000	1.2%
Long-term investments	450,000	4.8%	410,000	5.2%
Fixed assets (net)	6,556,000	70.1%	5,420,000	69.0%
Total assets...	$9,350,000	100.0%	$7,850,000	100.0%
Liabilities				
Current liabilities...	$1,090,000	11.7%	$1,050,000	13.4%
Long-term liabilities	2,150,000	23.0%	2,050,000	26.1%
Total liabilities..	$3,240,000	34.7%	$3,100,000	39.5%
Stockholders' Equity				
Preferred 5% stock, $100 par	$ 350,000	3.7%	$ 350,000	4.5%
Common stock, $10 par...................................	2,550,000	27.3%	2,550,000	32.5%
Retained earnings	3,210,000	34.3%	1,850,000	23.5%
Total stockholders' equity	$6,110,000	65.3%	$4,750,000	60.5%
Total liabilities and stockholders' equity.........	$9,350,000	100.0%	$7,850,000	100.0%

Voyageur Inc.
Income Statement
For the Year Ended December 31, 2006

	Amount	Percent
Sales	$12,800,000	102.4%
Sales returns and allowances	300,000	2.4%
Net sales	$12,500,000	100.0%
Cost of goods sold	7,550,000	60.4%
Gross profit..	$ 4,950,000	39.6%
Selling expenses...	$ 1,550,000	12.4%
Administrative expenses	825,000	6.6%
Total operating expenses..	$ 2,375,000	19.0%
Operating income...	$ 2,575,000	20.6%
Other income..	125,000	1.0%
	$ 2,700,000	21.6%
Other expense (interest)	150,000	1.2%
Income before income taxes..	$ 2,550,000	20.4%
Income taxes..	937,000	7.5%
Net income	$ 1,613,000	12.9%

PROBLEM 15-3

		Calculation	Final Result
a.	Working capital	$2,344,000 − $1,090,000	1,254,000
b.	Current ratio	$$\frac{\$2,344,000}{\$1,090,000}$$	2.2
c.	Quick ratio	$$\frac{\$1,380,000}{\$1,090,000}$$	1.3
d.	Accounts receivable turnover	$$\frac{\$12,500,000}{\left(\dfrac{\$680,000+\$575,000}{2}\right)}$$	19.9
e.	Number of days' sales in receivables	$$\frac{\$12,500,000}{365}=\$34,247 \qquad \frac{\$680,000}{\$34,247}$$	19.9
f.	Inventory turnover	$$\frac{\$7,550,000}{\left(\dfrac{\$860,000+\$740,000}{2}\right)}$$	9.4
g.	Number of days' sales in inventory	$$\frac{\$7,550,000}{365}=\$20,685 \qquad \frac{\$860,000}{\$20,685}$$	41.6
h.	Ratio of fixed assets to long-term liabilities	$$\frac{\$6,556,000}{\$2,150,000}$$	3.0
i.	Ratio of liabilities to stockholders' equity	$$\frac{\$3,240,000}{\$6,110,000}$$	0.5
j.	Number of times interest charges earned	$$\frac{\$2,550,000+\$150,000}{\$150,000}$$	18.0
k.	Number of times preferred dividends earned	$$\frac{\$1,613,000}{\$17,500}$$	92.2
l.	Ratio of net sales to assets	$$\frac{\$12,500,000}{\left(\dfrac{\$8,900,000+\$7,440,000}{2}\right)}$$	1.5
m.	Rate earned on total assets	$$\frac{\$1,613,000+\$150,000}{\left(\dfrac{\$9,350,000+\$7,850,000}{2}\right)}$$	20.5%
n.	Rate earned on stockholders' equity	$$\frac{\$1,613,000}{\left(\dfrac{\$6,110,000+\$4,750,000}{2}\right)}$$	29.7%
o.	Rate earned on common stockholders' equity	$$\frac{\$1,613,000-\$17,500}{\left(\dfrac{\$5,760,000+\$4,400,000}{2}\right)}$$	31.4%

		Calculation	Final Result
p.	Earnings per share on common stock	$$\frac{\$1{,}613{,}000 - \$17{,}500}{255{,}000}$$	$6.26
q.	Price-earnings ratio	$$\frac{\$29.75}{\$6.26}$$	4.8
r.	Dividends per share of common stock	$$\frac{\$250{,}000}{255{,}000}$$	$0.98
s.	Dividend yield	$$\frac{\left(\frac{\$250{,}000}{255{,}000 \text{ shares}}\right)}{\$29.75}$$	3.3%